UNDERSTANDING SOCIAL MOVEMENTS

This book offers a new and fresh approach to understanding social movements. It provides interdisciplinary perspectives on social and cultural protest, and contentious politics. It considers major theories and concepts, which are presented in an accessible and engaging format. Historical and contemporary case studies and examples from a variety of different countries are provided throughout, including the American civil rights movement, Greenpeace, Pussy Riot, indigenous peoples' movements, liberation theology, precarity protests, Occupy, Tea Party, and Arab Spring.

The book presents specific chapters outlining the early origins of social movement studies and more recent theoretical and conceptual developments. It considers key ideas from resource mobilization theory, the political process model, and new social movement approaches. It provides an expansive commentary on the role of culture in social protest and looks at substantive areas in chapters dedicated to religious movements, geography and struggles over space, media and movements, and global activism.

Understanding Social Movements will be a useful resource for undergraduate and post-graduate students across disciplines wanting to be introduced to or extend their knowledge of the field. The book will also prove invaluable for lecturers and academic researchers interested in studying social movements.

Greg Martin is a Senior Lecturer in the Department of Sociology and Social Policy at the University of Sydney, Australia. He has published on social welfare movements, subcultures and social movements, protest policing, and new social movement theory. His other research interests are in criminology and sociolegal studies, and he is co-editor of the book, *Secrecy, Law and Society* (Routledge, 2015). He is a member of the Editorial Advisory Board for the journal *Social Movement Studies*, and is an Associate Editor of *Crime Media Culture*.

There are only a handful of textbooks in social movements. This engagingly written book is unique in its interdisciplinarity, its comprehensive treatment of both American and European theories and its inclusion of movements in the global South, Europe, and the Middle East, along with recent US social movements, including the global justice, Occupy, and Tea Party movements.

−Verta Taylor, *Professor of Sociology, University of California, Santa Barbara, USA*

Often proclaimed dead, coopted, institutionalized − in the new millennium social movements have been instead confirmed as a driving force of change in our societies. In this deep and broad assessment of social movement studies, their contributions and pitfalls, Greg Martin provides us with a rich tool kit of concepts and theories that will help us read contentious politics in the past, the present, and the future.

−Donatella della Porta, *Director of Center on Social Movement Studies-Cosmos, European University Institute, Italy*

Greg Martin leads the reader ably from the origins of social-movement scholarship in crowd theory, right through to the most interesting concerns today: globalization, the media, the geography of protest, emotions, narratives, and more. His integration of religious movements into how we study other social movements is especially welcome.

−James M. Jasper, *teaches sociology at the Graduate Center of the City University of New York*

This book is packed with interesting examples, from the role of black churches in the US civil rights movement, to Pussy Riot − from the Zapatistas to the Comfort Women that really bring concepts and theories to life. It is clearly written and will really help students understand what is at stake in social movement studies, dealing as it does, not just with well-developed themes such as resource mobilisation and culture, but also new topics including emotions, media and space.

−Professor Kate Nash, *Department of Sociology, Goldsmiths, London*

Understanding Social Movements offers an unusually comprehensive approach to the processes that ordinary people undergo, as they try to remake the worlds they live in. It starts with the foundations and takes us through the prospects for meaningful change in the future. The book is an asset for students and a challenge for citizens.

−David S. Meyer, *Professor of Sociology, University of California, Irvine, USA*

In his new book, Greg Martin provides a concise yet comprehensive introduction to social movements. The numerous illustrations from outside Europe and North America, and the attention to cultural and symbolic challenges alongside more political ones, represent a distinctive feature of this interesting and useful volume.

−Mario Diani, *University of Trento and ICREA-UPF Barcelona, Spain*

UNDERSTANDING SOCIAL MOVEMENTS

Greg Martin

Routledge
Taylor & Francis Group

LONDON AND NEW YORK

First published 2015
by Routledge
2 Park Square, Milton Park, Abingdon, Oxon OX14 4RN

and by Routledge
711 Third Avenue, New York, NY 10017

Routledge is an imprint of the Taylor & Francis Group, an informa business

British Library Cataloguing-in-Publication Data
A catalogue record for this book is available from the British Library

Library of Congress Cataloging-in-Publication Data
Martin, Greg, 1951–
    Understanding social movements / Greg Martin. — 1 Edition.
        pages cm
    1. Social movements.   2. Social change.   3. Online social
networks.   4. Globalization—Social aspects.   I. Title.
    HM881.M37 2015
    303.48'4—dc23
    2014044751

ISBN: 978-0-415-60087-3 (hbk)
ISBN: 978-0-415-60088-0 (pbk)
ISBN: 978-0-203-83709-2 (ebk)

Typeset in Bembo
by Apex CoVantage, LLC

For the girls: Rebecca, Maya, Roxana

CONTENTS

10 Conclusion   250

FIGURES

BOXES

ACKNOWLEDGEMENTS

For their tremendous patience, I am grateful to the editorial staff at Routledge: Gerhard Boomgaarden, Emily Briggs, and Alyson Claffey. I would also like to thank Rebecca Scott Bray for help with image permissions and for believing that I could actually finish this book. Lastly, I am indebted to my grandparents, Walter and Eleanor Toomes, without whom I could not have achieved many things in my life.

CHAPTER 1

Introduction

This is a book about social movements. As we shall see, the field of social movement studies has a long history in the social sciences, and the idea of social movement as, broadly speaking, social and political change stretches back to the dawn of sociological thought. Hence, midway through the nineteenth century, Karl Marx famously pronounced, 'Philosophers have only *interpreted* the world in different ways; the point is to change it' (Marx, quoted in Thompson 1996: 175, original emphasis). And, in many respects, this captures the essence of what social movements are about. They are collective forms of protest or activism that aim to affect some kind of transformation in existing structures of power that have created inequality, injustice, disadvantage, and so on. This is not to say all social movements are necessarily positive or progressive in nature. For, as we will see occasionally in the book, movements can also be conservative, reactionary, or regressive. The rise of the Tea Party movement in the United States is a recent example.

SHOULD WE BE OPTIMISTIC ABOUT SOCIAL MOVEMENT RADICALISM?

As already stated, most social movements aim to affect transformations in politics and society. Indeed, the recent emergence globally of Occupy and of the Arab Spring across the countries of the Middle East was heralded as a beacon of hope for radical politics and democratic change in the contemporary period. Against this, it has been observed, many commentaries tell a rather gloomy and pessimistic narrative of depoliticization, apoliticality, and social movement deradicalization (Dean 2014). In some ways, this reflects sociological accounts of declining civic engagement, part of which involves disengagement from conventional forms of politics and government (Putnam 1995). It also echoes the view that the discipline of sociology itself has been cut adrift from its radical roots, such that, where once disciplinary transformations came from social movements, now we are all too familiar with the image of 'a conventional textbook on globalization, social change or modernity with a dramatic cover photo of protestors – and a complete absence of social movements *within* those same covers' (Cox 2014: 968, original emphasis).

In other ways, these developments reflect scholarly work about 'diminishing social movement radicalism and a narrowing of possibilities for egalitarian, radical democratic alternatives to existing structures of inequality and domination' (Dean 2014: 454). Essentially, what Dean alludes to here is the presence of a 'paradigm' (Kuhn 1962); that is, a set of beliefs shared by the political theory community (including social movement scholars), which, although highly persuasive, is not necessarily supported by empirical data. Such accounts of the prevalence of political disinterest and apathy are variously premised on a belief in the ubiquity, and indeed hegemony, of neoliberal capitalism and the operation of free markets, which have become key elements in the current political orthodoxy and consensus formed around centrist-right politics. In short, so the argument goes, we are now living out or reaping the consequences of the neoliberal restructuring projects of the Reagan-Thatcher era, wherein, Thatcher once infamously said in an interview for *Woman's Own* magazine in 1987 (and I paraphrase): 'There is no such thing as society, only individual men, women, and their families'. Inevitably, we are left with an impoverished public sphere, not only privatized industries, but privatized lives and selves, the end of 'the social' and concomitant rise of (antisocial) economic reductionism and self-interested individualism, and, ultimately, a hollowed-out, morally bankrupt remnant of 'society' (see Marquand 2014, for discussion).

The upshot for those who hold a pessimistic view of society and radical politics is that there is no alternative to the current status quo. However, according to Dean (2014: 455–456), such accounts tend to dismiss, or at least gloss over, the potential significance of, for example, the global anti-capitalist movement, which, among other things, was responsible for the successful disruption of the World Trade Organization (WTO) meetings in Seattle in 1999. To be sure, questions as to efficacy such as this lie at the heart of social movement studies. But to what extent do movements like the global justice movement, Occupy, and the Arab Spring *actually* change things, or 'make a difference'?

In a powerful interview with journalist Jeremy Paxman, broadcast in October 2013 on the British current affairs program *Newsnight*, comedian turned radical political commentator-cum-revolutionary Russell Brand talked of the essential irrelevance of mainstream party politics and politicians who continue to support bankers' 'right' to award themselves gratuitous bonuses. Indeed, while British Prime Minister David Cameron has attempted to reassure Britons that 'we are in this together', for the most part, this sentiment has added insult to injury, given the bank bailout following the (bank-instigated) global financial crisis (GFC) of 2008 was funded by 'austerity measures' subsequently imposed on ordinary citizens.

In a piece he wrote at the time for his guest-edited edition of the *New Statesman*, Brand quite rightly pointed out that the English riots of 2011 (which need to be seen in the wider context of the bank bailout) were far from nihilistic and materialistic, as those who condemned them would have us believe. Rather, he said, they were inherently political for the following reason: 'These young people have been accidentally marketed to their whole lives without the economic means to participate in the carnival' (Brand 2013: 26; see also Martin 2009, 2011a).

In the context of the austerity-funded bank bailout, it is easy to see why some lack optimism or hope for any genuine alternative. Indeed, what has been especially galling is the establishment's capacity to reinvigorate the ideology and institutions of neoliberal capitalism after the near collapse and widespread discrediting of the economic order following the GFC (Jones 2014). However, while to some, disengagement is the only option, others have become so enraged they feel there is no alternative *other than* to get involved in protest, demonstrations, marches, and the like. This proved to be the case with the Indignados in Spain, Occupy, and the Arab Spring.

What motivates people to become involved in collective action in the first place is of key concern to social movement scholars. Some believe people are motivated by emotions such as anger, indignation, and a sense of injustice; others reckon people are driven by thinking strategically about how they might best achieve political goals collectively. The matter of motivation, in turn, leads us to other areas of interest. For example, one of the principal dilemmas for activists is

© James May/Alamy

Figure 1.1 A man waves an Egyptian flag in Tahrir Square hours before President Mubarak steps down from office on 11 February 2011

how willing they are, or should be, to engage with established actors and organizations within the political system. In order to achieve their goals, should social movements engage with and harness the resources of professional organizations and political parties, or should they seek to be autonomous of the existing system and its constituents? Put simply, how far should social movements be willing to go to achieve their goals? Should they remain true to their original radical goals, or should they be prepared to compromise them to affect a modicum of change?

Important here, too, is the idea of social movement 'success'. Should we 'measure' success simply in terms of the attainment of policy or legal goals, such as facilitating the introduction of some anti-discrimination law, or should we conceive of success more broadly in terms of raising awareness, spreading knowledge, and disseminating information, or changing cultural values and attitudes? Movements like the women's movement and the American civil rights movement brought about widespread transformations across a broad range of spheres (social, cultural, political, legal, economic), while other movements have made more specific or piecemeal contributions.

SOCIAL MOVEMENTS IN SOCIETY

What we have discussed thus far are among the issues one confronts in the 'social movement society' wherein, Meyer and Tarrow (1998: 20) propose, 'social protest has become more common, more easily diffused and sponsored by increasing numbers and types of organizations'. If this is the case, Meyer and Tarrow (1998: 26) say, and 'states have become more adept at institutionalizing movements and activists are becoming both more professional and more interchangeable with interest groups in their activities, what will happen to those actors who refuse the blandishments of recognition and legitimation?' Here we confront a fundamental issue in social movement studies whereby some scholars focus on the relationship between social movements, the state, and wider political system, while others see social movements as eschewing conventional politics altogether.

Those who hold the former view tend to work within political process, resource mobilization, or contentious politics frameworks. Although these perspectives have different emphases, the common denominator is, as Scott (1990: 10–11) puts it, a belief that the telos of social movement activity is the integration of previously excluded issues and groups into the 'normal' political process. This is a perspective that was developed principally in the United States, and is one that still holds sway there. As we will learn, this approach can be juxtaposed with approaches developed in Europe, which, from the 1980s, identified the emergence of so-called, 'new social movements'. The argument here is that contemporary movements differ from the 'old' labour movement, in that they are concerned not with socioeconomic issues, but with 'post-material' values related to lifestyle and 'identity politics', which exist beyond old (i.e., class-based) politics. Unlike their American counterparts, who believe social movements seek to be included in the polity, new social movement theorists argue that movements strive to be autonomous of the political system.

In very broad terms, this rather polarized way of thinking has, and, in some sense still does, mark a distinction between North American and European ways of thinking about social movements. Again, speaking very generally, the distinction has been, and, to some extent still is, reflected in the approaches adopted by the two specialist journals in the field: the North American–based journal *Mobilization* (established in 1996), and the journal *Social Movement Studies* (established in Europe in 2002). A caveat is required, however, for although each of these journals has its own take on social movement research, there is nevertheless a lot of cross-pollination of ideas and a high degree of interdisciplinarity nowadays in social movement studies. Indeed, it is hoped that interdisciplinarity is something that comes across in this book – for example, in the inclusion of chapters dedicated solely to religion, space/geography, and media, which are topics that do not ordinarily feature so prominently in social movement textbooks.

Notwithstanding the increasingly interdisciplinary nature of social movement studies, as in other fields, there will still be those who have a preference for one set of ideas or one theory over others. It should be noted, however, that, for the most part, theories about social movements have been generated in the developed north of the globe, which, it has been argued, points to the essential ethnocentricity of social movement studies. Accordingly, it is said social movement studies has not taken seriously enough questions that are, for instance, posed by the global justice movement, such as how the prosperity of the First World has been achieved at the expense of the underdeveloped Third World. With its stress on post-materialism (and neglect of political-economic issues), the new social movement perspective is especially guilty of this. We will consider that and other criticisms of new social movement theory in the following pages. However, by providing case studies and examples of protest and social movements from around the world, it is one intention of this book to remedy, in some small way, the tendency towards ethnocentrism in the social movements literature. But there will undoubtedly be omissions.

DOING SOCIAL MOVEMENT RESEARCH

One thing we will not look at in this book is the area of methodology and researching social movements. Arguably, the prototypical approach to doing social movement research was devised by French sociologist Alain Touraine in the 1970s. Touraine's (1978: 182) method was one of 'sociological intervention', which he defined as, '[t]he action of the sociologist bringing social relationships to light and making these relationships the principal object of analysis'. During the 1970s and 1980s, Touraine and his colleagues conducted a number of interventions, including with French student and labour movements, the anti-nuclear movement, and Solidarity in Poland. Unlike other more conventional methodological techniques, 'sociological intervention does not aim at gathering data; it aims at reconstructing and exploring a struggle to become an actor' (McDonald 2002a: 249). For example, the sociological intervention with Solidarity:

    . . . pointed to a movement made up of actors involved in struggles for national independence, democracy and labour rights. These dimensions were in tension and at times in conflict, and the success and later fragmentation of Solidarnosc was a story of the construction and deconstruction of the synthesis of these identities.

(McDonald 2002a: 249)

The hope is that a sociological intervention will result in researchers being able to help a social movement 'move from *reliving* its experience to *analyzing* its experience' (McDonald 2002a: 255, original emphasis). Although he has criticized this approach for conferring on social researchers a role akin to that of a missionary (Melucci 1995: 58), Italian sociologist, and former student of Touraine, Alberto Melucci was nevertheless influenced by Touraine in developing his own research methodology (Melucci 1989: 236). As we shall see later in the book, for Melucci, the formation of a collective identity is crucial to social movements seeking to communicate clear and coherent messages to the broader society. However, more often than not, collective actors will be composed of a plurality of groups, interests, and orientations that can conflict or be in tension with one another. Here too researchers are called upon to intervene in the collective action of social movements. Indeed, although he is attentive to methodological issues, Melucci's (1989: 251) model nevertheless requires that researchers do not merely reveal the existence of plurality, conflict, and tension in collective action, but that they also play an active part in structuring the gestalt of contemporary social movements and their composite groups.

Over time, research and methods have become important areas of interest for social movement scholars, although it could not be said that there is, as yet, a coherent literature on the topic. Nonetheless, there have been a few journal special issues dedicated to the topic of research methods and social movements, including *Qualitative Sociology* 21(4) 1998 ('Qualitative Methods and Social Movement Research'); *Social Movement Studies* 11(2) 2012 ('The Ethics of Research on Activism'); and *Mobilization* 18(4) 2013 ('Frontiers of Social Movement Methodology'). There are also numerous individual journal articles on this and related areas, including, but not limited to, the following: Crist and McCarthy (1996); Earl (2013); Giugni and Yamasaki (2009); Harris (2012); Hug and Wisler (1998); Lofland (1997); and Walgrave and Verhulst (2011).

Various ways of approaching the study of collective action were considered in an early volume edited by Diani and Eyerman (1992). More recently, Klandermans and Staggenborg (2002) edited a collection, which includes chapters on classic research methods and techniques, such as surveys, interviewing, and case studies. More specialist texts include Joseph et al.'s (2007: 2) edited book on 'political ethnography', by which they mean an approach that 'draws upon close-up observation of politics in action to scrutinize the dispositions, skills, desires, and emotions of a variety of political actors and the meanings that they attach to their practices'.

Some textbooks on social movements do contain information on research methods, although this material can be somewhat limited and, to my knowledge, it never, if ever, appears as a discrete chapter. For example, in her text on social movements, Staggenborg (2011: 47–49) devotes some space to look at the use of different methods in social movement research, such as surveys, in-depth interviews, and participant observation. She notes, but does not consider in any detail, that each method has its strengths and weaknesses, concluding that 'the use of multiple methods within and across empirical studies has been critical to the development of social movement theory' (Staggenborg 2011: 49). I use this example only to illustrate the point that a consideration of research methodology in textbooks on social movements is largely lacking, and in that respect this book is, alas, no exception.

UNDERSTANDING SOCIAL MOVEMENTS

Given that social movements aim to change society for the good, it would seem logical that a fundamental task for us in this book lies in understanding social movements as collective agents of change. As we saw in the last section, some researchers believe they have a role to play here: intervening in social action to aid movements' quest for change. However, as noted earlier, not all social movements are progressive, which is a theme that arises in Chapter 2, when we explore some of the early attempts to understand social movements and other forms of collective behaviour. Some of the early collective behaviour theorists saw any kind of mass action as inherently irrational and ultimately dangerous, since it was associated, respectively, with the suppression of individual free will or with the emergence of fascism in twentieth-century Europe. As we shall see, though, not all of the early theories of social movements regarded collective behaviour as necessarily negative or bad.

In Chapter 3, we turn to consider the other extreme, if you will, of the collective action spectrum, when we look at theories of social movements as essentially *rational collective actors* (i.e., means-ends oriented). Hence, according to resource mobilization theorists, a movement's success is determined by its effective mobilization of resources (means) to achieve certain political goals (ends). As such, much of the material covered in this chapter falls under the political process umbrella mentioned earlier. In Chapter 4, we consider new social movement theory, which emerged partly as a critique of the overly rationalistic resource mobilization perspective and the overly political focus of the political process model, both of which, it is argued, have tended to ignore the hidden cultural dimensions of social movements. As with other approaches, new social movement theory has not been without its critics, and in this chapter we will consider those, addressing, among other things, the seemingly intractable question, 'what's new about new social movements?'

As a perspective that privileges the cultural over the political dimensions of social movements, new social movement theory can be seen as a product of the 'cultural turn' that occurred in the social sciences towards the end of the twentieth century. However, a concern for the cultural aspects of social movement activity is not limited to new social movement theory. So, in Chapter 5, we extend our cultural analysis of movements to examine other broadly cultural aspects of protest, looking, for instance, at the role of passion and emotion, storytelling and narrative, music, and other performative elements of collective action. Chapter 6 considers religious movements and social movements. It explores some of the similarities and differences between religious and social movements by looking, for example, at the religious or spiritual qualities of social movements and the political and emancipatory features of religion and religious movements.

Chapter 7 considers the confluence of geography and social movement studies. It looks at both the physical and nonphysical spaciality of social movements and protest, which includes issues relating to geopolitical space, social space, and cultural and identity space. It also examines how protest space is policed and controlled by state authorities. Chapter 8 looks at the relationship between social movements and media, which includes the mainstream mass media, new digital technologies such as the Internet and camera phones, and social media. Among other things, Chapter 9 considers globalization and transnational activism, and includes a look at the example of the global justice movement. (And here it should be stressed that, in each chapter of the book, examples of actual cases are provided to illustrate theoretical and conceptual points.) Chapter 10 is a concluding chapter, which draws together some of the main themes and perspectives that have figured prominently in the book. Our journey begins now though by looking at the origins of social movement studies in early works of social psychology and collective behaviour theory.

CHAPTER 2

Origins of social movement studies

█ INTRODUCTION

It is an intention of this chapter to provide an introduction to key theories and concepts in early studies of collective behaviour and social movements. The chapter begins by examining the early social psychological theories of crowd behaviour and mass psychosis of Le Bon and Freud. According to both perspectives, collective behaviour is a threat to the normal social order, although updated psychological research into crowd action suggests otherwise. The case of the Nuremburg rallies is used to illustrate the role of propaganda in collective behaviour. The chapter looks at the sociology of collective behaviour, much of which saw collective behaviour in a positive light. It examines the symbolic interactionist approach of Herbert Blumer, the emergent norm theory of Turner and Killian, and Neil Smelser's structural-functionalist account and value-added model.

The chapter evaluates symbolic interactionist and structuralist perspectives, and shows how these early theories of collective action continue to inform key debates and influence a number of areas of social movement studies today, including research into the 'dramaturgy' of social movements, and analyses of the performative role of colour in contemporary social protests. Accordingly, the chapter considers some of the ways in which earlier theories and studies of social movements connect to later theories and studies, which are examined in subsequent chapters.

Hence, towards end of the chapter, rational choice theory is discussed as a precursor to resource mobilization theory, which is examined in Chapter 3. And, in the conclusion, material presented in later chapters of the book is anticipated when we consider how older ideas, theories, and concepts remain pertinent today, as is evident, for example, in the influence of symbolic interactionism on the study of culture and processes of identity formation in new social movements (Chapter 4), the positive role of emotions in collective action and the performative dimensions of protest (Chapter 5), and connections between religious movements and social movements (Chapter 6).

SOCIAL PSYCHOLOGY OF CROWDS

In 1897, Gustave Le Bon published *The Crowd: A Study of the Popular Mind*. Writing from a social psychological perspective, Le Bon set out to establish the general characteristics of a 'psychological crowd', the most striking feature of which he said was the following:

> Whoever be the individuals that compose it, however like or unlike be their mode of life, their occupations, their character, or their intelligence, the fact that they have been transformed into a crowd puts them in possession of a sort of collective mind which makes them feel, think, and act in a manner quite different from that in which each individual of them would feel, think, and act were he in a state of isolation.
>
> (Le Bon, quoted in Evans 1969: 12)

For Le Bon, the individual in a crowd loses their ability to exercise free will and becomes an automaton; and they lose any sense of civilization and cultivation, becoming a barbarian guided by instinct. Thus, he concluded, 'the crowd is always intellectually inferior to the isolated individual' (Le Bon, quoted in Evans 1969: 14). However, while for Le Bon a crowd may be criminal, it can also be heroic: 'It is crowds rather than isolated individuals that may be induced to run the risk of death to secure the triumph of a creed or an idea' (Le Bon, quoted in Evans 1969: 14).

Updated accounts of crowd behaviour and collective action in social psychology offer a critical perspective on the older theories of people like Le Bon. For example, Drury and Reicher (2000) critique

Le Bon's idea that crowd behaviour is irrational and destructive. In accordance with theorists such as Turner and Killian (1987 [1957]), which are considered later, Drury and Reicher argue crowd action is socially meaningful. They are interested not only in how crowd action reflects social meanings, but also how it creates and develops new meanings. In so doing, they build upon research conducted by themselves and others, which elaborates a social identity model of crowd behaviour, positing that, contrary to Le Bon's theory, and the 'de-individuation' research it precipitated:

> . . . individuals in crowds do not lose their identity but rather shift from behaving in terms of disparate individual identities to behaving in terms of a contextually specified common social identity; hence, rather than losing control over their behaviour, crowd members judge and act by reference to the understandings which define the relevant social identification.
>
> (Drury and Reicher 2000: 581)

Significantly, Drury and Reicher (2000: 580, original emphasis) distinguish their work from much of the sociological research into social movements that forms the bulk of the content of this book, since, according to them, 'the precise role of such intergroup dynamics in bringing about psychological consequences for members of different groups is not examined in these accounts; these are *sociological* accounts which merely note psychological change rather than *psychological* accounts of such change'. Nonetheless, their approach chimes with key themes in the sociology of social movements. They stress the role of free will and agency, evidenced by, for instance, their preference for the use of the term crowd *action* over collective/crowd *behaviour*. Moreover, they emphasize cognitive processes and the rationality that is exercised by crowd members who have the ability to 'judge and act'. Finally, their use of the phrase 'common social identity' is reminiscent of the notion of 'collective identity', which is used in social movement studies, and especially in new social movement theory (see Chapter 4).

COLLECTIVE BEHAVIOUR THEORY

The work of Le Bon was an important launch pad for future research into collective behaviour. In a period marked by the emergence of fascism in Europe, many social scientists took a dim view of collective behaviour, which was regarded as irrational and pathological. Writing in the 1920s, Sigmund Freud (1945 [1921]) feared that as opposed to when they think and act as individuals, people in crowds behave irrationally and with a mob or herdlike mentality.

While he agreed that people in crowds and spontaneous gatherings think and act differently from individuals, Herbert Blumer (1969: 69) argued collective behaviour could also have productive and emergent qualities, the study of which, he claimed, concerns examining 'the ways in which the social order comes into existence, in the sense of the emergence and solidification of new forms of collective behaviour'. When he originally published his outline of collective behaviour in 1934, Blumer identified four 'elementary collective groupings': (i) the *acting crowd*; (ii) the *expressive crowd*; (iii) the *mass*; and (iv) the *public*.

The *acting crowd* is spontaneous and momentary. It lacks organization, leadership, identity, and a 'we-consciousness'. However, the distinguishing feature of the acting crowd is that attention is directed towards a common objective or goal. The *expressive crowd*, on the other hand, has no such goal or purpose: '[I]ts impulses and feelings are spent in mere expressive actions, usually unrestrained physical movements, which give release to tension without having any other purpose' (Blumer 1969: 82–83). For Blumer, examples of this kind of expressive collective behaviour include the carnival or the dancing crowds of primitive sects.

The *mass* is composed of people who participate in mass behaviour, 'such as those who are excited by some national event, those who share in a land boom, those who are interested in a murder trial which is reported in the press, or those who participate in some large migration' (Blumer 1969: 86). Finally, Blumer referred to the *public* as being a group of people who, first, are confronted by an issue; second, are divided in their opinion as to how to address the issue; and, third, are engaged in discussion about the issue.[1]

BOX 2.1 PROPAGANDA AND COLLECTIVE BEHAVIOUR: THE NUREMBURG RALLIES

On considering the role of propaganda in his outline of collective behaviour, Blumer noted the importance of social psychological processes that were apparent during the Nuremburg rallies, which may be observed at other mass gatherings:

In the area of public discussion and public consideration, propaganda operates to mould opinions and judgments not on the basis of the merits of an issue, but chiefly by playing upon emotional attitudes and feelings. Its aim is to implant an attitude or value which comes to be felt by people as natural, true, and proper, and, therefore, as one which expresses itself spontaneously and without coercion.

(Blumer 1969: 94)

The Nuremburg rallies, held in Germany between 1933 and 1935, are a good illustration of how the social psychology of crowds works in ways described by social scientists, as well as highlighting the dangers of mass behaviour. Footage of the rallies was recorded by Leni Riefenstahl whose documentary film, *Triumph of the Will*, depicted the 1934 National Socialist (Nazi) party congress (see Figure 2.1).

© Pictorial Press Ltd./Alamy

Figure 2.1 *Triumph of the Will* poster for the 1936 film about the 1934 Nuremberg Nazi party rally

Throughout Riefenstahl's film, which was us█
Adolf Hitler is presented as a charismatic lea█
minds of his devoted audience by means of █
relationship or connection exists betwee█
is hardly surprising Nazism has been d█
2007). Indeed, like a religious event, propag█
burg rallies utilized iconic symbols and imagery, █
suggesting Nazism was very much a 'cult of personality', █
authority of a charismatic leader, or what Max Weber (1947 [19█
as 'charismatic authority'.

SYMBOLIC INTERACTIONISM: BLUMER'S THEORY OF SOCIAL MOVEMENTS

Alongside his theory of collective behaviour, Blumer (1969: 99) developed a typology of social movements, which he defined as 'collective enterprises seeking to establish a new order of life'. He showed how in the career of social movements they typically begin as amorphous and poorly organized, after which they develop a culture and social organization. Blumer identified three kinds of social movements: (i) *general social movements*; (ii) *specific social movements*; and (iii) *expressive social movements*.

Examples of *general social movements* are the labour movement, the student movement, the women's movement, and the peace movement. These movements have brought about changes in values or 'cultural drifts', examples of which include 'the increased value of health, the belief in free education, the extension of the franchise, the emancipation of women, the increasing regard for children, and the increasing prestige of science' (Blumer 1969: 100). General social movements operate over a wide range of areas of society and have vague aims, such as the women's movement general aim to emancipate women. Accordingly, general social movements lack organization, an established leadership, and a recognized membership.

Importantly, general social movements form the basis for the development of *specific social movements*, which are the 'crystallization of much of the motivation of dissatisfaction, hope, and desire awakened by the general social movement and the focusing of this motivation on some specific objective' (Blumer 1969: 102). Here, Blumer uses the example of the anti-slavery movement, which was to some extent the individual expression of the broader nineteenth-century humanitarian movement.

Defining characteristics of specific social movements include a well-defined objective or goal, the development of organization and structure to achieve that goal, clear leadership, and a membership with a 'we-consciousness'. Blumer described the five ways in which specific social movements grow and become organized:

1. *Agitation* typically occurs in the early stages of a movement's development. It is a means of exciting people, functioning to stir them up and awaken in them new ideas and feelings of restlessness and dissatisfaction.
2. *Esprit de corps* is the development of a collective feeling of belonging and an important means of creating a sense of solidarity among members. This is achieved by the following means: the identification of an enemy; informal and communal association (e.g., singing, dancing, joking, and having fun); and ceremonial behaviour and ritual, such as using paraphernalia or sentimental symbols such as slogans, songs, poems, and clothing at meetings, rallies, demonstrations, and parades (see Box 2.2).
3. *Morale* is generated out of a set of convictions around the rectitude of the movement's purpose, faith that the movement will attain its goal, and belief in its 'scared mission' (Blumer 1969: 109). For Blumer, the development of morale is quasi-religious: members develop a sectarian attitude akin to a religious faith, movement leaders assume the status of religious idols, and sacred texts are adopted, such as Karl Marx's *Das Kapital* as the 'bible' of the communist movement.
4. *Ideology* consists of 'a body of doctrines, beliefs, and myths' (Blumer 1969: 110). It is the philosophy and psychology of a movement, whose purpose is to provide a set of values, convictions, criticisms, and defences.
5. *Tactics* play a role in gaining adherents and keeping them, and in reaching objectives.

BOX 2.2 SOCIAL MOVEMENT COLOURS: 'REBEL COLOURS'

Blumer argued that the paraphernalia of rituals is key to the development of a movement's esprit de corps. Although he did not expressly mention the use of colour here, other more recent studies illustrate how significant colour is for some social movements. Using data on the protests against the International Monetary Fund (IMF) and World Bank meetings held in Prague in September 2000, Chesters and Welsh (2004) show how the colours of particular marches reflected different collective identities, political perspectives, and protest repertoires (or tactics). They propose that the three 'Rebel Colours', Blue, Pink, and Yellow, acted as collective 'sense-making devices' or 'frames' (a concept discussed in more detail in Chapter 3, but for now we can take to mean, 'a collective definition of the situation' [Benford and Hunt 1992: 38]), which enabled individuals to orient to movements of which they were members and events in which they participated (Chesters and Welsh 2004: 318).

During a series of large international meetings, protesters developed the idea that separate marches could use different colours, which eventually became the modus operandi for the 'global day of action' that took place on 26 September (S26), when the IMF/Work Bank conference opened. Protestors agreed the coloured marches would reflect political affiliation, ideological position or affective ties (e.g., regional identity, language), or affinity with particular protest repertoires. However, the use of colours was not limited to protest repertoires, but extended, among other things, to politically significant 'playful engagement'. As such, '[i]t was agreed that where possible the colours assigned to the marches should avoid familiar political associations, thereby confusing the authorities and creating ambiguity around what might otherwise become fixed expressions of particular identities' (Chesters and Welsh 2004: 322). In a separate study, Marian Sawer (2007: 40) has shown how people's taken-for-granted emotional identification with political colours along party lines (e.g., red for labour, blue for conservative) has led to *cognitive dissonance* over recent years in the United States where conservative Republican states are described as 'red states', and Democrat states are 'blue states'. We will return to Sawer's research in Chapter 5 when we look at emotions and social movements.

As it is for many social movement scholars, Chesters and Welsh are concerned with how the S26 protesters – which formed part of a highly diverse global social movement – were able to coalesce for the duration of the marches. That is to say, how was unity, or what Blumer called a 'we-consciousness', achieved in the face of internal diversity? Their answer is that 'the Rebel Colours provided the framework that enabled diverse social movement groups and disorganizations to act in concert for the duration of the IMF and World Bank protests' (Chesters and Welsh 2004: 332). Moreover, insofar as 'the "Rebel" Colours indicate difference and pragmatism', according to Chesters and Welsh (2004: 331–332), 'they demonstrate an internal dialogue that is strongly opposed to homogenization of a political perspective, protest repertoire or tactical orientation'. In other words, the Rebel Colours were the means through which:

> . . . the complex set of orientations towards collective action exhibited by different individuals and groups were assimilated. Diversity of political perspective, preference for protest repertoire, distinctive cultures of resistance and strategic orientation were subsumed using a mechanism that allowed for difference, holding it in tension, both within the respective marches and between them.
>
> (Chesters and Welsh 2004: 326)

Chesters and Welsh unpack the various meanings of each colour to show how colour indicated political standpoint and protest repertoire preference, as well as serving as a common denominator between a diversity of people and groups. The Yellow March offered a critique both of the neoliberal approach of the IMF and World Bank, and of traditional modes of engaging with political and economic elites. The yellow frame was geared towards direct contact, as well as symbolic critique. Thus:

> . . . Yellow was Ya Basta! [Spanish meaning, 'enough is enough'] in their white overalls with their comic provocations of balloons and water pistols facing lines of riot police clad in black and armed with APCs and guns, a classic exploitation of the black/white binarism of good and evil, which was used to maximum effect.
>
> (Chesters and Welsh 2004: 327)

The blue frame was direct, confrontational, and without compromise, and although regarded as problematic, violence in defence was deemed acceptable, and sometimes regarded necessary in offence by those identifying with this frame. The Blue March drew upon various symbolic resources of anarchism, and it attracted most of the traditional anarchist groups of central Europe, many of whom were clad in black and wore masks to protect their identity (and offer some protection from tear gas in anticipation of confrontations with the police). Indeed, the blue frame is a familiar and recurrent one, associated with many social movements across both Europe and the United States, providing

> . . . an unapologetic rationale for engagement with few limits, it positively affirms the distinction between violence against property and violence against the person, yet maintains a pragmatic assessment of power which

suggests that violence against the person is a likely outcome of 'revolutionary activity'.

(Chesters and Welsh 2004: 328)

By contrast, the pink frame signified nonviolence. Even though the colour pink has long been associated with the gay and lesbian movement, interviewees Chesters and Welsh spoke with argued that pink was chosen for its lack of political connotations. The tactics used by those associated with the pink frame derived from the protest repertoires developed in the United Kingdom by Reclaim The Streets and Earth First!, which were involved in organizing anti-road protests, impromptu street parties, and ecologically oriented anti-capitalist direct actions (see Martin 2014). Moreover, the pink frame emphasized performative repertoires: playful, ludic, and carnivalesque forms of protest involving dance and theatre and the like. Tactical Frivolity were an influential group during S26 who, instead of wearing protective clothing (like those involved in the Blue March), developed an implicit critique of the routinized violence (i.e., clashes with police) that occurs at many protest events by, for instance, donning carnival costumes and wielding pink feather dusters.

Unlike specific social movements, *expressive movements* do not seek to affect social change. Rather, they constitute expressive forms of collective behaviour that can have profound effects upon individuals and the social order. The two kinds of expressive movements identified by Blumer are religious and fashion movements. The tension and unrest that give rise to the emergence of religious movements are released, not in purposive action, but in expression. Intense feelings of intimacy, exaltation and ecstasy, and the development of an esprit de corps are prominent features of religious movements, which include both cults and sects.

Fashion movements are expressive because they provide 'an opportunity for the expression of dispositions and tastes' (Blumer 1969: 118). Fashion not only relates to clothing, but also manners, the arts, literature, and philosophy. Although Blumer says the fashion movement is a genuine expressive movement, it differs significantly from other movements he examines. For instance, it does not develop a 'we-consciousness' and esprit de corps. No morale is built up among participants, and there is no ideology, no recognized leadership, and no tactics. The success of fashion simply depends upon the acceptance of a particular style or pattern.

BOX 2.3 EMERGENT NORM THEORY

Building on Blumer's symbolic interactionist perspective, Turner and Killian (1987 [1957]) developed what has become known as 'emergent norm theory'. They argued that most, if not all, social movement activists have an acute sense of what is just and unjust: 'A movement is inconceivable apart from a vital sense that some established practice or mode of thought is wrong and ought to be replaced' (Turner and Killian 1987 [1957]: 242). Gradually, members of a movement develop *new perspectives* by recognizing the injustice of prevailing conditions. An example would be the release of a best-selling book that crystal-lizes people's awareness of a particular issue, such as Betty Friedan's publication in 1963 of *The Feminine Mystique*, which 'crystallized the new perspectives on women's roles for the emerging women's movement' (Turner and Killian 1987 [1957]: 244). Another example mentioned earlier when we looked at Blumer's category of specific social movements is Marx's tome, *Das Kapital*.

The realization of a new perspective is often fuelled by *aroused indignation*, which typically occurs within a much shorter timeframe than the develop-ment of new perspectives. An example here would be when open conflict or antagonism takes place between activists who question existing conditions, and their opponents, as often happens at public protests and demonstrations. In sum, the positive effect of new perspectives combined with the negative effect of aroused indignation enables a movement to develop a revised sense of justice, or what Turner and Killian (1987 [1957]: 245) call, 'the emergent norm', which, they argued, is 'one essential aspect of any social movement'.

SMELSER'S STRUCTURAL-FUNCTIONALISM AND THE VALUE-ADDED MODEL

Like Blumer, Neil Smelser regarded collective behaviour as purposive behaviour whereby people attempt to reconstitute their social environ-ment. They do that in the name of a 'generalized belief', which Smelser (1964: 117) likened to a magical belief, in that, 'the world is portrayed in terms of omnipotent forces, conspiracies, and extravagant promises, all of which are imminent'. Smelser sought to explain collective behav-iour by employing a 'value-added' approach, which places each determinant of collective behaviour on a scale from *general* to *specific*. Smelser regarded each determinant as a necessary but not a sufficient condition for the occurrence of collective behaviour: taken together, each constitutes a necessary *and* sufficient condition for the occurrence of an episode of collective behaviour. Hence, for Smelser (1964: 120), the value-added approach 'is a logical patterning of determinants, each seen as contributing its "value" to the explanation of the episode'.

BOX 2.4 DETERMINANTS OF COLLECTIVE BEHAVIOUR: EXAMPLE OF A FINANCIAL PANIC

Smelser used the example of a financial panic to show how each element contributes incrementally to an episode of collective behaviour. The following five determinants (from general to specific) are necessary for collective behaviour to occur:

1. *Structural conduciveness* – this refers to the ability of people to dispose of resources at will. In the case of a financial panic, this might entail the free and rapid disposal of stocks and shares, which would make panic possible. However, that would only make panic *possible*, since structural conduciveness alone does not cause panic, but merely establishes a range of circumstances in which panic can occur, while ruling out others in which panic could not occur.

2. *Strain* – the threat of financial loss is an obvious strain in relation to financial panic (see Figure 2.2). However, as with structural conduciveness, the mere

© North Wind Picture Archives/Alamy

Figure 2.2 Depositors making a run on a bank during a financial panic in the 1800s

threat of financial loss will not, in and of itself, cause panic. Accordingly, strain operates within the scope of conduciveness.

3. *Growth of a generalized belief* – here the threat is exaggerated and seen as imminent and ominous. In the case of financial panic, this results in a hysterical belief or 'a cognitive restructuring of an uncertain threat into a definite prognostication of disaster'. Moreover, 'precipitating events', such as the closure of a bank, serve to reinforce this belief and provide 'evidence' to support it.

4. *Mobilize people for action* – mobilizing in the name of a generalized belief may take the form of a single spontaneous event initiated by a rumour about a 'panic sell' by a leading stockholder, or it may derive from a deliberate and highly organized social movement.

5. *Social control* – in a general sense, this refers to 'counterdeterminants' for the conditions of collective behaviour listed earlier. Counterdeterminants may be preventative (dealing with conduciveness and strain), or they may appear only after an incidence of collective behaviour has occurred. In a financial panic, for example, social control may occur either by spiking rumours or by preventing sellers from selling.

Source: Smelser (1964: 119–120)

In his book, *Theory of Collective Behaviour*, Smelser (1962) gives examples of five basic types of collective behaviour:

1. The *panic* or 'a collective flight based on hysterical belief' (Smelser 1962: 131). People accept a belief about a generalized threat and flee from established patterns of social interaction to preserve life, property, or power that are under threat. In this way, the panic meets all of the criteria for classifying it as an episode of collective behaviour: it is collective, uninstitutionalized, arises out of strain, and is based on a generalized belief. Actual settings where panic occurs include the battlefield, a sinking ship, and burning buildings.

2. The *craze* or 'mobilization for action based on a positive wish-fulfilment belief' (Smelser 1962: 171). Crazes can occur in many spheres of society. In the economic sphere, crazes might arise as speculative booms in securities or miscellaneous items such as tulips or mulberry trees. In the political sphere, crazes might manifest as 'unanticipated bandwagon surges' for candidates at political conventions (Smelser 1962: 172). In the expressive or cultural sphere, crazes include fad and fashion in clothes, architecture, vehicles, and art. In the religious sphere, sects or religious communes and other forms of revivalism constitute examples of crazes.

3. The *hostile outburst* is defined as 'mobilization for action under a hostile belief' (Smelser 1962: 226). Participants in an outburst attack someone who is blamed as responsible for a disturbing set of circumstances. Examples include a mob burning down the home of a local politician who has made an unpopular decision, or rioting strikers angry that 'scabs' (strike-breakers) have been hired by their employer to assume the work roles of the striking employees. Given that hostility is a key component of social movements, it should be no surprise that hostile outbursts often accompany large-scale social movements, such that normally peaceful protest may erupt into violence and confrontation with the authorities.

4. The *norm-oriented movement* 'is an attempt to restore, protect, modify, or create norms in the name of a generalized belief' (Smelser 1962: 270). Participants in norm-oriented movements might attempt to influence norms *directly*. Here, Smelser gives the example of feminist groups seeking to establish private education for women. Alternatively, norm-oriented movements may try to *induce* an established institution, authority, or body to affect norms – for instance, groups lobbying parliament to change public policy on particular matters. Such movements might try to affect any kind of normative transformation (e.g., economic, educational, political, religious), and can span the political spectrum, from reactionary, conservative, progressive, to radical. A norm-oriented movement may result in a 'normative innovation', such as a new law, custom, association, or political party faction (Smelser 1962: 170). Smelser (1962: 272) also makes the following important distinction:

> Many norm-oriented movements occur independently of value-oriented movements, which call for more sweeping changes. The agitation for shorter hours of labour (a norm-oriented movement) in the United States, for instance, has been limited to demands for normative change; on the whole it has not been attached to movements which challenge the values of the capitalist system.

Moreover, like Blumer, Smelser (1962: 273) distinguishes between norm-oriented movements and general social movements, the latter of which 'possess neither sufficiently crystallized beliefs nor a sufficient degree of mobilization to fall in the category of collective outbursts [but] provide a backdrop from which many specific norm-oriented movements emanate'.

5. The *value-oriented movement* is 'a collective attempt to restore, protect, modify, or create values in the name of a generalized belief'

(Smelser 1962: 313). Smelser distinguishes between religious and secular value-oriented beliefs. Examples of religious belief include various sects, such as Seventh Day Adventists, Methodists, Shakers, Mennonites, Christian Scientists, and Bahais. Secular value-oriented beliefs, on the other hand, include nationalism, communism, socialism, anarchism, and syndicalism (i.e., trade unionism). Significantly, beliefs frequently involve a mixture of religious and secular elements. An example would be Christian socialism.

For Smelser, each of these types of collective behaviour stands in a hierarchy of complexity and inclusiveness. So, while a norm-oriented movement may contain elements of panic, a panic cannot incorporate elements of a craze unless it becomes a craze. Thus, a higher level of collective behaviour may include a lower level of behaviour, but not vice versa.

EVALUATING BLUMER AND SMELSER

The main weakness of Blumer's approach derives from his focus on social psychological factors. He thus ignores structural factors and the contexts within which social movements emerge. This is something addressed by Smelser. However, in many respects, Smelser offers a mere inversion of Blumer's theory: 'He is stronger where Blumer is weak (structure) but weak where Blumer is strong, particularly in the question of agency' (Crossley 2002: 54). Despite the ostensible merit in wedding these two seemingly complementary theories, Crossley warns that Smelser's attempt to transcend Blumer's account tends only to highlight and reinforce the strengths of the latter and the former's weaknesses in two specific ways.

First, Smelser's neglect of agency coupled with his mechanistic and reductionist account of generalized belief formation highlights the need for an approach, like the one developed by Blumer, that focuses on the role of 'reasonable' communication and social interaction in the generation of movements and collective action:

Human agents collectively make social movements albeit in circumstances that are not of their choosing. Their generalized beliefs arise out of their interactions and discussions, and these same discussions serve to frame and channel their immediate emotional reactions to situations.

(Crossley 2002: 54)

2) Second, problems arising from Smelser's sole focus on the external factors that shape social movement formation might be remedied by recourse to Blumer, who emphasized the interactions between social movement participants and the wider outcomes of these interactions, such as the development of an esprit de corps, morale, ideology, and tactics.

THE ENDURING INFLUENCE OF COLLECTIVE BEHAVIOUR THEORIES AND SYMBOLIC INTERACTIONISM

In their introduction to social movement studies, della Porta and Diani (2006: 13) argue that '[t]he sociology of social movements owes many of its insights to students of the collective behaviour school', because, among other things, here, 'for the first time, collective movements are defined as meaningful acts, driving often necessary and beneficial social change'. Crossley (2002: 37), too, shows how one of Blumer's main contributions to the study of social movements has been his appreciation of movement cultures and the various functions they perform in creating solidarity and orchestrating mobilization. He goes on to say, quite rightly, that Blumer's pioneering work in this area is rarely recognized in contemporary social movement research, which only recently has re-established an interest in movement cultures and collective identity (see Chapters 4 and 5). In a rare instance of recognition, however, Johnston et al. (1994: 17) show how contemporary approaches to the study of collective identity 'acknowledge a strong symbolic interactionist influence', a tradition that 'points to interaction among social movement participants as the locus of research on identity processes' (see also Martin 2002: 85). An example of how both collective behaviour theory and symbolic interactionism has influenced subsequent research into social movements is presented in Box 2.5.

BOX 2.5 SOCIAL MOVEMENTS AS DRAMAS

As stated earlier, collective behaviour theory emerged largely to counter ideas about collective behaviour as irrational or pathological. Accordingly, much of the material we have looked at so far points to the potentially positive, creative, and productive qualities of collective action. During the 1970s, resource mobilization theory emerged also as a reaction against negative views of collective behaviour. It sought to 'recast movement participants as ultra-rationalistic actors devoid of feeling' (Benford and Hunt 1992: 50). However, as we will see in later parts of the book, resource mobilization theory has been criticized for overstating the rational aspects of collective action to the detriment of other elements that are regarded by some as equally important, such as social movement cultures and the emotional side of protest.

For example, Benford and Hunt have argued that since its ascendency, the pendulum has swung too far in the direction of resource mobilization theory, which has meant a strict focus on rationality and resources (e.g., people, money, ideas, services), and has caused social movement scholars to neglect the intersubjective and interpretative *processes* by which meanings are developed, sustained, and transformed. In short, by focusing on the objective factors associated with social movement mobilization, resource mobilization theorists have failed to look at subjective factors.

To understand the *dynamics* of collective action and thus show *how* collective action is achieved as an ongoing accomplishment, Benford and Hunt have developed a dramaturgical approach. Influenced by the pioneering work of sociologist Erving Goffman, they regard social movements as dramas 'in which protagonists and antagonists compete to affect audiences' interpretations of power relations in a variety of domains, including those pertaining to religious, political, economic or lifestyle arrangements' (Benford and Hunt 1992: 38). Attempting to understand power from the point of view of movement participants, Benford and Hunt (1992: 38) show 'how they collectively construct their images of power and how they struggle to alter extant power relations'. For them, movement actors define and communicate power by employing four dramatic techniques: (i) *scripting*, (ii) *staging*, (iii) *performing*, and (iv) *interpreting*.

Scripting refers to 'the development of a set of directions that define the scene, identify actors and outline expected behaviour' (Benford and Hunt 1992: 38). Social movement scripting starts with the development of dramatis personae, or a cast of characters, which includes roles for antagonists (e.g., 'capitalist pigs', 'male chauvinists', 'baby killers', 'warmongers'), victims (who feel a sense of injustice), protagonists (e.g., charismatic leaders like Martin Luther King, Jr.), supporting cast members (i.e., activists), and audiences (who may be recruited as supporting cast members). Benford and Hunt show how, once recruited, the cast's ongoing involvement depends on a 'vocabulary of motives', which provide adherents with compelling reasons for taking action and justifying that action in relation to movement goals. Among other things, this entails the scripting and staging of emotions (see Chapter 5), which dramatizes the exercise and/or abuse of power.

Benford and Hunt (1992: 41–42) give the example of a carefully orchestrated disarmament event held in 1985, where members of the audience wept as American air force personnel, who dropped nuclear bombs on Hiroshima and Nagasaki at the end of the Second World War, broke down and sobbed when reconciled with Japanese survivors. However, social movements cannot survive on emotion alone. To endure, they must have some level of organization: 'Too little passion with too much organization fails to inspire participants; but too much passion with too little organization reduces a potentially powerful group to an undirected crowd' (Benford and Hunt 1992: 42). One way organization is achieved is via the staging of movement performances.

Staging refers to 'appropriating, managing and directing materials, audiences and performing regions' (Benford and Hunt 1992: 43). That involves the maintenance and expansion of a movement organization's capacity to convey its ideas about power, which also requires it garner and manage money and other resources. From a dramaturgical perspective, staging entails developing and manipulating symbols, and making sure performances are consistent with the script. For instance, it would be inconsistent for peace campaigners to stage an event where some parts of the supporting cast displayed symbols of guns, clenched fists, and the burning of flags, because that would be antithetical to the nonviolent script of the peace movement.

Because social movement dramas require audiences, it is also important they promote and publicize their activities by, for instance, distributing newsletters, leaflets, posters, and press releases. Lastly, because staging is an interactive process, organizers and antagonists have to adjust to one another's actions. However, most often, antagonists attempt to limit the places movement performances can be staged by controlling physical spaces (e.g., erecting architectural barriers such as fences and restricting free assembly by issuing 'protest permits'). One reason for this is that antagonists are 'typically involved in managing their own dramas, including preventing counter-performances that might upstage or disrupt their performances' (Benford and Hunt 1992: 44).

Performing refers to 'the demonstration and enactment of power', which 'concretizes ideas regarding the struggle between protagonists and antagonists and reveals to audiences ways they can achieve or preserve desirable power relations' (Benford and Hunt 1992: 45). Performing involves 'dramaturgical loyalty' (performers are committed to a movement's definitions of a situation or 'emergent norms'), 'dramaturgical discipline' (espousing the appropriate 'vocabulary of motives', sustaining self-control to maintain a movement's affective line, and avoiding inappropriate behaviour such as disclosing secrets), and 'dramaturgical circumspection' (preparation in advance to adjust and improvise performances as and when unforeseen developments occur).

© Lee W. Nelson, www.iNeTours.com

Figure 2.3 Plowshares sculpture, UN Headquarters, New York

The plowshares sculpture was created by Evgeniy Vuchetic and is located in the grounds of the UN Headquarters in New York City. The sculpture was a gift from the Soviet Union in 1959, and features the following verse from the Old Testament, which acts as an inspiration to peace activists: 'And they shall beat their swords into plowshares' (Isaiah 2:4).

Jacobsson and Lindblom (2012) have recently shown how 'dramaturgical control' operates by examining the carefully choreographed actions of the Plowshares peace movement in Sweden (see Figure 2.3). Here, the action scripts are articulated clearly and are learned, rehearsed, and internalized via the use of repetitive role-playing, which prepares activists for collective action with no room for improvisation. Indeed, unpredictability would be dangerous, as other collective actors could become violent if they feel threatened. And, for this reason, argue Jacobsson and Lindblom (2012: 54), 'to be able to adhere to the script no matter what happens during the action, the activists practise poise under pressure'.

Interpreting refers to 'the process of individually or collectively making sense out of symbols, talk, action and the environment, or, more succinctly, determining what is going on' (Benford and Hunt 1992: 48). Accordingly, '[i]nterpreting is a never-ending social activity that makes movement scripting, staging and performance possible' (Benford and Hunt 1992: 48). For Benford and Hunt, interpretations are the very object of movement dramas. Performances attempt to affect the ways audiences interpret reality, which is interpretative work that essentially concerns relations of power:

> It identifies who has and who lacks power, portrays how it is wielded, presents an alternative vision of power arrangements and articulates how such transformations might be realised. Movement interpretive work thus stimulates audiences to redefine their situations as unjust and mutable so that existing power structures can be altered.
>
> (Benford and Hunt 1992: 48)

SUMMARY

Benford and Hunt's work on the dramaturgical aspects of collective action is interesting, not only for its substantive content, but also because it provides some insight into past and present directions in social movement studies. Hence, their ideas about the dramaturgy of social movements build upon collective behaviour theory, including Turner and Killian's emergent norm theory, and their notion that a sense of injustice is crucial to all social movements. Their work is also grounded in perspectives that continue to inform studies in social movements today, like the analysis of framing processes, which we will look at in Chapter 3, as well as ongoing interest in the 'dynamics of contention' (McAdam et al. 2001). Benford and Hunt's work alludes to what are now firmly established areas of research in social movement studies, which are covered in subsequent chapters of this book, such as concerns relating to emotions and 'passionate politics' (Chapter 5), and the social control and policing of protest (Chapter 7).

Moreover, the influence of symbolic interactionism, evident in Benford and Hunt's focus on the subjective, qualitative, and interpretive aspects of social movements, continues to inform qualitative research into social movements (see Chapter 1), such as approaches that see narrative (stories, tales, anecdotes, allegories) as important for social movement framing (Polletta 1998a: 420–422) – for example, 'how frames are expressed and made concrete [. . .] through the stories that members share, through the collective bundle of narratives that are treated as relevant to the movement ideology' (Fine 1995: 134). However, as we shall see in Chapter 5, even though the framing perspective offers an important corrective to the overly rationalistic and instrumental approach of resource mobilization theorists, it has been criticized by those interested in the emotional aspects of social movements – which includes storytelling and narrative – for overemphasizing cognitive processes in, for example, explaining what motivates people to become involved in collective action.

Benford and Hunt's article should also be seen in the context of the 'cultural turn' that occurred in the human sciences, and which had a profound effect upon social movement studies (Johnston and Klandermans 1995: vii; Martin 2002: 74). While the cultural turn affected the emergence of the framing perspective, which focuses 'on how organizations use values, beliefs, and general cultural trends to their advantages' (Johnston 2009: 3), most notably it influenced ideas about contemporary 'new' social movements, which, it is argued, are concerned principally with culture and lifestyle and processes of collective identity formation, unlike their older counterparts, which were essentially concerned with the strategic mobilization of resources to achieve political and economic ends. Like Benford and Hunt, new social movement theorists developed a critique of resource mobilization theory on the basis that it emphasizes the objective rather than the (inter) subjective factors involved in collective action. In Chapter 4, we consider new social movement theory after looking at resource mobilization theory and allied approaches in Chapter 3. However, before doing so, and considering our present focus on the origins of social movement studies, we will now look at some of the philosophical underpinnings of resource mobilization theory.

RATIONAL CHOICE THEORY AND THE FREE RIDER PROBLEM

Resource mobilization theory has its basis in rational choice theory. In 1965, American economist and social scientist Mancur Olson outlined a theory of collective action in his book, *The Logic of Collective Action.* Olson's ideas are based on neoclassical economics, which attempts to explain human action in terms of individual choices and preferences. It assumes individuals act rationally. That is to say, people seek to maximize the benefits and minimize the costs of their action. Olson reasoned that if these assumptions are correct, collective action would be implausible since rational, self-interested individuals will not act to achieve common interests or public goods. Rather, they would seek only to maximize their own self-interested ends. Far more plausible is the prospect that people will 'free ride', receiving all of the benefits of collective action without incurring any of the costs. Olson presented his basic premise in the introduction to his book as follows:

> Indeed, unless the number of individuals in a group is quite small, or unless there is coercion or some other special device to make individuals act in their common interest, *rational, self-interested individuals will not act to achieve their common or group's interests.*
>
> (Olson 1965: 2, original emphasis)

Collective bargaining provides a case in point. Collective agreements between trade unions and employers benefit all members of the workforce irrespective of union membership. For example, all workers in a particular factory will benefit from a pay award that union officials negotiate with employers. So, what is the benefit to the individual worker in paying fees to join the union when they appear to receive all of the benefits of union activity without incurring the cost of joining? According to Olson's logic, the massive scale of free riding would preclude the possibility for collective action in the first place.

That is why some kind of compulsion is required. This might take the form of coercion, such as the formation of a 'closed shop', that is, where union membership is mandatory. Another approach is to provide positive inducements for membership to offset the resources used by individuals in joining. Olson called these 'selective incentives', which in the case of trade union membership might entail things like offering members preferential prices on bank loans and insurance products, discounts on cinema tickets, or reductions on goods sold at retail shopping outlets.

Besides these 'fringe benefits' union members also stand to benefit from wage claims made by unions. Indeed, in his book about Britain during the mid- to late 1970s, Dominic Sandbrook (2012: 12) says that contrary to the popular belief that trade unionists then were 'bound together by working-class solidarity and a shared dream of a brave new world [. . .] most union members were interested only in their pay packets'. Seemingly, for most people:

> . . . the point of having a union card was not to gain entry level to some socialist paradise but 'to gain tangible rewards',

from a foreign holiday to a new kitchen. Younger workers were accustomed to the fruits of affluence; what they wanted from their union was not so much the New Jerusalem as a new [Ford] Cortina.

(Sandbrook 2012: 12)

CRITIQUES OF RATIONAL CHOICE THEORY

Rational choice theory, or 'rational actor theory', as it is also known, has been subject to criticism, not least because it is premised on a view of people as self-interested and essentially asocial. However, as Crossley (2002: 66) points out, acting strategically presupposes people's inherent sociality: people have 'empathic capacity' to second-guess the probable reactions of others, which is a skill acquired from interaction with and imitation of others. Moreover, Crossley (2002: 67) argues, it is important to ask why individuals participate in collective action from which they stand to receive no direct benefit, such as animal rights activists who advocate entirely on behalf of others, and, in this case, another species.

To be sure, a good deal of social movement activity operates beyond the peculiarities of problems posed by rational choice theory. For instance, solidarity and collective identity are concerns for a number of social movements, and not just contemporary 'new' movements (discussed in Chapter 4), but older movements, too, including the US civil rights movement, which emphasized black pride and identity, and labour movements, which, both historically and presently, emphasize working-class identity and consciousness (Crossley 2002: 67). Moreover, 'pride' has figured as a central motivating factor not only for black activists, but also for gay and lesbian activists (Gould 2001).

Hence, those scholars who are interested in the passionate and emotional aspects of social movements suggest it is ludicrous to postulate that rational calculation provides the impetus for getting involved in collective action. As we shall see in Chapter 5, that view overstates not only rational but also cognitive factors, and thus ignores the notion, recognized by Turner and Killian, that people are often motivated by a sense of injustice, which elicits strong emotional responses, such as anger, indignation, fear, or compassion (Polletta and Amenta 2001: 305). In Chapter 4, we will look at this in the context of what have become known as 'injustice frames' (Benford and Snow 2000).

CONCLUSION

The purpose of this chapter has been to provide an introduction to the origins of studies into collective behaviour and social movements. It is also intended that some of the material in the chapter be used as a platform from which to explore themes and perspectives developed in more detail in subsequent chapters. Accordingly, towards the end of the chapter we looked at rational choice theory because that inspired the development of resource mobilization theory, which we turn to examine in the next chapter.

Not only has it been the aim of this chapter to preempt material presented in later chapters of the book, but it is also intended that, in so doing, some legacies of earlier theories and approaches might be highlighted. In some cases, later work in the field negates earlier theories of collective behaviour and social movements, while, in other cases, as we shall see, older theories continue to be relevant. In Chapter 5, for instance, we will look at how, in contrast to early social psychological and collective behaviour theories, contemporary social movement scholars view as positive the emotions, passion, feelings, and affectivity that are involved in protest and activism. We will also see how festival, carnival, drama, theatre, and performance are key to some forms of collective action, which, as we saw earlier, are features Blumer associated with the *expressive crowd* that has no goals or purpose.

Throughout this chapter we have also seen how religious movements, sects, and cults have been incorporated into early theories and conceptual frameworks, although they are not accorded the status of social movements. For instance, Blumer regarded cults and sects as examples of *expressive social movements*, which, like fashion movements, do not seek social change. Similarly, Smelser saw sects and religious communes as examples of *crazes*, equivalent to fads and fashion in clothes, or otherwise as *value-oriented movements*. In Chapter 6, we return to examine this topic in greater depth by considering, among other things, why social movement scholars have tended to resist including religious movements in their analyses of social movements, as well as exploring connections that have been identified between new religious movements and new social movements.

Finally, it is intended that some of the material presented in this chapter feed into the discussion of new social movement theory in Chapter 4. As mentioned earlier, this and other approaches that are concerned with culture and the *process* of collective identity formation owe a debt of gratitude to symbolic interactionism, and especially the

33

pioneering work of Blumer. Indeed, in certain respects, symbolic interactionism paved the way for the emergence of the 'cultural turn' in social movement studies. That not only spawned interest in new social movements, but also generated broad interest in the cultural aspects of protest, which we examine in subsequent parts of this book.

SUGGESTED READINGS

The following texts and resources can be used to explore issues raised in this chapter.

Books

Any textbook on social movements will provide coverage of most of the issues examined here. These are some examples:

Buechler, S. M. (2011) *Understanding Social Movements: Theories from the Classical Era to the Present.* Boulder, CO: Paradigm Publishers.
Crossley, N. (2002) *Making Sense of Social Movements.* Buckingham: Open University Press.
della Porta, D. and Diani, M. (2006) *Social Movements: An Introduction* (2nd ed.). Oxford: Blackwell.
Staggenborg, S. (2011) *Social Movements.* Oxford: Oxford University Press.

The following is a very useful resource for understanding key concepts considered in this chapter, and throughout the book:

Chesters, G. and Welsh, I. (2011) *Social Movements: Key Concepts.* London: Routledge.

NOTE

1   Blumer's view of the public is comparable to what social philosophers like Hannah Arendt and Jürgen Habermas refer to as the 'public sphere' (Crossley 2002: 28).

CHAPTER 3

Political opportunity, resource mobilization, and social movement organization

INTRODUCTION

This chapter builds upon material presented in the last chapter by first considering how resource mobilization theory emerged as a critique of collective behaviour theory and rational choice theory. Rather than seeing social movements as irrational or composed of disaggregated individuals, resource mobilization theorists view social movements as *rational collective actors*, and focus on the role played by formal organizations in determining *how* social movements effectively mobilize resources to achieve their goals.

The chapter examines the political process model, which itself is critical of classical approaches that considered social movements as psychological phenomena, but is also critical of resource mobilization theory for being apolitical and presenting a static model of collective action. Key to the political process model is the concept of 'political opportunity structure', which is discussed and evaluated. The cases of New Zealand's anti-nuclear weapons movement and US anti-corporate activism are used to show how the political opportunity structure concept has been extended and modified.

holars concerned with *how* movements mobilize have also studied
᠆tics of social movements, or 'repertoires of contention'. Further-
᠆ore, social movement tactics have been linked to 'cycles of protest',
which are periods of intense collective action that emerge in response
to political opportunities. Insofar as a focus on social movement organization has implications for social movement outcomes, the chapter
considers the ways original movement goals might be compromised
by incorporation or co-optation into the formal political establishment, as well as the contribution made to movement outcomes by
informal organizations and social networks. It is shown, for example,
how black churches provided organizational networks and resources
vital to the success of the civil rights movement in America (see Box 3.6).
Moreover, in developing a 'master frame' around the principle of equal
rights and opportunity for all, the black movement provided a diverse
range of other movements in that protest cycle with a vehicle to articulate their own grievances and challenges.

The chapter ends by considering the impact of the 'cultural turn' on
resource mobilization theory by looking at the analysis of framing
processes in social movement studies. The chapter's conclusion antici-
pates material presented in Chapter 4 by considering briefly the
influence of resource mobilization theory on some 'cultural' approaches
to understanding social movements, which are interested in 'structuralist' questions as to *why* social movements occur, yet retain a concern for
how everyday networks and informal organizations contribute to collective mobilization, and thereby examine the *processes* by which
collective identities are formed.

RESOURCE MOBILIZATION THEORY

In considering social movements as *rational collective actors*, resource
mobilization theorists articulate a critique of both Olson's rational
choice theory, which they deem too individualistic, and collective
behaviour theory, which depicts collective behaviour as irrational.
Resource mobilization theory emerged in the United States during the
1970s. By way of comparison to collective behaviour theory, theorists
attached to this school of thought see social movement activity as part
of a normal process to secure political power. Unlike structuralist
accounts of social movements, which are concerned with *why* social
movements come into being (see Chapter 4), resource mobilization
theory is interested in *how* movements effectively mobilize resources to
successfully achieve their organizational goals, where resources are

taken to mean, 'anything from material resources – jobs, incomes, savings, and the right to material goods and services – to nonmaterial resources – authority, moral commitment, trust, friendship, skills' (Oberschall 1973: 28).

Although resource mobilization theorists tend to be critical of Olson's rational choice theory, some have been more influenced by it than others. Crossley (2002: 78) remarks that Anthony Oberschall (1973) is the most explicit in his acceptance of Olson's basic proposition that people are rational and self-interested, as well as his idea of 'selective incentives', which are seen by Oberschall as 'more than sufficient to draw a rational actor into a collective struggle'. Crossley (2002: 86) shows how the influence of Olson is also present in McCarthy and Zald's work and, in particular, the economistic logic that informs Olson's framing of the problem of collective action.

For McCarthy and Zald (1977), social and political problems are analogous to economic problems, which are solved by entrepreneurs prepared to exploit a gap in the market, and which they are able to profit from. Social movement organizations (SMOs) therefore act like other organizations in society inasmuch as they are formal organizations attempting to implement the preferences of a social movement or 'countermovement' (see Box 3.1). McCarthy and Zald (1977: 1219) extend the economic analogy when they say that all SMOs operate as part of a broader social movement industry (SMI), where '[t]he definition of SMI parallels the concept of industry in economics'. Here, SMOs are the equivalent of firms within an industry. However, it is not an unproblematic task to group SMOs into SMIs, as some SMOs might have target goals that are narrowly stated, whereas others will have broadly stated goals. For example, we may speak of:

> . . . the SMI that aims at liberalized alterations in laws, practices, and public opinion concerning abortion. This SMI would include a number of SMOs. But these SMOs may also be considered part of the broader SMI commonly referred to as the 'women's liberation movement', or they could be part of the 'population control movement'.
>
> (McCarthy and Zald 1977: 1220)

No matter to which social movement they are attached, all SMIs operate within a society's 'social movement sector' (SMS); a concept derived from the pluralist view of political power in the United States, which sees politics as 'a matter of competing interest groups, none of which can dominate completely over any of the others since all have

▍BOX 3.1 DEFINING 'SOCIAL MOVEMENT'

McCarthy and Zald (1977: 1217–1218) define a *social movement* as 'a set of opinions and beliefs in a population representing preferences for changing some element of the social structure or reward distribution, or both, of a society'. A *countermovement*, on the other hand, refers to 'a set of opinions and beliefs in a population opposed to a social movement' (McCarthy and Zald 1977: 1218). A simple example here might be the fight by anti-vivisectionists to stop experimentation on animals (a social movement), which is met with resistance from research scientists (a countermovement), claiming that animal vivisection is needed to find cures for human diseases and life-threatening illnesses (see Figure 3.1).

Although McCarthy and Zald (1977: 1218) are careful to provide an 'inclusive' definition of the term social movement, which 'allows the possibility that a social movement will not be represented by any organized groups but also allows for organizations that do not represent social movements at formation', the resource mobilization perspective has been criticized for focusing on formal organization, as well as relying on economistic language (e.g., rewards, preferences, resources), which tends to make its analysis of movement mobilization lack both a spontaneous and a normative element. By contrast, in

© sinisterpictures/Citizenside

Figure 3.1 Anti-vivisection activists march on Downing Street, London

Chapter 2 we saw how Turner and Killian's (1987 [1957]) 'emergent norm theory' placed a sense of injustice at the centre of all social movement activity. Moreover, we saw how activists frequently respond emotionally, rather than rationally, to injustice. However, McCarthy and Zald's definition does have features in common with other theories of social movements, including a focus on networks of relations between a plurality of actors, collective identity, and conflictual issues (Diani 1992).

A concern with networks of informal interactions is evident in the social movement sector concept, and McCarthy and Zald's more recent concept of 'micro mobilisation context', which is defined as 'any small group setting in which processes of collective attribution are combined with rudimentary forms of organization to produce mobilization for collective action' (McAdam et al. 1988: 709). Mario Diani (1992: 8) says that although McCarthy and Zald's reference to 'a set of opinion and beliefs' in their definition of a social movement 'does not necessarily imply the presence of shared feelings of belongingness' (i.e., collective identity), their more recent work does 'testify to their growing concern for interactive processes of symbolic mediation which support individuals' commitment'. Finally, even though resource mobilization theorists see social movements as involved in processes of social change, they nevertheless 'acknowledge that as promoters or opponents of social change social movements become involved in conflictual relations with other actors (institutions, countermovements, etc.)' (Diani 1992: 8).

access to resources of different kinds' (Nash 2000: 17). Thus, to McCarthy and Zald (1977: 1224), '[i]n any society the SMS must compete with other sectors and industries for the resources of the population'. A measure of the success of SMOs is whether they can compete successfully to achieve their 'target goals', which are defined as 'a set of preferred changes towards which [each SMO] claims to be working' (McCarthy and Zald 1977: 1220).

Individuals and organizations control resources that are vital to a SMO attaining its goals. Any social movement has 'adherents', or individuals and organizations believing in a movement's goals. Those providing resources for a SMO are described as 'constituents'. The 'bystander public' refers to nonadherents who are indifferent to a social movement or SMO and merely witness social movement activity. 'Potential beneficiaries' are those who would benefit directly if a SMO achieved its target goal. However, a SMO may attempt to mobilize adherents who are not potential beneficiaries. This category is divided into 'conscience adherents', or individuals and groups that are part of a social movement but do not stand to benefit from the goal accomplishment of a SMO, and 'conscience constituents', or direct supporters of a SMO not standing to benefit directly from its successful goal accomplishment. McCarthy and Zald also distinguish a 'classical SMO' from a 'professional SMO', where the former refers to a SMO that focuses on beneficiary adherents for resources, while the latter denotes organizations directing resource appeals primarily at conscience adherents, and which use few constituents for organizational labour.

POLITICAL PROCESS MODEL

Opinion appears to be divided as to which political model has most influenced resource mobilization theorists. Chesters and Welsh (2011: 148) suggest the theory implies adherence to 'the pluralist system of political expression in the USA', which was explained earlier. In his critique, however, McAdam (1982: 36) argues the resource mobilization perspective 'implies adherence to the elite model of the American political system', which 'rests on the fundamental assumption that wealth and power are concentrated in America in the hands of a few groups, thus depriving most people of any real influence over the majority decisions that affect their lives'. Social movements are therefore seen 'as rational attempts by excluded groups to mobilize sufficient political leverage to advance collective interests through noninstitutionalized means' (McAdam 1982: 37).

Ironically, and notwithstanding these seeming differences of opinion as to the political grounding of resource mobilization theory, critics have said that a major problem with the theory is its *apolitical* nature. For example, Dalton et al. (1990: 9–10) argue:

> The theory appeared indifferent to the political or ideological content of a social movement; it was applied in an almost mechanistic way to organizations of widely differing political and ideological scope, without incorporating these factors within the workings of the model.

By contrast, European approaches to 'new' social movements (examined in Chapter 4) tend to give more weight to ideological factors – not only asking *how* social movements mobilize, but also asking *why* they do so. Moreover, other approaches place little emphasis on the mechanistic aspects of mobilization, stressing instead the crucial role emotions play in activism and social protest (see Chapter 5).

POLITICA

In his early critique of existing perspectives on s including resource mobilization theory, Doug M the political process model, which he claimed i with a Marxist view of power, in that it believes cal power of excluded groups, who with sufficient orga.. capable of realizing their own power and goals, without the patro.. age of elite groups. This view was born of McAdam's empirical work on black insurgency and the civil rights movement in the United States, which did not require an injection of external resources, but largely relied upon preexisting indigenous networks and structures (e.g., black churches and community organizations) for its strength.

The term 'political process' captures the essence of McAdam's approach, namely that 'in contrast to the various classical formulations, a social movement is held to be above all else a *political* rather than a psychological phenomenon' and that 'a movement represents a continuous *process* from generation to decline, rather than a discrete series of developmental stages' (McAdam 1982: 36, original emphasis). Thus, the political process model stands in sharp contrast to resource mobilization theory for: (i) emphasizing the political dimension of social movements; and (ii) stressing 'dynamism, strategic interaction, and response to the political environment' (McAdam et al. 2001: 16).

STRUCTURE OF POLITICAL OPPORTUNITIES

Central to the political process model is the concept of 'political opportunity structure', which refers to the degree of openness or closure of the formal political system (della Porta and Diani 2006: 16). As Meyer notes, the first explicit reference in the literature to a 'political opportunity' framework was made by Eisinger (1973) who was interested in whether the openness of urban governments to more conventional forms of citizen participation was likely or not to precipitate city riots. Eisinger (1973: 12) argued, 'it would seem reasonable to suspect that the incidence of protest [. . .] is related to the nature of the opportunity structure', which he defined in terms of the relative openness or closure of municipal governments in US cities. He concluded that '[c]ities with extensive institutional openings pre-empted riots by inviting conventional means of political participation to redress grievances; cities without visible openings for participation repressed or discouraged dissident claimants to foreclose eruptions of protest' (Meyer 2004: 128).

The relative openness or closure of the prevailing political system depends to a great extent upon the willingness of elite groups to include powerless groups in the polity. Ordinarily, excluded groups, or *challengers*, have little power due to their weak bargaining position relative to established polity *members*; although, as McAdam (1982: 40) points out, 'opportunities for a challenger to engage in successful collective action do vary greatly over time'. A good example of how the relative openness of political opportunity structures varies over time and according to the willingness of political elites to include excluded collective voices in the polity is evident in the Australian context. It has been observed that under the administration of Prime Minister John Howard (1996–2007) debate was stifled and dissent silenced (Hamilton and Maddison 2007; Maddison and Martin 2010), whereas soon after his election in 2007, Prime Minister Kevin Rudd (2007–2010, 2013) made a deliberate attempt to consult with a range of people and groups from across the community, holding the 2020 Summit in Canberra, 19–20 April 2008, in an effort to help shape a long-term strategy for the nation's future.

While resource mobilization theorists depict segments of the elite as willing, and sometimes aggressive, sponsors of social insurgency, the political process model is premised on a view 'that political action by established polity members reflects an abiding conservatism', meaning '[t]hey work against admission to the polity of groups whose interests conflict significantly with their own' (McAdam 1982: 38). To generate a social movement – and thus realize its latent potential – it is not sufficient for a powerless group or aggrieved population to be simply presented with a favourable structure of political opportunities. Rather, it 'must be able to "convert" a favourable "structure of political opportunities" into an organised campaign of social protest' (McAdam 1982: 44).

Although for many scholars political opportunity structure remains a useful concept, which has been extended and applied in numerous contexts (see Boxes 3.2 and 3.3), it has been critiqued too. For example, Meyer (2004: 141) has criticized political opportunity theory for tending to produce research that is 'conceptualized broadly but operationalized narrowly'. Moreover, James Jasper (1997: 35) is critical of the circularity that is often involved in the use of the term political opportunity structure, saying that 'whatever "provides incentives" for collective action seems to be a political opportunity structure'. Jasper also highlights the catch-all nature of the concept when he states, '[a]nything that, in retrospect, helped a movement mobilize or win a victory tends to be labelled a political opportunity structure' (Jasper 1997: 35). Finally, he argues, '[t]he term *structure* misleadingly implies relatively fixed entities, so that attention is often diverted away from open-ended strategic inter-play. If the point is to highlight strategic political opportunities, adding the word *structure* creates an oxymoron' (Jasper 1997: 36, original emphasis).

BOX 3.2 POLITICAL OPPORTUNITY AND NESTED INSTITUTIONS: THE CASE OF NEW ZEALAND'S ANTI-NUCLEAR WEAPONS MOVEMENT

Given the increasing influence of international factors on nation-states and protest movements, it is unsurprising that social movement scholars have turned their attention to the ways that interactions between domestic and international factors impact upon the claims and possible effects of movements (see also Chapter 9). Using the case of the anti-nuclear weapons movement in New Zealand, David Meyer (2003) examines the relationship between the global and the local by explicitly extending the concept of political opportunity structure. He argues that 'national political opportunity structures are *nested* in a larger international environment that constrains or promotes particular kinds of opportunities for dissidents within the state' (Meyer 2003: 19, original emphasis).

Smaller organizations and social networks may be tightly or loosely nested within larger social and political institutions. Essentially, '[t]he more tightly nested an institution is, the more constrained are its policy options and politics' (Meyer 2003: 24). In the New Zealand case, though, 'the geographic and political distance afforded the state sufficient autonomy such that a social movement could achieve policy changes unthinkable elsewhere' (Meyer 2003: 24). During the 1980s, the Western security alliance, headed by the United States, was critical of New Zealand's anti-nuclear policy. However, New Zealand's Labour government was able to capitalize on this loose nesting of the state within wider international politics, which 'created a great deal of slack, and afforded politicians a range of policy options unavailable to allied states facing equally determined peace movements' (Meyer 2003: 30).

New Zealand's nuclear-free stance enabled it to carve out a distinct international identity, as well as a different and less marginal position in the international political arena. And even when the United States imposed restrictions on the extent of cooperation and flow of intelligence between the two nations, the New Zealand government was able to work that to its advantage. The United States' harsh rhetorical response to New Zealand's anti-nuclear policy, coupled with minimal sanctions, helped New

© Greenpeace/John Miller

Figure 3.2 The *Rainbow Warrior* in Mardsen Wharf, Auckland Harbour, after the bombing by French secret service agents in 1985

Zealanders to see the nuclear issue as a matter of self-determination and national independence: 'A nuclear-free New Zealand became a point of public pride, and not simply an exit from existing security arrangements' (Meyer 2003: 30–31). And, Meyer (2003: 29) says, this sense of nationalist pride was reinforced when the Greenpeace ship, *Rainbow Warrior*, was blown up and sunk by French intelligence agents in Auckland Harbour in 1985, killing a crew member in the process (see Figure 3.2). The New Zealand anti-nuclear movement was also buoyed by peace movements elsewhere, which was a reciprocal affair insofar as 'activists in the Western alliance attempted to adapt the nuclear-free-zone concept to their own political purposes' (Meyer 2003: 31).

BOX 3.3 OPPORTUNITY STRUCTURES IN ANTI-CORPORATE ACTIVISM

In her book about anti-corporate activism in the United States, Sarah Soule (2009) shows how in addition to a domestic opportunity structure, there exists a transnational or international political opportunity structure, which affects the operation of social movements. Drawing on the ideas of Van der Heijden (2006), Soule (2009: 44) shows how at the global level the notion of political opportunity structure 'may be thought of as the set of international governmental associations (e.g., UN, EU, WTO, World Bank), which establish treaties, agreements, and norms'. We will consider these ideas in more detail in Chapter 9, when, among other things, we look at them in the context of the emergence of a 'global civil society'.

In relation to her work on anti-corporate activism, however, Soule argues that the international political opportunity structure may be particularly significant for some corporations operating within multinational enterprises, which are governed by international agreements and treaties. In fact, she states:

> . . . multinational enterprises exist within a domestic opportunity structure, the opportunity structure of the host country in which they operate, and the transnational opportunity structure, thus social movements against such corporations and their outcomes are governed by multiple levels of opportunity.
> (Soule 2009: 44)

Soule (2009: 39–40) also notes some modifications of the 'political opportunity structure' concept, including 'cultural opportunity structure', 'legal opportunity structure', and 'gendered opportunity structure'. However, she argues, only the notion of gendered opportunity structure has helped develop our understanding of social movement *outcomes* (as opposed to social movement mobilization):

> The gendered opportunity structure includes the characteristics of the political system that might make political actors more or less favourable to claims by women. For example, favourable public opinion about women's roles and women legislators has been used to operationalize this concept.
> (Soule 2009: 40)

Soule argues that the pressure put on American universities during the 1970s and 1980s to divest in South African-related companies in protest of the racist policy of apartheid was helped greatly by the fact that the American public was appalled by what was going on in South Africa. In this way, the beliefs and opinions of the larger society, she contends, 'might be thought of in terms of the broader cultural opportunity structure' (Soule 2009: 91). Moreover, the prodivestment pressures emanating from the US Congress, which passed several pieces of anti-apartheid legislation during the mid-1980s, 'may be thought of as part of the broader political and legal opportunity structure' (Soule 2009: 91).

REPERTOIRES OF CONTENTION

A concern with *how* social movements mobilize has led some to examine 'repertoires of contention', or 'the tactics groups employ in their struggles with one another' (McAdam 1995: 235). Charles Tilly (1986: 4, original emphasis) developed the concept of repertoire, which he defines as follows: 'With regard to any particular group, we can think of the whole set of means it has for making claims of different kinds on different individuals or groups as its *repertoire* of contention'. Tilly argues that most of the time the forms of social movement claims making in any given place bear a strong resemblance to previous forms. This is not to say, however, that repertoires are merely repetitive, since protest tactics are always adapted to context. Indeed, Tilly (2006: 41) notes that movement participants are engaged in 'unceasing small-scale innovation', although this tends to be 'innovation within the script':

> Any population has a limited repertoire of collective action: alternative means of acting together on shared interests. In our time, for example, most people know how to participate in an electoral campaign, join or form a special-interest association, or organize a letter-writing drive, demonstrate, strike, hold a meeting, and build an influence network.
>
> (Tilly 1986: 390)

The existing repertoire, therefore, circumscribes collective action. However, as Rhys Williams (2004: 96) points out, the metaphor of the 'repertoire' not only constrains collective action, for it combines *structure* and *agency* – choices are made – but 'within structured options', thus leaving room for agency and strategic decision making while acknowledging the cultural and historical circumstances constraining choice:

> The dictionary definition of 'repertoire' plays on both the structuring and agentic aspect of the term. It defines repertoire as the plays or operas a company is prepared to perform, as a list of skills an individual or group possesses, and as a complete supply of devices or ingredients used in a particular field or practice. Thus it is both the storehouse of available elements, as well as those that actors have the knowledge and capacity to use.
>
> (Williams 2004: 96)

Tilly (1986: 390) also makes a music analogy, saying the repertoire in question will resemble the improvisation of jazz artists: 'people know the general rules or performance more or less well and vary the performance to meet the purpose at hand'. For Tilly, repertoires 'do not descend from abstract philosophy'; they are 'learned cultural creations' emerging from struggle:

> People learn to break windows in protest, attack pilloried prisoners, tear down dishonored houses, stage public marches, petition, hold formal meetings, organize self-interest associations. At any particular point in history, however, they learn only a rather small number of alternative ways to act collectively.
>
> (Tilly 1995: 26)

In his historical study of popular action in France, Tilly shows how there was a shift in the repertoire of contention from about the 1850s. The repertoire before that time tended to be *parochial* in scope (i.e., focused at the local level) and relied heavily on *patronage*, that is, 'appealing to immediately available powerholders to convey grievances or settle disputes' (Tilly 1986: 391). Examples included seizure of grain, field invasions, destruction of tollgates (see Box 3.4), and attacks on machines.

BOX 3.4 THE REBECCA RIOTS

The Rebecca Riots were a series of protests, taking place between 1839 and 1843, where Welsh tenant farmers and farm workers destroyed turnpikes (see Figure 3.3). Turnpikes were gates built across roads by landowners, which prevented people from passing through unless a toll was paid. Previously, passage was free. Believing the tollgates threatened their livelihood since they would be charged to take their livestock and crops to market, protestors from an already impoverished rural population set about destroying the gates. The protestors comprised men dressed up as women and were named, 'Rebecca's Daughters', reputedly after a verse in the Biblical book of *Genesis* (24:60): 'And they blessed Rebekah, and said unto her, Thou art our sister, be thou the mother of thousands of millions, and let thy seed possess the gate of those which hate them'.

ing a single offender. Thirty veteran pensioners went down from Carmarthen to St. Clear's on Tuesday week, and a troop of lancers are daily expected on the spot. Judging, however, from the past abortive attempts to suppress the lawless movement, people are not very sanguine in their expectations of a speedy restoration of the supremacy of the law. Indeed, the Captain Rock-like proceedings in Pembrokeshire and Carmarthenshire seem, from all we can learn, to assume daily a more threatening complexion.

THE WELSH RIOTERS.

© Illustrated London News Ltd./Mary Evans

Figure 3.3 During the Rebecca Riots, tollgates were attacked in South Wales. Many of the male rioters dressed as women and called themselves 'Rebecca and her daughters'.

The repertoire that emerged in the mid-nineteenth century, on the other hand, was generally *national* in scope and relatively *autonomous*, meaning people instigated their own grievances and demands independently of existing powerholders. The social movement that emerged during the mid-1800s comprised a 'series of challenges', usually against the national authorities, and the new repertoire consisted of 'concrete actions' that combined 'various elements', including 'public meetings, demonstrations, marches, strikes, and so on' (Tilly 1986: 392). Examples of this new repertoire and the operation of social movements were the 'vast linked demonstrations of Languedoc's winegrowers in 1907 and the coordinated road-blocking and potato-dumping of Brittany's farmers in 1961' (Tilly 1986: 393) (see Box 3.5). For Tilly, this coordination of complex collective action to produce the appearance of a unified social movement was 'virtually unknown in Western nations until the nineteenth century' (Tilly 1986: 394).

BOX 3.5 REVOLT OF THE LANGUEDOC WINEGROWERS

In 1907, winegrowers and vine workers in the Languedoc region of southern France mounted a revolt in protest at a glut in the wine market that had the effect of driving down the price of wine, lowering wages, and threatening jobs (see Figure 3.4). The oversupply of wine was caused by the increasing use of industrial wine-making methods and 'fraudulent' wine production techniques (i.e., using sugar, chemicals, and industrial alcohols), which departed from the production of 'natural' wines. Echoing the rhetoric of the union movement, the winegrowers and vine workers demanded a 'right to work' or, as the leader of the movement, Marcelin Albert, put it, a 'right to live from the vine' (Harvey Smith 1978: 110). The collective organization of the Languedoc winegrowers and vine workers supports Tilly's (1986) account of repertoires employed by national mass movements from the mid-nineteenth century, since the movement engaged successfully with the French government that enacted a law, 'which strictly regulated the use of sugar in wine making, and discouraged other forms of fraud by requiring every grower register the size of his vineyard and his annual wine harvest' (Harvey Smith 1978: 120).

© Mr. Sallis-Bouscarle

Figure 3.4 French winegrowers' revolt led by Marcelin Albert in Narbonne, 1907

So why did the repertoires change? Tilly explains the shift from a local repertoire based on patronage to a newer national repertoire based on autonomy according to the process of the concentration of capital and political power that occurred from the mid-nineteenth century:

> As capitalism advanced, as national states became more powerful and centralized, local affairs and nearby patrons mattered less to the fates of ordinary people. Increasingly, holders of large capital and national power made decisions that affected them. As a result seizures of grain, collective invasions of fields, and the like became ineffective, irrelevant, obsolete. In response to the shifts of power and capital, ordinary people invented and adopted new forms of action, creating the electoral campaign, the public meeting, the social movement, and the other elements of the newer repertoire.
>
> (Tilly 1986: 395–396)

While marches, boycotts, occupations, and so forth still largely characterize the modern repertoire of collective action, campaigns for global justice signal a changing context, and with it a changing repertoire. Transformations in global capitalism have meant capital is concentrated less in national industries and more in multinational corporations; the power of nation-states is now checked by that of supranational bodies and organizations such as the United Nations and World Bank; and the harnessing of new media (especially the Internet) by social movements means mobilizations tend increasingly to have a transnational rather than national orientation (della Porta and Diani 2006: 170). We will return to look at the effect of new media technologies on the scope of both local and global activism in the contemporary world in Chapters 8 and 9.

CYCLES OF PROTEST

Sidney Tarrow has employed a variant of the political process model to examine what he terms 'cycles of contention' or 'protest cycles', which are intensified periods of collective action. Tarrow (1998: 10) shows how cycles of protest emerge in response to changes in political opportunities and constraints, which people build upon using known repertoires, and are based on dense social networks and consensual, action-oriented 'cultural frames' (which are discussed in more depth later in this chapter). The convergence of all of these factors facilitates sustained conflict with powerful opponents. Only in such cases does a social movement exist, and 'when contention spreads across an entire society, as it sometimes does, we see a cycle of contention' (Tarrow 1998: 10). An example would be the various social movements that emerged out of the 1960s counterculture, which initially started in the United States but eventually spread to other countries.

In one sense, the concept of cycles or waves of protest stands in stark contrast to the notion of repertoires of contention, discussed earlier, because while the former represent intensified periods of protest, the latter change very slowly via long evolutionary processes (Tarrow 1995: 91). Nevertheless, Tarrow proposes a resolution to this apparent paradox, saying:

> . . . moments of madness do not transform the repertoire of contention all at once and out of whole cloth, but contribute to its evolution through the dynamic evolution of larger cycles of mobilization in which the innovations in collective action that they produce are diffused, tested, and refined in adumbrated form and eventually become part of the accepted repertoire. It is within these larger cycles that new forms of contention combine with old ones, the expressive encounters the instrumental, traditional actors adopt tactics from new arrivals, and newly invented forms of collective action become what I call 'modular'. Cycles of protest are the crucibles in which moments of madness are tempered into the permanent tools of a society's repertoire of contention.
>
> (Tarrow 1995: 91–92)

della Porta and Diani (2006: 189) show how the idea that mobilization ebbs and flows, proceeding in waves, has consequences for repertoires of contention. Moreover, they argue, as a protest cycle develops, movements may change tactics, which, in turn, affects changes in the external environment. Thus, they say, disruptive tactics are often used during the initial stages of protest, which may be met with hostility by the authorities, especially where the political opportunities are closed. Later in a protest cycle, the authorities might decide that 'instead of calling out the troops or allowing the police to wade into a crowd' it is better to 'infiltrate dissenting groups and separate leaders from followers' (Tarrow 1994: 112). Alternatively, participation may be channeled into organizations, and, in such cases, movement actors might adopt a more political logic whereby they engage in implicit bargaining with those in authority

(Tarrow 1994: 168). However, as we shall see later, that approach might affect positively the efficacy of a social movement, or it may result in the co-optation of a movement into the political system, which could mean it compromises its original values and goals.

BOX 3.6 THE IMPORTANCE OF PREEXISTING NETWORKS FOR BLACK INSURGENCY AND THE US CIVIL RIGHTS MOVEMENT

Previously, it was stated that of all resource mobilization theorists, Oberschall is the most explicit in his appropriation of Olson's ideas. However, his work departs from Olson's in an important way. Oberschall (1973: 117) is critical of Olson's 'assumption that the members of a large collectivity are unorganized individual decision makers similar to the numerous, small, independent producers in the market of the classical economist'. Rather than seeing collective action as a problem analogous to the economic decision making of atomized individuals, Oberschall proposes a *sociological* theory of mobilization, which assumes collective action is grounded in pre-existing networks of everyday life, local communities, and small organizations, all of which provide valuable resources for protest movements.

Many accounts of black insurgency and the civil rights movement in the United States have adopted this general approach, arguing that black churches, in particular, provided organizational networks and resources (such as leadership and supporters) essential to the success of the black protest movement (e.g., McAdam 1982; Morris 1984). However, Aldon Morris (1984: 281) has been critical of Oberschall's approach to the civil rights movement for overemphasizing the role of outside support from 'Northern white liberals, the federal government, courts, mass media, philanthropic foundations, and white college students'. While Oberschall does acknowledge the black community and especially black churches 'provided an important pre-existing mobilization and resource base for the movement [. . .] because his approach assigns heavy weight to outside elites and events, it does not reveal the scope or the capacity of the movement's indigenous base' (Morris 1984: 281). In contrast, Morris (1984: 281) states his research 'demonstrates that the overwhelming majority of local movements were indigenously organized and financed'.

HOW ORGANIZED SHOULD A SOCIAL MOVEMENT BE?

From the analysis presented in Box 3.6 regarding the importance of indigenous networks of social relations and local communities for collective mobilization flows a key criticism of resource mobilization theory, namely that it overemphasizes the role of formal organizations and tends to allot little or no significance to informal and less organized social groups (Crossley 2002: 92). However, this also highlights a fundamental dilemma lying at the heart of much collective action, which was identified some time ago by Alberoni (1984) when he argued that 'movement' and 'institution' ought to be considered, theoretically speaking, as two very different social states. In empirical work, this is reflected in a concern for the effects on social movements of processes of co-optation, incorporation, and professionalization.

As we saw earlier, for adherents of the political process model, social movement activists must somehow attempt 'to "convert" a favourable "structure of political opportunities" into an *organized* campaign of social protest' (McAdam 1982: 44, emphasis added). In other terms, they must seek to connect their demands to 'institutionally imminent possibilities' (Giddens 1991a: 155). However, for some social movement commentators, incorporation into the political system is regarded as undesirable, since, they believe, to be effective, collective actors must seek to be autonomous of established political institutions. For others, such as Tilly, 'integration into the political system [. . .] may facilitate the realization of a movement's aims, rather than representing its co-option and neutralization' (Nash 2000: 131). Indeed, during periods in which it may be hard to mobilize support, formalized social movement organizations may find it easier to maintain themselves as 'they have paid leaders who create stability because they can be relied on to perform ongoing tasks necessary to organizational maintenance' and they 'have structures that ensure that tasks are performed despite a turnover in personnel' (Staggenborg 1988: 599).[1]

A further illustration of the conundrum of organization and institutionalization that is faced by many activists is provided in McAdam's work on the black civil rights movement. Crossley (2002: 92) makes the point that for McAdam, external sponsorship, and the formal organizational structure that frequently comes with this, can act as a conservative force in the sense that 'formality breeds accountability and thus deference towards the political establishment, when real change sometimes requires radical actions which offend the sensibilities of the establishment'. On the other hand, a loss of organization contributed to the eventual demise of the 1960s civil rights movement:

> Without the 'conscious planning or centralized direction' needed to link together the growing collection of autonomous protest units, the black movement had, by the decade's end, become a largely impotent political force at the national level. Lacking the strong centralized organizational vehicles required to sustain the disruptive campaigns that earlier had supported federal action, the movement was increasingly confined to limited efforts at the local level.
>
> (McAdam 1982: 186)

ASSESSING SOCIAL MOVEMENT SUCCESS

Talk of the demise of social movements begs the question: how might we ascertain whether or not a social movement has been successful? While one might consider this a fundamental line of inquiry in social movement studies, not least because 'one of the raisons d'être of social movements is to bring about changes in some aspects of society', it is, however, a relatively neglected area of study (Giugni 1999: xv). Nonetheless, there is research that deals with the impact, outcomes, and consequences of social movements.

For example, in their study of social movements as bearers of new ideas, which we will look at further in Chapter 5, Eyerman and Jamison (1991) consider social movements as transitory phenomena whose success is paradoxical: 'The more successful a movement is in spreading its knowledge interests or diffusing its consciousness, the less successful it is likely to be as a permanent organization' (Eyerman and Jamison 1991: 3–4). Moreover, the longer a movement exists outside or on the fringes of the political system, the less influential it is likely to be. In the short run, the success or failure of a movement will depend on its ability to mobilize resources or exploit political opportunities to achieve its goals. However, its success, historically speaking, will depend on 'the effective diffusion of its knowledge production; but diffusion depends upon there being sufficient time and space for a movement identity to be articulated' (Eyerman and Jamison 1991: 64). Thus, movements are successes in one way, yet failures in another, which is a point that applies to social movements as bearers of new knowledge as well as movements seeking political inclusion. A similar point has been made by Alan Scott (1990: 10–11) who says if a telos of social movement activity is the normalization of previously excluded issues and groups, then 'success' is 'quite compatible with, and indeed overlaps, the disappearance of the movement as a movement'.

A discussion about social movement success also has implications for the aforementioned concept of 'political opportunity structure'. In discussing the effect of social movement activism on public policy, Meyer says that policy changes affect the conditions in which activists mobilize. He states, '[a]s policy makers respond to social movements, the environment in which the movement makes claims – the "structure of political opportunities" in particular – changes, advantaging and foreclosing particular claimants and strategies of influence' (Meyer 2005: 19). Governments may respond to movements in a number of ways. They may do so only by defining narrow policy outputs; they may do so on a rhetorical level; they may officially recognize movement groups or individual activists within the domain of policy; or they may appoint activists to official positions within a bureaucracy:

> Thus, the feminist campaign against rape as the most threatening and egregious element of patriarchy was turned into a public safety effort. From eliminating oppression of women, activists and government established a working relationship, in Matthews's (1994) terms, with the goal of 'managing' the problem of rape. At the same time, government's appropriation of the campaign against rape, using its resources to control the image of the issue and to enlist and employ activists as service workers, made it more difficult for activists to mobilize.
>
> (Meyer 2005: 19)

THE 'CULTURAL TURN' IN RESOURCE MOBILIZATION THEORY: FRAMING PROCESSES AND COLLECTIVE ACTION

A development in resource mobilization theory that is a precursor to some of the material presented in the next chapter to do with the emergence of 'new' social movements concerns what Kate Nash (2000: 123–131) describes as the 'cultural turn' in resource mobilization theory. Specifically, she is referring to the development of frame analysis in the study of social movements, which we touched upon in Chapter 2.

In an effort to remedy the criticism that resource mobilization theory proffers an atomistic and overly rationalistic model of the individual, certain scholars have attempted to account for subjectivity and culture in collective mobilization processes. Influenced by the work of American sociologist Erving Goffman and, in particular, his book, *Frame Analysis* (Goffman 1974), social movement scholars have developed a perspective that seeks to link social psychological and resource mobilization views about movement participation. Accordingly, Snow et al. (1986: 464) talk of 'frame alignment processes', which they take to mean 'the linkage of individual and SMO interpretative orientations, such that some set of individual interests, values and beliefs and SMO activities, goals, and ideology are congruent and complementary'. Put more simply, frame alignment entails 'achieving a common definition of a social problem and a common prescription for solving it' (Goodwin et al. 2001: 6).

Goffman (1974: 21) originally used the term 'frame' to denote 'schemata of interpretation', which enable individuals 'to locate, perceive, identify, and label' occurrences in their life space and the world at large. By helping to make events and occurrences meaningful, frames function to organize experience and guide action – both individual and collective action. Therefore, to Snow et al. (1986: 464), 'frame alignment is a necessary condition for movement participation, whatever its nature or intensity'.

Like the frames Goffman refers to, 'collective action frames' perform an interpretive function by simplifying and condensing elements of the 'world out there', though in ways 'intended to mobilize potential adherents and constituents, to garner bystander support, and to demobilize antagonists' (Snow and Benford 1988: 198). Hence, 'collective action frames are action-oriented sets of beliefs and meanings that inspire and legitimate the activities and campaigns of a social movement organization' (Benford and Snow 2000: 614).

Collective action frames are constituted through a set of 'core framing tasks' whereby:

> . . . movement adherents negotiate a shared understanding of some problematic condition or situation they define as in need of change, make attributions regarding who or what is to blame, articulate an alternative set of arrangements, and urge others to act in concert to affect [sic] change.
>
> (Benford and Snow 2000: 615)

Benford and Snow refer to processes of identifying problems and attributing blame as 'diagnostic framing', studies of which tend to focus on 'injustice frames' that 'call attention to the ways in which movements identify the "victims" of a given injustice and amplify their victimization' (Benford and Snow 2000: 615). It will be recalled from Chapter 2 that Turner and Killian (1987 [1957]) believed a sense of injustice is central to all social movement activity. Likewise, Gamson (1992: 68, original emphasis) has asserted that all 'collective action frames are *injustice* frames'. However, Benford and Snow (2000: 615) reject sweeping generalizations such as this because, they say, '[i]n the case of many religious, self-help, and identity movements, for example, it is questionable whether a well-elaborated collective action frame need include an injustice component'.

BOX 3.7 MASTER FRAMES AND CYCLES OF PROTEST

Previously, we saw how Tarrow (1998: 10) argues that in periods of intense mobilization, or 'protest cycles', people 'draw on consensual and action-oriented cultural frames', where a cycle of protest is taken to mean the existence of conflict or contention across an entire society. To accommodate the idea that social movements operate within cycles of protest, Snow and Benford (1992) have developed the notion of 'master frames', which perform the same functions as movement-specific collective action frames, but on a larger scale.[2] In short, a master frame 'allows numerous aggrieved groups to tap it and elaborate their grievances in terms of its basic problem-solving schema' (Snow and Benford 1992: 140). They give the example of the US civil rights movement, which developed a master frame that accentuated the generic 'principle of equal rights and opportunities regardless of ascribed characteristics and articulated it with the goal of integration through nonviolent means' (Snow and Benford 1992: 145).

Master frames such as this have widespread appeal, providing a variety of movements within a protest cycle with a vehicle to mobilize their own challenges. In the case of the US civil rights movement, Snow and Benford (1992: 149) argue:

> . . . the flowering of movements such as those associated with women, Chicanos, American Indians, the aged, and the disabled on the heels of the black movement was precipitated in part by the extension of the principle of sexual rights and opportunities from the domain of black America to the situation of the other groups.

However, just as master frames might play a central role in initiating cycles of protest, so, Crossley (2002: 146) observes, it follows that 'cycles may come to an end when a particular master frame loses its appeal'.

CONCLUSION

McAdam et al. (1996) have attempted to provide an integrated and dynamic model of social movements by looking at the relationships between political opportunities, mobilizing structures, and framing processes. However, this has met with criticism from Nash for, among other things, McAdam et al. exaggerate the degree to which movement actors control definitions and opportunities. Citing Tarrow (1992), Nash (2000: 128) argues, 'social movement leaders do not have complete control over how the collective frames of action they propose will be received, nor over how far their supporters will be prepared to follow their leads'. As Tarrow (1992: 191) himself puts it, 'framing is less like a completed symphony than like improvisational jazz: composers provide the initial "head" for a jam session, but the improvisations depend on a group of players over whom they have little control'.

Moreover, Nash (2000: 128) contends, McAdam et al.'s approach reveals a wider problem associated with the cultural turn of resource mobilization theory, namely that '[t]he understanding of actors' motivations for collective action as socially constructed cannot simply be grafted on to the resource mobilization theory approach, as if its premises in rational choice theory were irrelevant'. Furthermore, resource mobilization theorists 'tend to see culture simply as a resource, to be manipulated by an actor who is somehow outside it, using it rationally as the best means to reach a given end' (Nash 2000: 128). To Nash, this avoids addressing the fundamental question the cultural turn intends to address; that is, to provide an explanation as to how it is that people become involved in collective action in the first place.

Indeed, while there are some similarities between the framing approach and culturalist perspectives in social movement studies, as we shall see in the following two chapters, there are also significant differences. Hence, Benford and Snow's (2000) concern with the role of beliefs and meanings in inspiring individuals to get involved in collective action, as well as their interest in the processual aspects of protest whereby activists negotiate a shared understanding of a problematic situation or condition, is reminiscent of Alberto Melucci's approach to social movements (examined in the next chapter), which, he says, consist of a plurality of meanings and orientations that must be reconciled if a coherent collective identity is to be formed. Moreover, as we will see in Chapter 5, since it is an offshoot of resource mobilization theory, the framing perspective may be criticized not only for treating some of the cultural aspects of social movements (e.g., songs and music) as mere resources to build solidarity, but also for overstating rationality and cognition, and understating the role of emotions in motivating people to become involved in collective action. As we have already established, often it is a sense of injustice that spurs people to act, and it is usually emotions (e.g., anger, indignation, fear, or compassion) that underpin this response, rather than rational or cognitive processes.

In the next chapter, we will start to examine what might be described as more culturally oriented approaches to the study of social movements, some of which combine resource mobilization theory's concern with *how* movements mobilize resources to achieve their goals and 'structuralist' accounts of *why* social movements emerge. Apparent in this work is the influence of Oberschall's notion that preexisting networks in everyday life form the basis of much collective action, which is an idea that now informs a whole body of research into social movements and networks, and involves the empirical study of a range of social protest – from local grass-roots activism to global social movements.

SUGGESTED READINGS

The following texts and resources can be used to explore issues raised in this chapter.

Books

McAdam, D., McCarthy, J. D., and Zald, M. N. (eds.) (1996) *Comparative Perspectives on Social Movements: Political Opportunities, Mobilizing Structures, and Cultural Framings.* Cambridge: Cambridge University Press.

McAdam, D., Tarrow, S., and Tilly, C. (2001) *Dynamics of Contention.* Cambridge: Cambridge University Press.

These two texts provide detailed explorations of some of the key ideas presented in this chapter dealing with movement dynamics, political opportunities, and framing approaches.

McAdam, D. (1982) *Political Process and the Development of Black Insurgency 1930–1970.* Chicago: The University of Chicago Press.

Morris, A. (1984) *The Origins of the Civil Rights Movement: Black Communities Organizing for Change.* New York: Free Press.

These books provide detailed accounts of the US civil rights movement. McAdam's book is particularly significant, as it contains some early ideas on structures of political opportunity and the political process model.

Journals

Diani, M. (1992) 'The Concept of Social Movement' *The Sociological Review* 40(1): 1–25.

In this article, Mario Diani develops a synthetic definition of 'social movement', which he derives from a variety of social movement sources.

Benford, R. D. and Snow, D. A. (2000) 'Framing Processes and Social Movements: An Overview and Assessment' *Annual Review of Sociology* 26: 611–639.

Meyer, D. S. (2004) 'Protest and Political Opportunities' *Annual Review of Sociology* 30: 125–145.

These two articles provide useful overviews of the framing and political opportunity perspectives.

Buechler, S. M. (1993) 'Beyond Resource Mobilization? Emerging Trends in Social Movement Theory' *The Sociological Quarterly* 34(2): 217–235.

McCarthy, J. D. and Zald, M. N. (1977) 'Resource Mobilization and Social Movements: A Partial Theory' *American Journal of Sociology* 82(6): 1212–1241.

McCarthy and Zald's article constitutes a classic pronouncement on resource mobilization theory. Meanwhile, in a relatively early critique, Steven Buechler draws on his own research into the US women's movement to identify a number of emerging theoretical trends, which, he says, pose challenges to the resource mobilization framework. These include some of the ideas and issues discussed in the next chapter and the one after that, such as collective identity, movement diversity, and processes of cultural construction.

NOTES

1   The ability of social movements to sustain themselves in fallow periods is discussed in some detail in Chapter 4 when we look at the concept of 'abeyance structures'.

2   This is similar to the distinction Herbert Blumer (1969) makes between general and specific social movements, which we considered in Chapter 2.

Social movements, old and new

INTRODUCTION

From the 1960s, people began to talk about the emergence of 'new social movements'. These movements are referred to as 'new' for a number of reasons, which we will explore in this chapter, but the main reason they have been described as such is because they raise issues and make demands about identity, lifestyle, and *difference* that are quite distinct from the class-based, socioeconomic claims and demands of the labour movement. However, as we shall see, the novelty of these movements has been the subject of much debate and contention, which is one of the reasons why the word *new* is sometimes placed in inverted commas in this chapter.

Throughout the chapter, we consider key ideas and concepts underpinning perspectives on new social movements, including the notions of 'post-materialism' and 'recognition'. We also look at important critiques of new social movement theory and consider key concepts associated with those analyses, such as 'post-Fordism'. During the course of the chapter, we look at a number of case studies and examples to illustrate points that are made about new social movement theory and its critics. Similar to what we did towards the end of the last chapter, we finish this chapter by looking at proposals to synthesize European and North American approaches to social movements, which, in an effort to reconcile divergent perspectives, attempt to show

how social movements form collective (cultural) identities and achieve (political) goals, as well as addressing structural concerns as to *why* movements arise in the first place.

NEW SOCIAL MOVEMENTS IN PROGRAMMED SOCIETY

Alain Touraine was among the first to refer to the emergence of a new social movement. Writing from a neo-Marxist perspective, Touraine's views are premised on a particular theory of society, which he sees as dominated by a central class conflict. Thus, just as industrial society was defined by the conflict between capital and labour, so, Touraine believes, 'post-industrial society' will be defined by a social conflict between two opposing classes.

For Touraine (1985: 778), the central conflict in society consists of a struggle for the control of 'historicity', which he defines as 'the capacity to produce historical experience through cultural patterns'. In any given society, it is the ruling class that controls historicity, or the main cultural patterns (i.e., knowledge, investment, and ethics), which they impose upon the subordinate class, who fight to define their own cultural patterns. For Touraine, then, historicity and class conflict are inextricably linked, which is reflected in his definition of a social movement as: '*the collective organized action through which a class actor battles for the social control of historicity in a given and identifiable historical context*' (Touraine 1981: 31–32, original emphasis).

Touraine sees social movements as a central force in society; they are not marginal or exceptional events. He regards both powerful and powerless adversaries as social actors capable of being 'identified with the central cultural values and norms' (Touraine 1985: 774–775). However, neither class is able to exercise complete, 'hegemonic' domination over the other, since the struggle between them is inexorable.

Like Karl Marx, Touraine argues a new 'societal type' evolves within the womb of the former society. Accordingly, there are aspects of post-industrial society evolving within industrial society, which have not disappeared altogether. Moreover, although the labour movement is in decline, industrial conflicts still exist. However, whereas industrial society was organized around work and the relations of production, class domination in the new post-industrial societal type or 'programmed society' takes the form of technocratic management and control of data and information processing.[1] Accordingly, while social justice was key to the workers' struggles in industrial society, the new social movement of the programmed society seeks 'self-management' against the growing hold technocratic control has over more and more areas of social life.

BOX 4.1 POST-MATERIALISM

The concept of 'post-materialism' is a cornerstone of new social movement theory. It derives from Ronald Inglehart's (1977) famous study of changing values and political styles among Western publics. Using mass surveys, Inglehart proposed that a shift in 'value priorities' was taking place in Western societies as they moved into a post-industrial phase of development. According to Inglehart, less emphasis is placed on material well-being and security and more emphasis is placed on the meaning and quality of life. Moreover, Inglehart's data suggested value priorities correspond to generations or age cohorts. Drawing on the work of Abraham Maslow, Inglehart (1971: 991) argued the age cohorts that had experience of wars and scarcity in the period preceding the 'economic miracles' that occurred in Western Europe would give a relatively high priority to economic security and what Maslow called, 'safety needs'. For the younger cohorts, on the other hand, 'a set of "post-bourgeois" values, relating to the need for belonging and to aesthetic and intellectual needs, would be more likely to take top priorities' (Inglehart 1971: 991–992).

As is evident from this, Inglehart's ideas were premised on the work of Maslow (1943) and, in particular, his notion that there is a 'hierarchy of human needs'. According to Maslow, human beings are motivated to meet the following basic needs: physiological, safety, love, esteem, and self-actualization. These needs are organized hierarchically whereby 'the appearance of one need usually rests on the prior satisfaction of another' (Maslow 1943: 370). The requirement to satisfy physiological needs is the most fundamental human drive: 'A person who is lacking food, safety, love, and esteem would most probably hunger for food more strongly than for anything else' (Maslow 1943: 373). Maslow argued the need for self-actualization rests upon the prior satisfaction of the physiological, safety, love, and esteem needs. However, he said, often even if all of those needs are met:

... a new discontent and restlessness will soon develop, unless the individual is doing what he is fitted for. A musician must make music, an artist must paint, a poet must write, if he is to be ultimately happy. What a man *can* be, he *must* be. This need we may call self-actualization.

(Maslow 1943: 382, original emphasis)

The need for self-actualization and its connection to quality of life is central to thinking about the emergence of new social movements. The idea here is that the establishment across Europe after the Second World War of various forms of social security and, in particular, the welfare state – partly an accomplishment of the 'old' labour movement – created conditions of relative prosperity and affluence. Under these circumstances, where basic material needs are largely met, people seek to satisfy post-material needs.

As stated earlier, Inglehart argued there is a generational dimension to this process. Thus, many of the social movements that emerged during the 1960s were driven by young people who had been born in the post-war 'baby boom', and had been raised in a period of unparalleled economic security and prosperity, which was a far cry from the 'age of austerity' in which their parents had grown up between the First and Second World Wars. Consequently, new forms of politics emerged during the 1960s that moved beyond struggles traditionally associated with working-class concerns over material security, reflecting the post-material values of an emergent and aspiring new middle class as the chief constituents of new social movements.

SOCIAL MOVEMENTS AND SOCIAL CLASS

In Box 4.1 we saw how the concerns of new social movements reflect the post-material values of the new middle classes. Frank Parkin (1968) provided an early explanation of why the Campaign for Nuclear Disarmament in Britain was composed largely of young and educated middle-class radicals. Subsequent analyses have drawn on Pierre Bourdieu's (1984) ideas to argue that 'cultural competence' explains why the educated middle classes tend to be more involved than people from other class locations, not only in new social movements and other types of 'identity movements', but also in politics and protest more generally (Crossley 2002: 173–177; Husu 2013; see also Eder 1993; Maheu 1995). According to this line of argument, the savoir-faire of middle-class activists derives from their possession of capital (e.g., economic forms of capital, such as money and ownership, and cultural capital, evident in taste and lifestyle) and a certain habitus (i.e., internalized dispositions, patterned ways of understanding and acting in the world arising from a particular structural position). Given its emphasis on the cognitive and social psychological aspects of activist involvement in social movements, it has been observed that Bourdieu's ideas share significant similarities with the framing perspective (Husu 2013: 272), as well as some elements of resource mobilization theory (Crossley 2002: 174–177), both of which were discussed in Chapter 3.

Interestingly, although Offe is frequently cited to support proposi-
tions connecting middle-class activism and new social movements, he
in fact regarded the social bases of those movements as more diverse.
For him, the social base of new movements corresponds to three segments of the social structure: the new middle class; elements of the old
middle class; and peripheral or 'decommodified' groups, such as unemployed workers, students, housewives, and retired persons (Offe 1985:
831–832). This view, then, would seem to chime with those scholars,
considered later, who criticize new social movement theory for looking only at those movements that are based on the post-material values
of the new middle classes.

SOCIAL MOVEMENTS AS 'NOMADS OF THE PRESENT'

Insofar as the transformations identified by Inglehart correspond to the
decline of industrialism (in the West, at least) and the emergence of
'post-industrial society', Alan Scott (1990: 70) has argued Inglehart's
thesis 'is essentially an empirical rendering of Touraine's theoretical
analysis'. To be sure, Touraine's work has been criticized for operating
at a high level of abstraction, which does not consider the meanings
activists themselves assign to their collective action, and does not reflect
the reality of contemporary movements as heterogeneous and not
fixed on a core class conflict (Martin 2004: 34).

Although the works of Melucci and Touraine share several themes
in common (which is unsurprising given that Melucci was a one-time
student of Touraine), unlike Touraine, Melucci is not concerned with
identifying *the* central social movement of post-industrial society. In
fact, he is critical of approaches that reify social movements and por-
tray them as epic figures moving on the historical stage. That is because
Melucci sees collective action as the *outcome* of a series of processes; it
is a social product and thus should be treated as a set of social relationships, rather than as a definite datum, metaphysical reality, or a 'thing'
with a 'real' essence (Melucci 1988: 247; 1996: 76–77).

To Melucci, social movements are complex collective phenomena
consisting of a plurality of meanings and orientations, which must be
reconciled if social actors are to develop a *collective identity*. Collective
identity then 'is as much an analytical tool as an object to be studied'
(Melucci 1996: 72). So, like resource mobilization theorists, Melucci is
interested in *how* social movements construct a collective identity out
of the diversity, tension, and conflict that characterize social movement
activity as a collective, human enterprise. But observers of 'new' social
movements are also interested in discovering *why* the formation of

65

Why collective identities are key

collective identities is so important for activists in contemporary societies. In short, they are concerned with the structural determinants of collective action, which, for Melucci, as for Touraine, are explained by recourse to a theory of society.

Both Touraine and Melucci ground their theories of social movements on the idea that there has been a fundamental shift from industrial to post-industrial society. However, whereas Touraine's ideas are premised on the notion of the emergence of a programmed society, Melucci's ideas are premised on the view that we now live in what he calls a 'complex society'. While industrial society was defined by material production, complex societies produce signs, symbols, and social relations. And, in such societies, social movements are themselves complex, fragile, and heterogeneous (Bartholomew and Mayer 1992: 142). Moreover, unlike 'old' social movements of the industrial period, 'new' movements are not focused on issues relating to socioeconomic class, but are instead focused on culture and are identity based. Hence, the emergence of 'identity politics', or what Giddens (1991b) refers to as 'life politics', which he regards as the antithesis of 'emancipatory politics' that defined social conflict in the industrial era.

Similar to Touraine's idea that the new social movement of a programmed society seeks to resist technocratic control over social life via self-management is Habermas' (1981: 36) notion that (new) social movements 'arise at the seam between system and life-world' to resist or stave off what he sees as the 'colonisation' of the latter by the former. Habermas extends Max Weber's thesis that the modern world is increasingly subject to processes of rationalization, which are evident in the growth of reason and the application of scientific knowledge to modern technology, as well as the growing influence of bureaucratic organization in modern society.

Rationalization and the concomitant process of 'internal colonization' are perhaps most clearly apparent in relations between citizens and the state. Hence, while the welfare state provides citizens with great benefits, it also exercises surveillance, regulation, and control over more areas of social life. For Habermas, new social movements arise to resist such intervention by the state into the lives of ordinary citizens: they are not concerned with issues of resource allocation and material (re)distribution, which preoccupied the 'old' labour movement, but with post-materialist concerns 'to do with the grammar of forms of life' (Habermas 1987: 392). Hence, he distinguishes the 'old politics', which, among other things, addresses economic and redistributive problems of modern capitalism, from a 'new politics' which relates to new problems of late capitalism that 'have to do with quality of life, equal rights, individual self-realization, participation and human rights' (Habermas 1987: 392).

Melucci's (1989: 175) ideas are similar to those of Touraine and Habermas insofar as he proposes contemporary social movements act as 'revealers' by exposing power that is increasingly hidden or masked by operational codes, formal rules, and bureaucratic procedures and decision-making processes. As such, they pose 'symbolic challenges' to the system – which attempts to homogenize complexity – by claiming the right to be recognized as *different*. That is why collective identity is so important, for it is through their culture or organizational form that these social movements communicate their message of difference to the wider society. And building a collective identity enables them to communicate a *coherent* message.

For these reasons, Melucci is critical of past analyses that have tended to focus on the public face of social movements, which equates collective action with mass mobilizations and demonstrations. Not only do these approaches suffer a 'myopia of the visible' (Melucci 1989: 44), but they also limit social movement activity to interactions with the state and other political actors, institutions, and movement organizations. Adopting a more expansive view of power, similar to Foucault's notion of the dispersal of power beyond politics and the state (Bartholomew and Mayer 1992: 147), Melucci considers as significant the cultural face of movements, or the 'pre-political' dimension of collective action, which resides in everyday life, social networks, and civil society. Like Oberschall (1973), whose work was discussed in Chapter 3, this perspective recognizes the importance for collective action of cultural networks and community organization. Moreover, as we shall see when we discuss social movement continuity and 'abeyance structures', movement cultures and networks are sometimes crucial for sustaining social movements in dormant periods of relative inactivity.

BOX 4.2 WOMEN'S SELF-HELP MOVEMENTS

Among other things, Melucci (1992: 53) acknowledges the influence in his work of 'the "feminine" perception of the world', which is no coincidence given the women's movement is regarded one of the key 'new' social movements. Indeed, some feminist scholars, and most notably, Verta Taylor, have criticized resource mobilization theory and political process approaches for emphasizing male-oriented, rational collective action in the public domain and ignoring the efficacy of social movements with a 'feminine logic' that are less instrumental than they are 'internally oriented [. . .] following an identity logic of action' (Taylor 1999: 10). Moreover, it has been observed that the women's movement demonstrates generally how formal, bureaucratic organization is not necessary for a social movement to operate effectively (Charles 2000: 49–50), although it has also been argued that collectivist forms of organization based on substantive or value rationality (as opposed to instrumental or formal rationality) is actually a common feature of *all* social movements (Rothschild-Whitt 1979). Of course, and as we shall see in Chapter 5, instrumental and expressive elements will often coalesce in any one social movement.

Nevertheless, according to Taylor (1999: 18), the locus of women's self-help is in submerged networks and social movement communities, and, as such, these movements are 'heavily cultural and revolve around disputed meanings and contested identities' (Taylor and Van Willigen 1996: 128). Thus, the formation of a collective identity is a vital aspect of a 'prefigurative politics', for '[b]y building a collective identity, self-help groups are able to connect women's personal experiences to the general problem of gender subordination' (Martin 2001: 378). Postpartum support and breast cancer movements and the self-help communities they form provide examples because they 'strive to exemplify a better way of organizing society by constructing a distinctive women's culture of caring in which participants can find emotional support as well as receive practical information to understand and overcome their problems' (Taylor and Van Willigen 1996: 135).

In Chapter 3, we saw how some commentators believe that in order to be successful, social movements must develop an organizational structure and have strategies that enable them to connect their demands to 'institutionally imminent possibilities' (Giddens 1991a: 155). By contrast, Melucci and other observers of 'new' social movements place a premium on social movement *autonomy*; that is, independence from the state and established political actors. Melucci says that the demands of contemporary social movements 'exist beyond political mediation and independently of its results' (Melucci 1996: 216). What he calls the 'democratization of everyday life' is signaled by the recognition and acceptance of *difference*, which occurs through the establishment of autonomous social movements:

A new political space is designed beyond the traditional distinction between state and 'civil society': an intermediate *public space*, whose function is not to institutionalize the movements nor to transform them into parties, but to make society hear their messages and translate these messages into political decision making, while the movements maintain their autonomy.

(Melucci 1985: 815, original emphasis)

For Melucci, social conflicts in complex societies are played out in the present, and are transitory. Unlike traditional forms of collective action, contemporary actors have no program, no future, and 'are not guided by a universal plan of history; rather, they resemble "nomads who dwell within the present"' (Melucci 1989: 55). Moreover, rather than 'measuring' collective action in terms of its 'effectiveness', as resource mobilization theory tends to do, Melucci (1989: 56) is concerned to show how contemporary collective actors set out to challenge or reverse dominant cultural codes, which attempt to standardize experience in differentiated, complex societies via the establishment of mass markets, as well as 'call into question the implementation of goals which have been decided by an anonymous impersonal power'. Since power lies increasingly in codes regulating information flow, the organizational form and solidarity of collective actors become an important means by which a message of difference is transmitted to the wider society. To Melucci, the women's movement is a good example of a movement that:

> . . . involves more than the affirmation of new rights and the demand for equality. It also claims the importance of difference, the need for alternative codes which demand recognition. Women raise the question of difference for the whole society, and urge that everyone be recognized as different.
>
> (Melucci 1989: 56)

Melucci's ideas differ significantly from those of resource mobilization theorists who regard social movements as rational (i.e., means-ends oriented) collective enterprises. For him, collective identity formation is not merely a vehicle used to achieve certain ends, but is a goal in itself: 'Since the action is focused on cultural codes, the *form* of the movement is a message, a symbolic challenge to the dominant patterns [. . .] The medium, the movement itself is a new medium, is the message' (Melucci 1984: 830, original emphasis). In other terms, 'movements are not qualified by what they do but what they are' (Melucci 1985: 809). It is for these reasons that Melucci stresses the importance of *social movement cultures*, and is critical of approaches prone to what he calls, 'political reductionism'. Again, the women's movement provides a case in point:

> . . . there was the creation of a women's culture, which was submerged and woven into the fabric of daily life, and which sustained and nourished women's mobilizations. But this conflict has moved

away from strictly political spheres, in which it intervenes occasionally on single issues, and operates instead predominantly in the sphere of symbolic codes. In this way, the women's movement supplies alternative definitions of otherness and communication, and transmits to the rest of society the message of possible difference.

(Melucci 1989: 95)

'Indignados' (M. Castells)

CRITICISMS OF NEW SOCIAL MOVEMENT THEORY

Unsurprisingly, theories of new social movements have been subject to criticism. Melucci (1996: 5) himself has said he 'watched with dismay as the category has been progressively reified', and that all of the critics 'commit the same epistemological mistake: they consider contemporary collective phenomena to constitute unitary empirical objects, seeking then on this basis to define the substance of their newness or to deny or dispute it'. However, for Melucci (1995: 110), rather than treating contemporary actors as personages or epic characters moving on the stage of history, they should be seen as comprising a variety of components, or as 'socially constructed collective realities'.

Steinmetz (1994: 179) has identified what he refers to as a small academic cottage industry that has grown up around attempts to prove new social movements are not really new. Essentially, critics of new social movement theory occupy two camps. First, there are those who employ historical analyses to demonstrate that new movements share features in common with past movements. So, for example, Kenneth Tucker (1991) shows how the formation of a collective identity and a sense of autonomy were central features of French syndicalism in the nineteenth century. Similarly, D'Anieri et al. (1990) argue the values of new social movements are not unlike those of the nineteenth-century Chartists; the Oneida community of the same period; and West German peace movements of the 1950s, 1970s, and 1980s. Moreover, Craig Calhoun (1994: 22) accuses new social movement theory of being 'historically myopic' for not recognizing that supposedly novel features of contemporary movements were formerly present in movements of the past. Identity politics, for instance, is nothing new:

In the early nineteenth century, labour movements were engaged in identity politics, presenting the case that the 'worker' was an identity deserving of legitimacy, calling for solidarity among those

As criticism of S.M.

sharing the identity, demanding their inclusion in the polity, and so forth.

(Calhoun 1994: 22)

Thus, for Calhoun (1994: 23), identity politics is not novel, nor is it limited to post-materialist ideologies, but 'has been part and parcel of modern politics and social life for hundreds of years'. Indeed, while it is often seen as one of the most significant 'new' social movements of the late twentieth century, Calhoun (1994: 23) argues the women's movement, in fact, 'has roots at least 200 years old'. Furthermore, he says, the nineteenth- and early-twentieth-century working-class movement was more multidimensional, and less univocal, than new social movement theorists seem to recognize; it was concerned not only with mobilization around wages, 'but also over women and children working, community life, the status of immigrants, education, access to public services, and so forth' (Calhoun 1995: 179). Finally, Calhoun (1995: 174) argues, while some movements eventually undergo institutionalization, incorporation, and co-optation, all have radical grassroots organization and eschew conventional politics to begin with. Hence, the supposed novel organizational features of new social movements are, in fact, features of *all* social movements in their nascent stage of development.

Other critics of new social movement theory argue that a variety of contemporary social struggles appear more old than new. Instead of being concerned with post-material issues and quality of life, these movements articulate more 'traditional' concerns and demands to do with material well-being, political opposition, and citizenship rights. As shown in Box 4.3, the disability movement is one such movement arguably less concerned with post-material values than with liberation, continuing inequality, and access to political and economic power (Martin 2001: 367).

BOX 4.3 DISABLED PEOPLE'S FIGHT FOR EQUAL RIGHTS AND ANTI-DISCRIMINATION LAWS

As we will see throughout this book, legal change is an important outcome of social movement activity. Indeed, in Chapter 3 we saw how the US civil rights movement developed a 'master frame' around equal rights and

© Marion Bull/Alamy

Figure 4.1 Disabled rights protesters at Parliament, Westminster, England (1999)

opportunity for all, which also became a central motif for other social movements. Importantly, formal equality for black people in the United States was achieved and became enshrined in laws banning racial discrimination, including the outlawing of discriminatory voting practices under the Voting Rights Act of 1965.

In the United Kingdom, civil rights have been demanded by a variety of groups, including women, lesbian, gay, bisexual and transgendered people, black, and disabled social movements (Annetts et al. 2009: 191). Although discrimination has not necessarily ended in practice, many of these movements have successfully achieved equal rights, in a formal sense, at least, by putting pressure on the British government to enact anti-discrimination legislation. Hence, the *Disability Discrimination Act 1995* (UK), for example, makes it unlawful to discriminate against disabled persons in employment and in the provision of goods and services, education, and transport, although employers and businesses only have to make 'reasonable adjustments' to accommodate the needs of disabled employees (Annetts et al. 2009: 192).

While the disability movement has sought to establish equality and end discrimination via the more traditional means of political inclusion and legislative reform, it has also made claims that resemble those of a new social movement. Thus, disability studies scholars have shown how the movement combines a concern for material deprivation and social disadvantage with newer concerns around autonomy and independent living (see Martin 2001: 370–371). The disability movement, therefore, is an example of a social movement that contains a mix of 'new' and 'old' elements, which is a point we take up later when we look at the coexistence of struggles for recognition and struggles for (re) distribution in 'social welfare movements'.

While some social movements are concerned with *continuing inequality,* other movements raise issues about new (and negative) forms of exclusion and discrimination in contemporary society. Thus, a variety of new movements have emerged as a reaction to 'post-Fordist' restructuring processes (see Box 4.4), which in many Western democracies elicited a 'neoliberal' response from governments (see Box 4.7). On this view, a 'crisis of Fordism' occurred in the latter part of the twentieth century. Formerly, under 'Fordism', the state intervened to ameliorate some of the worst effects of capitalism, which were most frequently suffered by the working-class citizenry. Hence, after the Second World War a number of nations introduced some version of a welfare state, which acted as a form of compensation (and safety net) for the working-class by providing such things as social security, free health care and education. Accordingly, a Keynesian form of the state became 'a necessary counterpart of the Fordist form of intensive accumulation' (Hirsch 1988: 48). Importantly, many of the concessions granted during the post-war 'golden age' of the welfare state were the ultimate outcome of hard-fought-for historical struggles over civil rights and social justice (Annetts et al. 2009).

However, from the mid-1970s, globalization, intensifying international competition, and fiscal crises, among other things, meant governments could no longer foot the bill for an extensive (and expensive) welfare state. Accordingly, from that time, neoliberal and monetarist policies were introduced to 'streamline' the welfare state, which effectively reversed many of the labour movement's past accomplishments (Turner 1986: 104–105). Perversely, much of the dismantling of welfare and state service provision in key areas such as education and health has been carried out by the 'baby boomer' generation, which benefitted the most from the free provision of those very services in the post-war era of prosperity and certainty that enabled them to participate in the (post-material) counterculture movements of the 1960s (Roszak 1970).[2]

As a result of post-Fordist restructuring, a growing number of marginalized groups could not be 'socially incorporated in the traditional (i.e., welfare state) ways' (Mayer 1991: 109). While the new social movements of the 1960s and 1970s were able to build upon the economic and political achievements of past movements to express post-material concerns, from the 1980s onwards, a growing number of social movements emerged 'for whom the quality of life [had] to do not with traffic congestion but with structural unemployment, drugs, crime, and struggles for affordable housing' (Mayer 1991: 120). Under post-Fordist conditions, then, 'old' issues resurface, including issues linked to increasing flexibility, casualization, and polarization in the workforce, which are some of the issues raised by the precarity movement (discussed later).

BOX 4.4 FROM FORDISM TO POST-FORDISM

Ash Amin (1994: 5) has argued that 'the post-Fordist debate is a confrontation of diverse viewpoints, a heterogeneity of positions which draw on different concepts to say different things about past, present and future'. Given such a position, it would be futile to provide a definitive account of post-Fordism, or Fordism, for that matter. Nevertheless, it is possible to discern some key features of each.

Fordism is so-called for its association with Henry Ford's system of automobile production, which characteristically divided labour into discrete tasks in an automated assembly line. However, according to David Harvey (1990: 125–126), what was most distinctive about Ford 'was his vision, his explicit recognition that mass production meant mass consumption'. Hence, in 1914, he introduced a five-dollar, eight-hour day, not only to 'secure worker compliance with the discipline required to work the highly productive assembly-line system', but also 'to provide workers with sufficient income and leisure time to consume the mass produced products the corporations were about to turn out in ever vaster quantities' (Harvey 1990: 126).

Under Fordism, the state assumed the role of resolving conflicts between capital and labour – such as conflict over wages – and established the necessary social conditions for capitalist production. Hence, the emergence soon after the Second World War of the Keynesian state, with its central tenet of universal welfare provision, which was, in essence, a concession to the working class, whose labour capitalists exploited and profited from. However, it must be remembered that '[t]he tense but nevertheless firm balance of power between organized labour, large corporate capital, and the nation state, and which formed the power basis for the postwar boom, was not arrived at by accident', but 'was the outcome of years of struggle' (Harvey 1990: 133).

According to Harvey (1990: 140), the Fordist-Keynesian system started to break up in 1973 when a sharp recession 'shattered that framework' and 'a process of rapid [. . .] transition in the regime of accumulation began'. Although it played out differently in different countries, the structural crisis of Fordism was a consequence of a number of factors, including declining productivity due to workers being resistant to rigid forms of Fordist work organization; globalized mass production, which made national economic management difficult; and increasing consumer demand for variegated products that could not be produced in standardized, mass-produced ways (Nielsen 1991: 24).

Whereas Fordism was driven by 'intensive accumulation', the driving force of post-Fordism is 'flexible accumulation'. The rise of flexibility is clearly apparent in work regimes and labour contracts where there has been a 'move away from regular employment towards increasing reliance upon part-time, temporary or sub-contracted work arrangements' (Harvey 1990: 150). To Richard Sennett (1998: 51–52), this '[f]lexible specialization is the antithesis of the system of production embodied in Fordism' because, for example, 'in the making of cars and trucks today, the old mile-long assembly line [. . .] has been replaced by islands of specialized production'. Just as work in post-Fordism becomes increasingly flexible or, more appropriately, 'precarious', so the power of organized labour is undermined; hence, we observe 'the rolling back of trade union power' (Harvey 1990: 150), which is a key component of neoliberalism, as the political expression of post-Fordism.

Although he is careful to stress we are living in a period of historical *transition*, which may never be entirely complete, Harvey (1990: 124) says 'the contrasts between present political-economic practices and those of the postwar boom period are sufficiently strong to make the hypothesis of a shift from Fordism to what might be called a "flexible" regime of accumulation'. Characteristics of this new epoch include 'new systems of production and marketing, characterized by more flexible labour processes and markets, of geographical mobility and rapid shifts in consumption practices', and 'the revival of entrepreneurialism and of neo-conservatism, coupled with the cultural turn to postmodernism' (Harvey 1990: 124). Indeed, if recent protests against precarity and austerity measures in Europe (discussed shortly) are anything to go by, the post-Fordist project would seem ever nearer completion.

Bartholomew and Mayer (1992) are particularly critical of Melucci's conception of 'complex society', which, they say, cannot explain these post-Fordist transformations, and the movements that emerge in their wake, because Melucci does not conceive of complex societies as organized hierarchically. Hence, his theory is unable to account for and include movements that arise on society's margins; that is, movements for civil rights, which have redistributive goals and react to negative forms of economic and social restructuring:

> Especially this sector, characterised by a newly flexibilized, unprotected workforce and out-of-workforce, seems hidden in his conception of complex society and, consequently, there is no direct attention paid to movements which reflect and develop their collective identity around unemployment, homelessness or similar newly relevant survival issues.
>
> (Bartholomew and Mayer 1992: 150)

Bartholomew and Mayer also argue that in his effort to avoid politically reductionist approaches, Melucci falls prey to 'cultural reductionism', which 'causes him to miss what is "old" or traditional in contemporary "new" social movements, such as struggles for citizenship rights and the continued existence and relevance of material issues' (Martin 2004: 38). This is a version of the idea, mentioned earlier, that social movements must connect their demands to 'institutionally imminent possibilities' (Giddens 1991a: 155), which itself reflects a more widely held view that the telos of social movements is the political inclusion of previously excluded groups and issues (Scott 1990: 10). Accordingly, it believed serious problems flow from the denial of politics in new social movement discourse, evident in its use of apolitical concepts such as autonomy and identity, in its placement of movements beyond issues of equality and welfare, and in its rigid distinction between cultural and political-economic issues (Plotke 1990: 100). Similar sentiments are expressed by Mooers and Sears (1992: 64) who are critical of Melucci's overemphasis on the symbolic aspects of social life in complex societies wherein material production is replaced by the production of signs and social relations; they ask, rather sardonically, 'one wonders what people might eat in such societies [. . .] Of course, they eat signs'.

Although they might more appropriately be referred to as a 'scene' rather than a social movement (Leach and Haunss 2009), this kind of argument has been applied to New Age Travellers, which Martin (1998) has observed were differentiated by generation. On the one hand, the older generation adopted a traveling way of life out of *choice* and expressed post-material values tied to new social movements, such as the green and peace movements, as well as new age spirituality (see Chapter 6). On the other hand, the younger generation was *forced* to move onto the road, having suffered homelessness and unemployment, which were just some of the negative social effects of neoliberal and neoconservative policies introduced in a post-Fordist context, and embraced by Thatcherite governments in Britain during the 1980s and 1990s.

Melucci has responded to his post-Fordist critics, arguing that although their analyses contribute to knowledge about new forms of domination, they are nonetheless imprisoned by old categories and outdated thought, as well as their obstinate adherence to 'post' notions. This prevents them from developing new understandings, which Melucci (1996: 90) says he tried to do via 'the working notions of "complex society" and "information society"'.

SOCIAL WELFARE MOVEMENTS: RECOGNITION OR REDISTRIBUTION, OR BOTH?

Critiques of new social movement theory, like that of Mooers and Sears (1992), who have wondered what people might eat in Melucci's complex societies, indicate that struggles for material improvement, or what Annetts et al. (2009: 7) call quaintly, the 'politics of the belly', have not disappeared, but persist in contemporary societies. Indeed, in their book about British social welfare movements, Annetts et al. offer accounts of both older welfare movements and 'new welfare movements'. The former were organized around what the 1942 Beveridge Report considered the 'five evils' of disease, want, squalor, ignorance, and idleness. Accordingly, Annetts et al. examine movements of the unemployed, the women's health movement, urban social movements, and social movements focused on the making of modern education.

Whereas these older welfare movements were instrumental in building the modern welfare state, new welfare movements 'operate in and around an already established welfare state system to preserve, extend, deepen and improve service delivery' (Annetts et al. 2009: 10). Included here are lesbian, gay, bisexual and transgendered activism, anti-racist movements, and eco-welfare movements, which, in Britain, have involved, respectively, the fight to secure civil partnership legislation, race riots in the north of England, and anti-road protests and the 'greening' of social welfare policy. Annetts et al. also consider movements for global social justice to be new welfare movements. Indeed, they argue, these movements could be regarded new social welfare movements par excellence, because 'when neoliberal antipathy to state welfare has been central to government social policy making, these movements have mobilized to defend the very principle of social welfare itself' (Annetts et al. 2009: 10–11).

Social movement resistance to neoliberalism is a topic to which we turn towards the end of this chapter, and the response of activists to globalization is considered in more depth in Chapter 9. For now, however, it is worth considering the argument that *all* contemporary social movements, to some degree or other, raise issues about the recognition of identity, culture, and difference *as well as* material inequality, redistribution, and exploitation. This relates to what, in a seminal essay, Nancy Fraser (1995: 69, original emphasis) terms the redistribution-recognition dilemma, which she resolves by proposing 'justice today requires *both* redistribution *and* recognition'. Accordingly, she talks of 'bivalent collectivities', which are 'hybrid modes' of collective action 'located in the middle of the conceptual extremes' that combine 'injustices that are traceable to both political economy and culture simultaneously'; in sum, bivalent collectivities 'may suffer both socioeconomic maldistribution and cultural misrecognition' (Fraser 1995: 78).

This idea has, in turn, been applied to contemporary welfare movements, which, not unlike new social movements, build upon the material-welfare accomplishments of past movements, but do so from the perspective of different lifestyles and identities. An example here would be the aforementioned women's self-help and postpartum depression movements, which combine redistribution and recognition, since they 'pose challenges to symbolic codes and institutional practices that may transform social policy' (Martin 2001: 376). Thus, through 'speak-outs', for instance, 'the movement brings postpartum illness into the public eye and challenges images of femininity that tie women to the private realm of the home and to motherhood' (Martin 2001: 377). Furthermore, by encouraging the partners of women suffering postpartum depression to participate in housework and childcare and to provide support and understanding, the movement challenges gendered views of care in society (Taylor and Van Willigen 1996: 136).

PROTESTING PRECARITY: NEW WINE, OLD BOTTLES?

As we have seen, a number of critics of new social movement theory cite issues of precariousness, or precarity, associated with post-Fordist restructuring to highlight the fact that not all social movements in contemporary societies are concerned with post-material values. In this section, we consider in more detail how precarity has become an important site of protest in ways that are reminiscent of the socioeconomic and material struggles most often associated with the 'old' labour movement. Indeed, as we shall see, it is debatable whether precarity itself is an entirely novel phenomenon.

In order to understand the precarity movement, it is essential first to grasp what is meant by the term 'precarity' and consider its contemporary significance. Classically, precarity has been seen as a feature of forms of employment that emerged from the mid-1970s, when jobs started to become increasingly temporary, casualized, and 'flexible'. By contrast, under the Fordist-Keynesian model (see Box 4.4), workers could reasonably expect to have stable jobs or 'a job for life', union representation, and a social safety net in the shape of the welfare state. Precarious workers suffer a double whammy: not only has job security disappeared, but under neoliberal post-Fordist regimes the welfare state has been dismantled and the power of trade unions has diminished. Indeed, while the destruction of unions has been part of the political project of neoliberalism, the demise of unionism is also connected to the changing nature of work in post-industrial societies.

At one time, people in the industrial West tended to work together en masse in large factories geared to the mass production of goods. People also tended to live in the communities where they worked. These conditions were conducive to the establishment of trade unions and collective mobilization around improving working conditions. Precarious and flexible forms of work, on the other hand, militate against this kind of collective organization: many people now work from home, work part-time or on short-term contracts, or they work in virtual or networked environments. Therefore, more people have less contact with their coworkers. As the workforce has become fragmented in this way, so the possibilities for collective action have dwindled. However, this has not stopped alliances and networks forming between a diversity of groups to protest against precarious work.

Who then are precarious workers, or the 'precariat' (Standing 2011), as they have come to be known? The people adversely affected by negative forms of flexibilization tend largely to be young people, migrants, and women. Examples include high-tech and new media workers in the United States (Brophy 2006), and cultural workers in France's film and television industries (Bodnar 2006). And, in these sectors, it is not only temporary workers who are affected by precarity.

Brophy shows how in the information technology (IT) business, the advent of offshore outsourcing has impacted upon upper-tier, full-time, permanent staff, who are now threatened by the same conditions that once affected only their 'permatemp' coworkers; for example, endless short-term contracts punctuated by periods of unemployment. Hence, according to Ross (2008: 43), as 'offshore outsourcing has climbed into white-collar sectors and is taking its toll on the professions, the plight of garment workers, onshore and offshore, can no longer be viewed as a remote example of job degradation, unlikely to affect the highly skilled'. Consequently, we witness the emergence of a global 'anti-sweatshop movement', which is 'an agile, international coalition to confront the power of large corporations' and push for labour rights.

A note of caution should be sounded here, though, since some researchers have pointed out that precarious work is not solely connected to what Hardt and Negri (2000) call 'immaterial labour'; that is, workers who produce commodities that are not material, but immaterial, such as information, knowledge, and communications. While the precarity movement in Europe has tended to be composed of young middle-class professionals (De Sario 2007: 27–8; Neilson and Rossiter 2008: 57), precarity itself is not limited to this class of people, and, indeed, it extends beyond the realm of employment. Precarious workers include Latino immigrant cleaners in the United States as well as highly skilled migrant IT workers on temporary work visas (Neilson and Rossiter 2008: 60–1). It also encompasses the Sans-papiers (discussed in Chapter 7) and other noncitizen migrants who are employed in precarious jobs:

> Precarity, then, does not have its model worker. Neither artist nor migrant, nor hacker nor housewife [. . .] Rather, precarity strays across a number of labour practices [. . .] it traverses a spectrum of labour markets and positions within them.
>
> (Neilson and Rossiter 2006: 11)

Because precarity equals instability and uncertainty, it affects areas of peoples' lives beyond work. For instance, being employed on a short-term contract has an impact upon housing, in that it affects one's prospects of securing a mortgage. Precarity also influences relationships, family life, and even fertility; for instance, women may delay having children until (if ever) either they or their partner attain stable employment. It is for these kinds of reasons that scholars have argued precarity is rapidly becoming common to all: a generalized condition of living in post-industrial societies in the twenty-first century (De Sario 2007: 28, 36).

However, Neilson and Rossiter (2008) question whether precarity is actually new at all. They propose Fordism was in fact an exceptional blip in capitalist development, which for a short period only provided people with certainty, stability, and security. Before and after this phase of capitalism, precarity has tended to define peoples' lives: 'If we look at capitalism in a wider historical and geographical scope, it is precarity that is the norm and not Fordist economic organization' (Neilson and Rossiter 2008: 54).

Notwithstanding the fact that precarity affects people's lives beyond employment, most of the protest has revolved around precarious work. Indeed, since precarious employment touches people 'in a multitude of different sectors' (Bodnar 2006: 688), the Meluccian challenge for activists is how to articulate their demands and convey their messages in a clear and coherent collective voice. In the beginning, the precarity protests that took place across Europe from 2001 fed off the wider anti-globalization movement and campaigns against the Iraq war (see Bodnar 2006: 685; De Sario 2007: 25, 26; Neilson and Rossiter 2008: 57). In this sense, the precarity movement was a 'spin-off' movement, drawing its impetus and inspiration from an 'initiator' movement (McAdam 1995).

The movement then came to be associated with the EuroMayDay events. Scholars have documented the repertoires used by the European precarity movement, which include what Chesters and Welsh (2004: 328) call 'carnivalesque forms of protest' (discussed in Chapter 5), although Rucht (2005) has argued that since its beginnings in 1890, May Day has mostly been both a 'day of struggle' *and* a 'day of festivities'. Thus, tactics include the use of performance, street parades and festivals, visual images and counter images on posters, and the adoption of the colour pink to express affinity with queer politics and global justice protests (see De Sario 2007; Mattoni and Doerr 2007). In her analysis of the visual images used by the European precarity movement, Nicole Doerr (2010) provides an example of a poster that appeared in the Italian city of Milan in 2008, which stresses the connection between precarity and migration (Figure 4.2.1). To protect precarious workers everywhere, the precarity movement has even invented its own saint, San Precario (Figure 4.2.2), whose 'image appeared for the first time during a direct action organized in a Milanese supermarket on 29 February 2004, a date that lacked a saint in the official calendar of the Italian Catholic Church' (Mattoni and Doerr 2007: 131).

BOX 4.5 SYMBOLS OF PRECARITY PROTESTS

Figure 4.2.1 May Day poster – liberazione

© Designed by Chainworkers.org CreW and inspired by the work of the artist Chris Woods

Figure 4.2.2 San Precario (santino) – patron saint of precarious workers

More recently, the precarity movement has shown signs of developing collective identities (à la Melucci), despite the diversity of groups adversely affected by precarity. For example, Bodnar (2006: 688) shows how, rather than defining themselves by their sector or industry, workers in France have organized under the generic category of 'intermittent and precarious' workers. In the process, alliances have been forged between cultural workers and precarious workers in fast food chains, supermarkets, and retail stores. Similarly, Brophy (2006: 622) shows how the rise of precarity provides an opportunity for mobilization by creating 'powerful affinities between figures as diverse as the software tester, the call centre worker and the undocumented nanny'. In an interview conducted by Doerr (2010), one European precarity protestor shows how a collective identity is emerging around migration and precarity. For them, migrants are the most precarious of all workers. And although the situations of all precarious workers are diverse, they say:

> . . . we are united in the need to find new ways to counter the ever increasing capitalist claims on our lives [. . .] we ask for uncondi-tional basic income stability, a European living wage, full legalization for migrants, self-organizing and unionizing rights freed from repression, access to culture, knowledge, and skills, the right to cheap housing.
>
> (Doerr 2010)

According to Andrew Ross (2008), however, people should not be overly optimistic about the power of the precariat. First, he doubts 'there is enough commonality to forge a political coalition of interests against the class polarization associated with economic liberalization' (Ross 2008: 41). For instance, the imbalance in social capital enjoyed by the range of constituents makes it likely those occupations with the most cachet would expect to play a central role while sidelining the others. Second, although many precarious workers do indeed desire the security of full-time, permanent employment, for others, intermit-tent and part-time work can be used to one's advantage by, for instance, helping to 'finance other interests, like acting, writing, travel or recre-ation' (Ross 2008:42). Therefore, because precarity is 'unevenly experienced', precarity in and of itself 'cannot be thought of as a com-mon target, but rather as a zone of contestation between competing versions of flexibility in labour markets' (Ross 2008: 42).

Similarly, Neilson and Rossiter (2008: 65) argue precarity does not furnish 'a pre-given cause for contemporary labour struggles'. They provide the example of a strike that was mounted by Indian taxi drivers in the Australian city of Melbourne following the fatal stabbing of a fellow taxi driver in a racist attack. The taxi drivers, who demanded better safety and working conditions, were also international university students whose visas allowed them to work only twenty hours per week. In this and similar 'organized networks', suggest Neilson and Rossiter (2008: 67), the common cause defies 'any straightforward transposition into state politics and cannot be confined within a single channel of political communication'. And, in this way, it resembles very much the heterogeneity of social movements discussed by Melucci:

> It is not a matter of building lasting alliances between, say, taxi driv-ers, university students and migrants [. . .] That participants in the blockade were simultaneously workers, students and migrants does

not mean that these three groups, when constituted separately, share interests, social outlooks or experiences of precarity.

(Neilson and Rossiter 2008: 67)

For Ross, there is also a gulf between the individualistic outlook of creative and knowledge workers and the enthusiasm shown by other precarious groups (e.g., migrants) for traditional trade union ways of organizing. Indeed, 'microserfs' working in the IT sector have been reluctant to enlist the support of trade unions, partly because unions are seen as archaic and undemocratic (Brophy 2006: 631), and partly because IT workers identify as 'professionals' and associate trade unions with manufacturing or craft labourers (Brophy 2006: 628). Likewise, the activities of intermittent workers in the French film and television industries 'increasingly took place outside the realm of union activities – and sometimes in direct opposition to union activities' (Bodnar 2006: 687). However, despite that reticence, in 1998, IT workers in the United States formed the WashTech union – an affiliate of the Communication Workers of America – and did so 'in the teeth of industrial cultures that promote an individualistic professional ethos' (Ross 2008: 42: see also Brophy 2006).

Thus, while immigrant campaigns such as the Service Employees International Union's Justice for Janitors 'has played a large, ongoing role in renovating the trade union movement' (Ross 2008: 42), the collective organization of workers in the IT sector is seen as an instance of the formation of 'new labour associations' (Brophy 2006: 624). Similarly, Bodnar (2006) argues the actions of cultural workers in France are the basis for a 'new labour movement', and De Sario (2007: 27) claims the EuroMayDay precarity actions constitute a strange kind of 'neo-trade unionism'.

This begs the question whether the precarity movement is a 'new' social movement, or a reincarnation of the 'old' labour or union movement. Research into social welfare movements discussed earlier (Annetts et al. 2009), including the contentious politics of unemployment in Europe (Giugni 2009), certainly indicates precarity born of being out of work is nothing new. Moreover, if we accept Neilson and Rossiter's (2008) argument that Fordism was a momentary phase of capitalist development and that precarity is the norm, it is not hard to draw parallels between the past and present. Indeed, echoing Tucker's (1991) critique of new social movement theory (discussed earlier), Bodnar (2006: 691) concludes, 'the precariat may well be the contemporary equivalent to industrial syndicalism movements of the past century'. Nor is the diversity of the precarity movement fundamentally novel, for, as we have seen, the historical labour movement was multidimensional and only provisionally and partially unified (Calhoun 1994: 179). On balance, then, it would seem the precarity movement represents the reemergence of older struggles organized around work, albeit its grievances and demands are made in new times.

We will look more at the question of novelty when we consider the various protests that have sprung up, particularly in Europe, as a response to austerity measures introduced by governments after the global financial crisis (GFC) of 2008. Before doing so, we consider how what appear to be novel issues can actually be the reemergence of older issues, albeit in a new context, as well as how social movements sustain themselves over time during periods of relative inactivity, when they seem to have disappeared, having, for example, been confronted by a hostile political environment.

ABEYANCE STRUCTURES

We have seen how new social movement theory has been criticized for falsely claiming to be novel features of contemporary movements that were present in movements of the past. One way of explaining 'movement continuity' over time is via Verta Taylor's (1989: 761) concept of 'abeyance', which 'depicts a holding process by which movements sustain themselves in nonreceptive political environments and provide continuity from one stage of mobilization to another'.

Taylor (1989: 772) sets out to challenge the 'immaculate conception' interpretation of social movements, highlighting the 'sources of continuity between cycles of movement activity'. She questions the view held by most researchers that the American women's rights movement emerged out of the US civil rights movement, which reputedly provided a 'master frame' for it and other social movements (see Chapter 3). Instead, she argues, like Calhoun (1994: 23), that the women's movement of the 1960s had its 'roots in an earlier cycle of feminist activism that presumably ended when suffrage was won' (Taylor 1989: 761). When in 1920 the vote was finally won (see Figure 4.3), the women's movement split into two branches: militant and moderate suffragists. In a sense, the success of the suffragettes was also their undoing, as feminists were left with no unifying goal.[3] And even though feminist activism continued during the 1920s and 1930s, cooperation between the two camps of suffragists was minimal and limited.

In the years after the Second World War (1945–1960) the women's movement faced an inhospitable social and political environment and, consequently, entered a period of relative hiatus. The 1950s are often portrayed as a period of calm after the turbulence of the war. An aspect of this was manifest culturally in ideas about a return to traditional family life, which, among other things, sought to affirm women's role as homemakers. Taylor (1989: 765) shows how women who deviated from this norm were regarded as sick, immoral, and neurotic – a view that was reinforced by the media, which 'denounced feminism, discredited women who continued to advocate equality, and thus thwarted the mobilization of discontented women'. Perhaps not surprisingly, the lifestyle and demographic characteristics of the militant suffragette members of the National Women's Party (NWP) did not match up to the normative cultural ideal. Many were educated, employed in middle-class professional and semi-professional jobs, and unmarried. However, although the hostile political and social environment meant members of the NWP were alienated, marginalized, and isolated, the NWP nevertheless 'provided a structure and status capable of absorbing these intensely committed feminists and thus functioned as an abeyance organization' (Taylor 1989: 765).

Taylor argues that despite being in the doldrums from 1945 to the mid-1960s, the NWP did have an impact upon a revitalized movement for gender equality in the late 1960s, thereby contesting the

Figure 4.3 English suffragist, Millicent Fawcett (1847–1929) addresses a rally at Hyde Park, London in 1913

view the women's movement had its roots in the 1960s civil rights movement. In particular, she considers the role members of the NWP played in founding the National Organization for Women (NOW) in 1966 and considers three ways in which the NWP shaped later feminist activism by providing: (i) preexisting activist networks; (ii) an existing repertoire of goals and tactics; and (iii) a collective identity.

Taylor's arguments demonstrate her eclectic use of social movement theory. First, she relies heavily upon a central premise of resource mobilization theory (discussed in Chapter 3), namely that 'political opportunities and an indigenous organizational base are major factors in the rise and decline of movements' (Taylor 1989: 761). In examining the significance of preexisting links and organizations for women's collective action, Taylor shows how many women who participated in struggles for women's rights throughout the 1940s and 1950s became active in the resurgent women's movement of the 1960s. The NWP, in particular, provided an underground feminist network and resources vital to the formation of NOW.

The NWP movement also influenced the goals and tactical choices of the resurgent movement. Applying Tilly's (1979) concept of 'repertories of contention' (see Chapter 3), Taylor (1989: 771) suggests 'the array of collective actions that a movement develops to sustain itself should influence the goals and tactics adopted by the same movement in subsequent mass mobilizations'. The NWP abandoned many of its more radical strategies after suffrage was won, but it retained constitutional amendment as a key goal. And largely because of NWP pressure, NOW voted in 1967 to endorse the Equal Rights Amendment to the US Constitution (proposed to guarantee nondiscrimination on account of sex), 'which became the most unifying goal of the movement by the 1970s' (Taylor 1989: 771). NOW also aped many of the NWP's institutionalized tactics; for example, lobbying, letter writing, and pressurizing political parties.

Second, in accordance with theorists of 'new' social movements, and Melucci in particular, Taylor shows how the NWP affected the development of group identity and consciousness in the American women's rights movement. The NWP provided the 1960s women's movement with a sense of being connected to the past, which, Taylor argues, is crucial to forming a collective identity. Because of its ties to suffrage, the NWP stood as a powerful symbol of women's long history of oppression and resistance.

SUMMARY

What is impressive about Taylor's account of abeyance structures and social movement continuity is that it draws upon several perspectives, discussed here and in Chapter 3. First, it is influenced by the political process model and resource mobilization theory, demonstrating the importance of political opportunities and preexisting organizations and networks for movement mobilization. Second, it helps explain the rise and decline of movement mobilization, or what Sidney Tarrow (1998) calls 'cycles of protest'. Third, Tilly's concept of 'repertoires of contention' is used to show how some of the tactics and goals of earlier activism are adopted in subsequent campaigns. Fourth, Taylor's work gives the lie to the idea of 'new' social movements by proposing that contemporary movements are always, to some extent or other, manifestations of deep-seated historical processes.

BOX 4.6 ABEYANCE STRUCTURES AND SOCIAL WELFARE: THE INFANT WELFARE MOVEMENT

Infant mortality, or infant death, was a problem in the early part of the twentieth century in places like Britain, since in a period of intensifying international economic, military, and imperial competition, it meant the number of potential workers and soldiers would dwindle (Dwork 1987). The infant welfare movement sought to reduce infant and child mortality by educating mothers about basic food hygiene and proper sanitation. The movement was made up of medical professionals (doctors and nurses), voluntary workers, and philanthropists. In schools and welfare centres, young mothers were taught autonomy and self-help and instilled with a sense of individual maternal responsibility, which was supported by a relatively conservative 'ideology of motherhood rooted in the nineteenth century doctrine of spheres, which made women's proper place the home' (Lewis 1980: 476–477). The movement also provided many women with 'information, companionship and a measure of assurance' (Lewis 1980: 485). Interestingly, the infant welfare movement provides an example of the operation of abeyance structures as described by Verta Taylor (1989).

Farmer and Boushel (1999: 86–88) argue that the strength of the movement during the nineteenth century might be explained by the relative weakness of the feminist movement during that period. Their argument is that, at times, women have played a vital role in various campaigns to force the state to be more active in the protection of children. For instance, when the feminist movement has been strong, it has been able to draw attention to the physical and sexual violence of men within the home. However, when the feminist movement has been less active, society has concerned itself with issues of 'neglect', which is usually taken to mean poor mothering. The implication here is that during these periods, women's activism has tended to be more 'defensive' and hidden or submerged in communities and everyday networks, that is, abeyance structures. These arguments suggest that far from being a 'new' social movement, the 1960s women's movement was but the latest manifestation of long-term feminist activism; hence, the reason why '[s]ome trace the movement further back than the current [twentieth] century, citing parallel activities in connection with sexuality, prostitution, child sexual abuse, marriage, education, employment and health in the 1850s' (Pascall 1998: 202).

SOCIAL MOVEMENTS SURVIVING NEOLIBERALISM

As discussed earlier, the 'crisis in Fordism' elicited a neoliberal response from numerous governments, mainly in the Western world. In many respects, neoliberalism might be regarded the political counterpart of the post-Fordist regime of 'flexible accumulation'. Since each regime of accumulation requires a corresponding mode of social and political regulation, neoliberalism is to post-Fordism what Keynesianism was to Fordism. While much has been written about the role of working-class movements in establishing the welfare state, the new movements that built upon that achievement, and social struggles against the negative effects of post-Fordist restructuring, few have considered the effects of neoliberalism on social movements and the ways social movements have responded to neoliberalism. Moreover, while Annetts et al. (2009: 232–233) show how 'neoliberal globalization' has been the target of global social justice campaigns (discussed in Chapter 9), there is scant research exploring how the relationship of neoliberalism to social movements has played out in particular places.

However, Maddison and Martin (2010: 104) do show how this happened in Australia from 1996–2007, when progressive social movements were greatly restrained by the government of Prime Minister John Howard, which combined neoliberalism and neoconservatism 'in an appeal to nationalism, moral righteousness, family values and antagonism to new social movements'. Contributing to scholarship on both political opportunity *and* movement continuity, Maddison and Martin show how Australian social movements persisted in a hostile political climate bereft of opportunities via a number of *survival strategies*, which were complex and sometimes contradictory. For example, parts of the Australian environment movement embraced neoliberalism. In the face of the Howard government's anti-green sentiment and skepticism towards claims about the manmade origins of climate change and global warming, environmental groups, such as Earthshare, sought to combat government funding reductions by working 'within and without the business community' (Doyle 2010: 166). They did so by 'approaching big business corporations to participate in a payroll deduction scheme as a means of raising funds for its activities' (Maddison and Martin 2010: 114).

By contrast, a resurgent labour movement opposed legislation intended to deregulate the labour market and erode worker rights in a campaign that in no small part led to the ultimate downfall of John Howard and his government (Muir and Peetz 2010). However, during the years of the Howard government, the labour movement sometimes worked with and sometimes appeared to work against social movements in Australia. On the one hand, the Australian Council of Trade Unions withdrew its support for 'sheltered workshops' (employing disabled people) to be registered through the national industrial relations regulatory body (Soldatic and Chapman 2010: 146). On the other hand, the union movement worked with advocates for refugee rights 'in refusing to refuel planes that were to deport asylum seekers, allowing sufficient time for legal injunctions to stop the deportations' (Tazreiter 2010: 211).

BOX 4.7 AUSTERITY AND PROTEST

Following the GFC that occurred in 2008, a number of Western governments introduced 'austerity measures', which were public spending cuts (e.g., cuts in education, health, housing) designed to tackle the accumulation of national debt and compensate for the huge public cost of bailing out the banks. Given that the banks were responsible for precipitating the GFC, many groups emerged to protest against austerity measures. In Britain, for example, UK Uncut have contested the proclamation of Prime Minister David Cameron that, 'we are all in this together', highlighting the fundamental contradiction in that statement: 'Ordinary people must accept savage public spending cuts, whilst rich corporations can avoid paying billions and billions in tax' (www.ukuncut.org.uk).

Groups protesting against austerity are outraged by the fact that bankers continue to reward themselves excessive bonuses while politicians stand idly by, since this is seen as just one example of the injustices endemic in capitalism. Hence, the emergence globally of the Occupy movement, which, to many:

> ... was the moment when resistance to the inequalities of capitalism finally emerged: a tipping point in which the unfairness of bank bailouts juxtaposed against rising personal poverty triggered a moment of clarity of the absurdity of the current economic and political system.
>
> (Pickerill and Krinsky 2012: 279)

More localized reactions to austerity have occurred across Europe (Flesher Fominaya and Cox 2013), including the protests in Spain of the Indignados (the outraged) who have mobilized against some of the adverse consequences of austerity politics, such as home evictions (Hughes 2011; Romanos 2014); although it has been argued that the Indignados are a direct precedent and inspiration for the Occupy Wall Street movement in the United States (Castañeda 2012), which itself became a movement with an international reach (Pickerill and Krinsky 2012: 284).

The origins of the GFC lay in the deregulation of financial markets, which has been a key tenet of neoliberalism. Given the project of neoliberalism is 'to re-establish the conditions for capital accumulation and to restore the power of economic elites' (Harvey 2005: 19), it is apt to consider austerity as the end game of neoliberalism. As stated earlier, neoliberalism is the political expression of post-Fordism. So while the negative consequences of post-Fordist restructuring processes (discussed earlier) may indeed give rise to 'newly relevant survival issues' (Bartholomew and Mayer 1992: 150), these issues, and the movement about which they revolve, are not new in themselves. Rather, what is new is the context within which these issues emerge and movements operate. As such, many ostensibly novel issues and new movements are simply the latest manifestations of older issues raised by movements of the past, including issues to do with precarity, unemployment, inequality, and injustice.

SYNTHESIZING APPROACHES

In the introduction to this book, we saw how the field of social movement studies is sometimes seen as being spilt between American and European approaches, although that division has become less rigid over time. Indeed, some of the earlier attempts to reconcile US and European approaches made explicit reference to the geographic origins of those perspectives (Klandermans 1991; Klandermans and Tarrow 1988; Tarrow 1991). Broadly speaking, North American approaches, such as resource mobilization theory, have tended to focus on strategy and the political effects of social movement activity, while European approaches, such as new social movement theory, have focused on identity and institutional change within civil society (Cohen 1985). Furthermore, while the former perspective views social movements as offensive attempts at 'inclusion within and expansion of political society', the latter tends to see them as seeking to defend and democratize civil society (Foweraker 1995: 21).

Foweraker (1995: 21) agrees with Cohen (1985) that it is possible to synthesize these two seemingly divergent approaches to treat social movements as both *expressive* and *instrumental*, which has also been recognized by other social movement scholars, as we shall see in the next chapter. Cohen's argument is that instrumental-strategic activity and collective identity formation can coexist in a single movement, and therefore, movements may involve struggles for political inclusion *as well as* struggles for the democratization of civil society. Social movements then have a dualistic character:

> . . . the civil rights movement (in the United States) sought both civil rights and the removal of traditional norms of social control, while the feminist movement aspires to change patriarchal institutions as well as winning economic and political power.
>
> (Foweraker 1995: 21)

Although this argument is reminiscent of those who are critical of new social movement theory for ignoring the role of identity and culture in historical movements (see earlier), Cohen is critical of analysts like Craig Calhoun who appear to believe social movements develop in linear stages, 'with the first stage creating identity and the second focusing on strategic action' (Foweraker 1995: 22). Rather, says Foweraker (1995: 22), 'identity cannot simply be conceived as a precondition of strategic action, because the processes of organization and strategic choice contribute crucially to construct and shape this identity'.

The notion that social movements are simultaneously cultural and political resembles very much Fraser's (1995) arguments, discussed earlier, about 'bivalent collectivities', which combine injustices to do with political economy, or material *redistribution*, and cultural *recognition*. Moreover, these ideas invoke the discussion we had towards the end of Chapter 3 about the 'cultural turn' in resource mobilization theory, or the attempt by McAdam et al. (1996) to include a role for social constructivist framing processes in studies of social movements. It will be recalled that this model was criticized for relegating culture to the status of a resource (Nash 2000: 128). Steven Buechler (2011: 189) has recently expressed a similar view, arguing McAdam et al.'s (1996) synthesis is essentially 'a "makeover" of the political process approach'. Likewise, Goodwin and Jasper (1999: 42) regard the synthesis as an updated version of McAdam's (1982) political process model, which 'only recognises strategic framing, reducing it to yet another "resource"' (Buechler 2011: 191). For Buechler:

> The proposal thus anoints a hierarchy rather than producing a genuine synthesis. Resource mobilization and political process theory provide the core ideas. Framing is included as a junior partner. New social movement theory and cultural questions in general are marginalized despite nods in their direction.
>
> (Buechler 2011: 190)

The various attempts to produce a synthetic approach to the study of social movements demonstrate it is no easy task, and that a key problem is the forced fit of essentially incompatible ideas, which leads to '"conceptual stretching" that dilutes the clear and specific meanings of terms for the sake of incorporating other elements' (Buechler 2011: 191; see also Goodwin and Jasper 1999: 52). In contrast to these synthetic models are the more organic approaches of people like Alberto Melucci and Verta Taylor. We saw earlier how Taylor's account of feminist activism and abeyance structures has drawn eclectically on a range of social movement theories and perspectives, from resource mobilization theory to ideas about the significance of culture, which is central to thinking about 'new' social movements.

Similarly, the work of Melucci (1989: 21–22, original emphasis) goes beyond the dualism of, on the one hand, structural theories that 'explain *why* but not *how* a movement is established and survives', and, on the other hand, resource mobilization models which 'regard such action as mere data and fail to examine its meaning and orientation'. Thus, Melucci argues, to understand contemporary social movements, we must examine both the *how* and the *why* of collective action. By looking at the *how*, 'we discover the plurality of perspectives, meanings and relationships which crystallize in any given collective action' (Melucci 1989: 25). Looking at the *why* allows us to understand that 'contemporary movements, more than others in the past, have shifted towards a non-political terrain: the need for self-realization in everyday life' whereby they 'challenge the logic of complex systems on cultural grounds' (Melucci 1989: 23).

Indeed, in his own effort to reconcile US and European approaches, Sidney Tarrow (1991: 396) has recognized that '[o]f the European scholars associated with the new social movement approach, only Alberto Melucci and his collaborators have tried to devise methodologies fitted to the task of studying collective identity formation between the overly structural European approach and the highly individualistic American one'. A similar approach has been adopted by Melucci's former student, Mario Diani (1992: 13), who stresses the role of social networks, cultural conflicts, and processes of meaning and collective identity construction to arrive at a synthetic definition of the concept of social movement, which he regards as 'a network of informal interactions between a plurality of individuals, groups and/or organizations, engaged in a political or cultural conflict, on the basis of a shared collective identity'.

CONCLUSION

In Chapter 3, we looked mostly at those theories, perspectives, and concepts that fall within the *strategy* paradigm identified by Cohen (1985), which concentrates on the mobilization of resources and political processes. In that chapter, we also looked briefly at some of the ways culture has been incorporated into resource mobilization theory and the political process model via framing approaches. By contrast, this chapter has focused on ideas falling broadly within the *identity* paradigm (Cohen 1985), which is concerned, among other things, with social movement cultures, transformations of civil society, and the democratization of everyday life. Using historical and contemporary examples, we have examined some important critiques of theories about 'new' social movements and, as in Chapter 3, have ended by looking at how social movement scholars have attempted to reconcile these divergent approaches to produce a synthesis.

The next chapter builds on this one by providing an extended analysis of the cultural dimensions of social movements and collective action. It includes a look at the study of emotions and 'passionate politics', the role of narrative and storytelling in social movements, and the significance of music and other performative aspects of social protest, some of which we have considered here in this chapter when we looked, for instance, at the role of carnivalesque protest, festivity, and colour in European May Day events.

SUGGESTED READINGS

The following texts are useful to explore the issues raised by this chapter.

Books

Melucci, A. (1989) *Nomads of the Present: Social Movements and Individual Needs in Contemporary Society*. London: Hutchinson Radius.
Touraine, A. (1981) *The Voice and the Eye*. Cambridge: Cambridge University Press.

These two books are classics in the field of new social movement theory.

Scott, A. (1990) *Ideology and the New Social Movements*. London: Unwin Hyman.

Although now a little dated, Alan Scott's book remains a useful introduction to the study of new social movements. It also looks at perspectives we have considered elsewhere in the book (e.g., collective behaviour theory), provides a detailed account of the ecology movement, and considers the perennial problems associated with social movements becoming political parties.

Journals

Buechler, S. M. (1995) 'New Social Movement Theories' *The Sociological Quarterly* 36(3): 441–464.
Pichardo, N. A. (1997) 'New Social Movements: A Critical Review' *Annual Review of Sociology* 23: 411–430.
These articles provide useful reviews and evaluations of the new social movement paradigm.

Cohen, J. L. (1985) 'Strategy or Identity: New Theoretical Paradigms and Contemporary Social Movements' *Social Research* 52(4): 663–716.
Diani, M. (1992) 'The Concept of Social Movement' *The Sociological Review* 40(1): 1–25.
Cohen and Diani both provide overviews of the field, as well as synthetic approaches to conceiving of social movements.

NOTES

1 'Technocracy' refers to an elite of technical experts who use scientific methods to govern or control a society or industry.
2 Research published by Prudential Insurance in 2009 suggests 1948 was the 'luckiest' year in the twentieth century to be born, 'providing a generation with both a growing public sector to mitigate risks and unprecedented house-price inflation for those who bought property in the 1970s' (Davies 2011). Given that statistic, and the fact that the baby boomer generation has been

instrumental in abolishing the free provision of education and other services they themselves benefitted from, it is unsurprising that many young people feel alienated and aggrieved at having had their futures stolen by the baby boomers (Beckett 2010; Willetts 2010), and that commentators have predicted a civil war between the generations (Howker and Malik 2010). This might also help explain why some of the most prominent contemporary protests concerned with inequality and exclusion are composed of young people and students (Ibrahim 2011; Salter and Boyce Kay 2011).

3   Similarly, Staggenborg (2011: 42–43) notes that positive political outcomes may not be good for subsequent mobilizations, as activists can feel movement goals have already been achieved.

CHAPTER 5

Protest and culture

INTRODUCTION

Interest in the cultural aspects of protest and collective action is not limited to the study of new social movements, which we looked at in the last chapter. The methods and perspectives of cultural analysis have also been adopted in other areas of social movement studies, such as in the book, *Social Movements and Culture*, which the editors considered part of 'the general turn toward cultural analysis in the social sciences' (Johnston and Klandermans 1995: vii). Since the publication of that collection of essays, Hank Johnston (2009: 3) has edited another volume entitled *Culture, Social Movements and Protest*, which, he says, considers the 'important additions to the cultural canon'. That book seeks to build on the earlier volume, which, according to Johnston (2009: 3), 'brought together US and European perspectives to present several new analytical approaches from various social science fields: rhetorical analysis, sociology of culture, narrative analysis, social psychology, and cognitive sciences'. The stated intention of the later book is 'to move our understanding yet another step ahead, extending the scope of how a cultural perspective can inform protest analysis' (Johnston 2009: 3).

In his introduction, Johnston (2009: 3) notes how 'the framing perspective has been the primary vehicle of culture in protest studies'. Having looked in some detail at the framing approach in Chapter 3, in this chapter we will consider what, using a cultural lens, some consider are the major limitations of this approach. In short, critics argue that while the framing perspective attempts to overcome the rational and instrumental bias of political process and resource mobilization theories, it still ends up focusing on the rational and cognitive aspects of protest to the neglect of the affective or emotional dimensions of collective action. To that end, one of the key areas we look at in this chapter is the study of the emotional life of social movements and activists. But we also look at a counter example of animal rights activists who eschew emotion in favour of adopting more rational–instrumental strategies to achieve their goals. Moreover, we see how emotions can play out in social movement organizations, which, like other bureaucratic forms, have tended to be equated with hierarchical structures and instrumental rationality that exclude emotionality. We also look at other aspects of the cultural life of social movements, including narratives; cultures of resistance (such as oppositional subcultures); performance; and the place of music, art, ritual, and theatre. While Johnston (2009: 4) says these are less explored avenues for cultural analysis in social movement studies, they are nevertheless of interest to a growing number of researchers working in the field.

PASSIONATE POLITICS

A key aspect of the cultural turn in social movement studies has been a recognition of 'the value of "bringing emotions back into" social movement research' (Goodwin and Pfaff 2001: 301). The notion of *bringing back* emotions is important here, not only because it recognizes impliedly the role of emotions in collective action, which has, until recently, been neglected, but also because it acknowledges the fact that emotions were previously considered important by social movement scholars, and by collective behaviour theorists in particular (see Goodwin et al. 2000). As we saw in Chapter 2, collective behaviour theory has tended to view the role played by emotions in crowds, for example, in quite negative terms. Goodwin et al. (2001: 2) trace this line of thought back to the sociological theory of Max Weber (1978 [1922]), who famously juxtaposed rationality (or reason) and emotions, seeing the latter as essentially irrational or, at best, nonrational.

In Chapter 2, we saw how theories of collective behaviour and the social psychology of crowds were used to explain the behaviour of people in mass gatherings like the Nuremburg rallies, which took place in Nazi Germany during the 1930s. In such cases, it was argued, the collective will subordinates the individual will, which may be influenced by the authority of a charismatic leader, as supposedly happens in some new religious movements, cults, or sects where impressionable converts are 'brainwashed'. Fear of fascism, communism, and cultic forms of religion, therefore, led many early students of collective behaviour to regard it negatively (see Eyerman and Jamison 1991: 10–12; Goodwin et al. 2001: 3).

But the study of emotions in social movement research has been neglected not only because of its association with negative and dangerous forms of collective behaviour, but also because from the late 1960s social movement studies was dominated by resource mobilization theory, which, as we saw in Chapter 3, treats social movements as *rational* collective actors, and hence sees no role for (irrational) emotions in the analysis of collective action. Similarly, with its focus on political strategy, the political process model is also unable to accommodate emotional analysis.

To critics of the resource mobilization and political process schools of thought, social movements depend 'neither on political opportunities nor on prior networks' (Polletta and Amenta 2001: 306). Rather, 'moral shocks' are believed to generate 'such a sense of outrage in a person that she becomes inclined towards political action, with or without the network or personal contacts emphasized in mobilization and process theories' (Jasper 1997: 106). Accordingly, emotions enable people to be optimistic and believe with confidence that opportunities for effective insurgency are there. This relates to what McAdam (1982: 34) calls 'cognitive liberation' whereby people mobilize 'on the basis of some optimistic assessment of the prospects for successful insurgency weighted against the risks involved in each action'. But even here cognitive liberation is seen in instrumental terms (i.e., weighing upon the risks and benefits); hence, it is devoid of any emotional input. As Goodwin et al. (2001: 7) put it: '"Liberation" implies heady emotions that "cognitive" then denies'.

This criticism has also been leveled at the framing perspective, which was developed by political process theorists responding to the observation that 'collective actors are best understood as normative and communicative challengers seeking to influence social institutions by means other than instrumental politics' (Young 2001: 104). As we saw in Chapter 3, framing approaches are premised on the view that 'frame alignment' occurs when movement entrepreneurs successfully transform cultural schemas in preexisting social networks into mobilizing structures. However, as Young (2001: 104) points out, framing processes are unfortunately 'almost always treated as cognitive processes'. And, as Kemper (2001: 69) has also noted, this is what caused

James Jasper (1998) to argue the frame alignment approach 'must be more than simply cognitive, but also emotional to evoke social movement participation'.

Therefore, scholars concerned with the role of emotions in social movements have attempted to go beyond the false dichotomies created by past analyses that have juxtaposed rationality and emotion, instrumentality and expression. They argue that ostensibly instrumental movements also have emotional and expressive dimensions, and thus emotions and cognition often comingle (Goodwin et al. 2001: 15). There may be times when a social movement is more emotionally driven, and other times when it is more instrumentally focused. Nevertheless, argue Polletta and Amenta (2001: 305), emotions frequently *precede* collective action: 'people are often motivated by anger, indignation, fear, compassion, or a sense of obligation, not optimism about the possibilities of securing political concessions through extra-institutional protest'. Such is the case with 'new emotional movements', whose novelty, in part, at least, reflects a broader societal acceptance of the public expression of emotions (Walgrave and Verhulst 2006: 277). A key characteristic of these movements is that while they may be sparked initially by the emotion of fear, this eventually gives way to rational-instrumental protest, with political and policy goals (Walgrave and Verhulst 2006: 280).

There are many examples of collective action involving emotions. So, we will look briefly here at one we examined earlier in the book when, in Chapter 4, we looked at the case of the precarity movement. De Sario's (2007: 34) analysis of the collective actions of the precarity movement in the Italian city of Turin illustrates the significant role of the 'emotional setting' during each phase or constellation of the movement; that is, 'the fusion of common emotions that gives the opportunity for possible connections, and even before that provides the emotional basis for trust and mutual help between groups and people who previously did not know each other'. Another example of the role of emotions in framing collective action is provided in Box 5.1.

BOX 5.1 DISPASSIONATE POLITICS? NON-EMOTIONAL FRAMING IN ANIMAL RIGHTS ACTIVISM

Goodwin et al. (2001: 15) observe that it is not only social movement scholars who have tended to devalue and been suspicious of 'emotionality', but that protestors, too, are often reluctant to admit their emotions, which, they argue, reflects wider efforts in modern societies to 'frame emotions in pejorative ways'. Similarly, McAllister Groves' (2001) study of animal rights activism shows how activists have normative assumptions about gender, feeling, and rationality.

Despite the fact that the animal rights movement is comprised mainly of women, the activists McAllister Groves interviewed in one grassroots organization in the southeastern United States tended to shun emotionalism in the movement in favour of what they considered to be rational arguments regarding the philosophy of their organization. Most of the interviewees were professional women who, according to McAllister Groves, were trying to 'gain legitimacy for their cause in a patriarchal community that trivializes issues that have been traditionally associated with women' (McAllister Groves 2001: 213). They embraced emotional neutrality, science, and masculine ways of looking at the world. Moreover, they used the term 'emotional' in a political way to describe those individuals whose approach to animal protection they saw as lacking legitimacy. Accordingly, they did not frame themselves as animal lovers, but emphasized instead the rational, scientific, and intellectual arguments against animal cruelty, believing these to look more professional, and hence less amateurish or feminine. In this way, McAllister Groves' study provides a counter example to research on social movements that sees them as positively embracing emotion, since it shows how, for some animal rights activists, at least, *dispassionate politics* can be a strategic or rational choice.

Despite this 'non-emotional framing', activists talked of 'acceptable anger', which, McAllister Groves argues, acts as a means of legitimating violent forms of protest by alleged terrorists, such as the Animal Liberation Front, from within the animal rights movement. This enables a more militant wing of the movement to coexist with its more rational, professional, and scientific constituency. Interestingly, the example provided by McAllister Groves is of a social movement organization, which, although not feminist in orientation, is populated heavily by women who apparently do not have the distinctively gendered 'emotion culture' of feminist organizations, which typically 'conform to a feminine logic by treating emotional expressiveness and caring nurturant personal relationships as primary' (Taylor and Rupp 2002: 142).

THE ROLE OF POLITICAL COLOURS IN THE EMOTIONAL LIFE OF SOCIAL MOVEMENTS

In Chapter 2, we saw that Chesters and Welsh (2004) explain how during the 26 September (S26) protests in Prague in 2000, marchers used colour to reflect their different collective identities, political perspectives, and protest tactics or repertoires. Similarly, Sawer (2007) is interested in looking at how *political* colours figure in the repertoires of contention of social movements. Her focus is on how these colours serve as a visual identification of 'the cause' of a social movement or political party, how they act as an outward display of values, and how they are important for sustaining a movement's sense of community. In particular, Sawer is concerned with showing how, as well as performing more instrumental or rational purposes, colours and related symbols elicit emotional responses from activists: 'The wearing of political colours is a significant statement of identity and/or values. Such public displays help engender an emotional unity and can be an important resource in building social movements and other campaigns' (Sawer 2007: 46).

Moreover, the colours may be chosen because they have existing political meanings, although they can 'also develop new meanings as they become part of the vocabulary of collective action and cross oceans and time zones' (Sawer 2007: 46). The colour red, for instance, has long been associated with the international socialist movement. It was a symbol of radicalism during the French Revolution, where once the red flag signaled martial rule by the state, but was then appropriated by demonstrators, 'who inscribed their flag "Martial law of the people against the revolt of the court"' (Sawer 2007: 41). In Australia, the red flag became such an emotive symbol that its display was banned under War Precautions legislation in 1918. Social democrats the world over have adopted 'The Red Flag' as an anthem sung by delegates at party conferences. In 1986, the British Labour Party replaced the radical fist with the red rose, which has been interpreted by some 'as an attempt to move away from the masculine imagery in the context of the increasing role of women in the left' (Sawer 2007: 41).

The colour black and black flags were emotive signifiers for early anarchist demonstrations, and, more recently, 'black has been worn and black flags carried by anarchist and autonomist contingents involved in anti-globalization protests both in Northern Europe and in the USA' (Sawer 2007: 42). Moreover, it has been argued the anarchist symbol of a circle surrounding the letter 'A' is one of the most recognized political symbols (Peterson 1987: 4).

The historical association between anarchism and socialism has resulted in flags combining black and red, such as in the case of the anarcho-syndicalist movement in Spain before the First World War. However, black has also been appropriated by fascist movements, which effectively subvert the political meaning of that colour in ways similar to those identified by Chesters and Welsh (2004) in Chapter 2 (see Box 2.2). Examples here include Mussolini's Blackshirts who marched on Rome in 1922, and the British Union of Fascists who followed Mussolini in adopting black shirts, which led to 'the banning of the wearing of political uniforms under the Public Order Act of 1936' (Sawer 2007: 43).

Sawer shows how the colour <u>green</u> has a diversity of meanings, including being a colour of Islam and Islamic political parties, Irish nationalism, the Chartists in nineteenth-century Britain, and the twentieth-century environmental movement. Indigenous movements have also used colours in their campaigns. For instance, the Rastafarian colours of red, gold, and green have come to signify black pride, and, in Australia, the colours of red, black, and yellow, which form the Aboriginal flag, unite all indigenous people regardless of whether they come from urban or traditional community environments. The pink triangle was once used by the Nazis to identify homosexuals, but like other symbols mentioned here, the colour pink was 'appropriated by the oppressed as part of the new politics of pride' and 'became a signifier of gay identity' (Sawer 2007: 45).

Coloured ribbons have always been used by political parties, as they have by a variety of movement activists. For example, in the nineteenth century, white ribbons were worn by suffragettes in the Women's Christian Temperance Movement in Australia, Canada, and New Zealand. Nowadays the white ribbon is worn on the International Day for the Elimination of Violence against Women. Red ribbons are worn in support of those living with and affected by HIV/AIDS.

NARRATIVE AND STORYTELLING

Along with a focus on the role of emotions in social movements, another key aspect of the 'cultural turn' in social movement studies has been the development of an appreciation for the role of narrative and storytelling, which is itself part of a broader 'narrative turn' that has occurred in a variety of fields of human inquiry (Davis 2002b: 3). Indeed, narrative and stories are often seen as an important feature not only of the cultural life of social movements but also the emotional lives of movements and their participants (Goodwin et al. 2000: 76). Because they contain rhetorical devices and storylines, which link a particular experience or occurrence to others, narratives can orchestrate and amplify both the emotional experience and meaning of collective protest events (Eyerman 2005: 46).

For example, Kane (2001) uses the case of the Irish Land War of the late nineteenth century to show how political alliances were forged between diverse groups via the narrative construction of meaning. She describes how, in the early years of the movement, 'narratives of oppression were recounted', and how central to these were metaphors of humiliation, shame, and sorrow' (Kane 2001: 257). Latterly, oppression narratives – pertaining to the wretchedness of the landlord system and British rule in Ireland – gave way to 'narratives of indignation', which were founded on 'an emotion emerging from anger and humiliation' (Kane 2001: 259).

Conceiving of social movements as 'bundles of narratives', Fine (1995: 135) identifies three classes of stories – horror stories, war stories, and happy endings – each of which 'plays upon the emotions of participants'. To Fine (1995: 128), narrative is a technique that functions to cement social bonds within a movement, as well as strengthen members' commitment to shared organizational goals and a collective identity. Indeed, to the question, 'why do activists tell stories?' Francesca Polletta (2002: 48) answers, '[t]hey probably do so to sustain and strengthen members' commitment'. However, as well as performing an internal function, storytelling also has external effects. For instance, Meyer shows how 'stories of influence' can be considered a social movement outcome, in the same way a specific policy or legal outcome can. As such, stories of influence constitute a 'spillover effect' of movement activity (Meyer and Whittier 1994). An example of the wider influence of movements beyond specific policy outcomes is evident in the fact that while the Equal Rights Amendment was defeated in the 1970s, there was a dramatic transformation in cultural values and attitudes about women in politics and in the workforce during that same period (Meyer 2009: 59).

Another case involves the emotional responses of women during the campaign to elect Rosalie Wahl in 1977, who was the state of Minnesota's first female Supreme Court justice. To her surprise, Kenney (2010) discovered that women involved in the campaign were less motivated by narrow instrumental legal goals (e.g., rape shield laws, custody determined by the best interests of the child, equal pay) than by a sense of *pride* – an emotion important in other movements; for example, black pride, gay pride – at being part of a wider collective movement. Kenney (2010: 144) shows how Wahl was a symbol of all women and that her campaign and appointment invoked an emotionally intense response, which cannot be explained in terms of policy objectives: it 'touched a chord with women across the political spectrum and generated grassroots mobilization to hold her seat, sparking an emotional response that energized heretofore politically inactive women'.

Although, as we saw in Chapter 4, some movements are self-referential and internally oriented, most exist in some form of antagonistic relation to larger structures and values, which they set out to challenge and change. They do that partly by means of 'counternarratives', which are oppositional or alternative stories 'at odds with or precluded by pre-existing and dominant social narratives' (Davis 2002b: 25). For many, this is a crucial function of storytelling in social movements, just as it is for other oppositional groups and deviant subcultures.

Thus, Fine's description of a 'war story' (i.e., 'collective experiences within the movement [. . .] that speak to the value of community') has been applied in Britain to New Age Travellers (Martin 1998: 740–741), some of whom would recount their experiences of the Battle of the Beanfield (see Box 5.2) – when they clashed violently with police in 1985 at Stonehenge – '[l]ike soldiers after a battle' (Fine 1995: 136). On the one hand, collective memories and accounts of such 'iconic events' (Lofland 1995: 203) may serve a strategic function, such as to galvanize collective action, while, on the other hand, they may become incorporated into the culture of a movement, thus serving to promote cohesion and the formation of a collective identity.

Stories from the past can perform other cultural functions. For instance, Polletta connects Verta Taylor's ideas about how social movements are able to sustain themselves over time via 'abeyance structures' (discussed in Chapter 4) to stories that are told about past movements. Hence, insofar as storytelling evokes emotions, narratives of the past can help sustain movements in less active periods (Goodwin et al. 2001: 21). Like Taylor (1989: 772), Polletta (2002: 49) is skeptical of the 'immaculate conception' view of social movements, arguing that stories of past movements help us trace the longer-term cultural impact of movements, which is more difficult to capture than legislative or policy outcomes, although they may be as or more important than those formal outcomes. Narratives of the past also provide new activists with a ready-made script for contemporary collective action, as well as a means of understanding current political challenges (Polletta 1998b).

Along with fostering solidarity and commitment between activists, according to Benford (2002), narrative and storytelling can act as means of social control in social movements. While nearly all social movement scholarship about social control relates to the effects of external influences on social movement outcomes – such as the role of the police, media, the state, and countermovements – Benford's (2002: 55, original emphasis) focus is on 'attempts to control the course of social movements from *within*'. For Benford (2002: 57), myths or sacred narratives of the past have the capacity 'to inspire action and constrain individual and collective behaviour'.

Key

Collective identities are also socially constructed through story-telling (Benford 2002: 71). So, if individuals are to become socialized as movement adherents, they must learn to be conversant in the proper movement myths and narratives. If they do not, they risk disrupting a movement's framing activities, which may, in turn, damage its public image. Moreover, if a participant's individual narrative contradicts a movement myth or narrative, conflict may ensue between those participants and adherents who seek to preserve the 'official' movement rendition of past events. This is precisely what happened in the case of New Age Travellers, as discussed in Box 5.2.

BOX 5.2 BATTLE OF THE BEANFIELD: A WAR STORY

In Chapter 4, we saw how Martin (1998) has explained generational differences between older and younger groups of New Age Travellers in terms of the post-material values of new social movements adopted by the former and the impact of post-Fordism upon the latter. However, this is only one way Travellers were differentiated by generation. The older Travellers, who had experienced the Battle of the Beanfield (mentioned earlier), regarded that event as mythic, and constructed a sacred narrative around it. This narrative of the past was fundamental to the collective identity of the older generation of Travellers, who were 'bound together by nostalgia' (Martin 1998: 741). However, while younger Travellers knew of and were able to retell the story of the Battle of the Beanfield, most had not experienced it. Because of that, the older generation believed, many younger Travellers were indifferent about Travellers' negative public image, which was seen by older Travellers as a mark of disrespect, since it violated the sacred narrative of Travellers suffering injustice because they were victims of police brutality during the Battle of the Beanfield.

In this way, the younger Travellers 'violated fundamental movement norms' (Benford 2002: 66). Largely as a result of the anti-social behaviour of the younger generation of Travellers, the older generation believed, the British government introduced legislation in the 1990s that effectively criminalized their way of life. Hence, older Travellers were apt to recount the story of the Battle of the Beanfield and other mythic tales of struggle against the authorities with intense emotion, frustrated at their inability to exercise what Benford (2002: 68) calls 'frame control', whereby participants 'censor' a movement's public image by controlling its framing activities.

THE CONTRIBUTION OF NARRATIVE ANALYSIS TO THE CULTURAL CANON OF SOCIAL MOVEMENT STUDIES

As stated in the introduction to this chapter, the framing perspective, which was discussed in some detail in Chapter 3, has been a key influence in the study of culture and social movements. However, we also saw how the framing approach has been subject to criticism, not least by those interested in narrative analysis, which is itself an aspect of the cultural turn in social movement studies (Davis 2002b: 3–4; Fine 2002: 230). For Davis (2002b: 9), a fundamental problem of the framing perspective is that it tends 'to overemphasize cognitive factors'. Thus, the concepts of framing and frame alignment (see Chapter 3) give undue stress to logical persuasion and consensus of belief:

> In matters of recruitment, for instance, the framing perspective draws attention to the inherently moral claims of movements, but focuses on cognitive dynamics and provides little illumination of how specific moral responses are aroused. The perspective intimates the importance of emotions that mobilize and demobilize, yet concentrates on congruent and logical beliefs as organizing experience, building a sense of personal efficacy, and guiding action.
>
> (Davis 2002b: 9)

By contrast, narrative analysis 'illuminates persuasion and shared vision at more subtle, imaginative, and pre-prepositional levels' (Davis 2002b: 24). In short, activists must do more than simply agree upon a set of clearly articulated and coherent reasons to act collectively; 'they must be *moved* to act, to take risks, to get involved' (Davis 2002b: 24, original emphasis). And that entails not only acting rationally and instrumentally, but also imaginatively, intuitively, and emotionally. Narrative and storytelling are key aspects of these processes. It should also be remembered from what was said previously in this chapter that passion and emotion are not antithetical to political strategizing and rational action:

> Narratives' dual character – both strategically deployed and constitutive of people's understanding of strategy, interest, and identity – is evident in their relationship to emotions. Stories are used strategically by activists to elicit emotions, say, the righteous indignation that propels someone into a march, or the anguish that generates financial contributions. At the same time, people make sense of

their experience, and respond to it emotionally, based on familiar narratives.

(Polletta 2002: 48)

Just as the framing perspective has been influential in the study of social movements and culture, so, too, has new social movement theory. However, like the framing perspective, it has certain weaknesses and limits that some assert can be remedied by narrative analysis. Just as framing scholars' use of the concept of frame alignment stresses external threats to alignment and pays 'minimal attention to internal movement processes and the situated and negotiated nature of participant engagement and solidarity', so, for Davis (2002b: 9), a key problem of new social movement theory is its tendency 'to skirt the problem of meaning-making'. Thus, while new social movement theorists 'have emphasized the constructed nature of collective identity, they have not typically shown *how* activists themselves fashion their identities and interests' (Davis 2002b: 9, emphasis added). Narrative analysis, by contrast, illuminates internal movement processes, highlighting 'the power of stories to both create and strengthen movement community and collective identity', and, as Benford (2002) shows, it also demonstrates the ability of narratives to formulate and control models of appropriate behaviour *within* social movements (Davis 2002b: 25).

A focus on narrative is also relevant for contemporary movements 'in which the goal of self-transformation as much as political reform may see personal storytelling *as* activism' (Polletta 2002: 48, original emphasis). In this way, narrative analysis is a valuable addition to the cultural canon in social movement studies, which complements new social movement theory *and* the framing perspective:

> It too draws attention to mobilizing beliefs, ideas, and identities, and the interactive and negotiated nature of movement meaning-making and solidarity. It too focuses attention on internal movement dynamics and draws attention to diffuse expressions of social activism. It too provides a language for analyzing the social construction of collective action, a language that both overlaps and goes beyond the conceptual frameworks of these other theories.
>
> (Davis 2002b: 24)

Accordingly, it is important to recognize, as Fine (2002: 230) does, that understanding social movements through the storytelling of activists does not represent a totalistic attempt to explain all aspects of collective action and substitute preexisting approaches with the study of 'group narrative'. Nevertheless, for Davis, the study of narrative not

109

only provides a means of overcoming some of the aforementioned weaknesses of the framing perspective and new social movement theory, but also provides a window on some of the neglected cultural dimensions of social movements:

Indeed, it seems fair to say that all cultural elements, all symbolic expressive aspects of movements, can be related to narrative and illuminated by its study. Culture is more than stories, of course; and not all cultural features of movements necessarily involve narratives. But, and this is my point, these features *might* involve narratives – be it vocabularies of meanings, expressive symbols, music, film, rules, rituals, histories, sacred places, or so on. Attending to stories is *one* way – but not the only way – to bring these crucial features of movements into the foreground and explore their context and explanatory significance.

(Davis 2002b: 10, original emphasis)

BOX 5.3 DAVID AND GOLIATH: THE McLIBEL TRIAL

In Chapter 3, we touched upon Soule's (2009) research into anti-corporate activism, including her analysis of anti-apartheid student activism on American university campuses during the 1970s and 1980s. At that time, students were involved in various acts of civil disobedience to protest against universities who invested in companies with South African ties. In his research, Benford (2002: 58) shows how movements using civil disobedience and other forms of nonviolent direct action often make use of 'tales regarding the effectiveness of nonviolent direct action campaigns of other movements'. According to Benford, these mythical tales typically take the form of David and Goliath narratives where ordinary people are depicted obtaining peace and justice against all odds. While frequently linked to wider social movements, such as civil rights or anti-corporate protest, such tales invariably involve individuals pitted against larger forces. The now legendary McLibel trial is a case in point.

In 1985, six activists from a small anarchist group named London Greenpeace (no relation to the larger environmental organization) gathered outside a McDonald's restaurant in London's Strand where they distributed leaflets criticizing the fast food giant for such things as being complicit in Third World starvation, destruction of rainforests, selling unhealthy food, exploiting children with advertising, exploiting workers and banning trade unions, and torturing and murdering animals. Subsequently, McDonald's consulted the

© Nick Cobbing/Alamy

Figure 5.1 The McLibel two, Dave Morris and Helen Steel, on the steps of the Royal Courts of Justice after hearing the Court of Appeal's decision on 31 March 1999 regarding their long-running case against McDonald's Corporation

Special Branch of London's Metropolitan Police (usually responsible for matters of national security and counterterrorism), and engaged the services of two private-eye agencies to infiltrate the group and gather information before finally serving writs for libel on five of its members (Vidal 1997: 193).

Three out of the five apologized to McDonald's after it became apparent any trial would be time consuming and costly. Two members of the group refused to apologize and represented themselves without legal aid, which is excluded in defamation cases in England in order to prevent 'frivolous petty suits' (Nicholson 2000: 9). The trial commenced in 1994. In a matter that arguably ended up being about censorship by big corporations, Morris and Steel claimed McDonald's had taken advantage of Britain's libel laws to silence (by threatening to sue) its critics, including 'the BBC, Channel 4, *The Guardian*, Today and many other vegetarian, green and labour movements' (Lloyd 1999: 342).

Eventually, Steel and Morris were found to have libeled McDonald's regarding 'rainforest destruction, packaging, food poisoning, starvation in the third world, heart disease and cancer and bad working conditions' (Lloyd 1999: 341). However, in a partial victory for the defendants, the trial judge said they had proved that 'McDonald's advertising exploits children, falsely advertise their food as nutritious, risk the health of their long-term regular customers, are "culpably responsible" for cruelty to animals reared for their products, are "strongly apathetic to unions", and that they pay their workers low wages' (Lloyd 1999: 341). McDonald's was awarded damages of £60,000. An appeal by Steel and Morris failed, although the Court of Appeal did hold that 'the allegations relating to pay and conditions were [fair] comment', and 'it was true to allege that, if one eats enough McDonald's food, one's diet may well become high in fat, etc., with the very real risk of heart disease' (Hudson 2005: 305). Accordingly, damages were reduced to £40,000.

After their application seeking leave to appeal to the House of Lords was refused, Steel and Morris took their case to the European Court of Human Rights, claiming their right to a fair trial had been violated because they had been denied legal aid. On 15 February 2005, some twenty years after the original leaflet campaign, the European Court found in their favour, ruling that the original case had breached Article 6 (right to a fair trial) and Article 10 (right to freedom of expression) of the European Convention on Human Rights. The British government was ordered to pay the pair £57,000 in compensation.

EMOTION IN STORIES OF PROTEST

In Chapter 3, we saw how the American civil rights movement depended for its success upon the support of black churches. Student sit-ins were a key repertoire used by civil rights activists in 1960. Like the broader civil rights movement, Morris (1984: 200) has argued, the 'sit-ins were largely organized at the movement churches rather than on the campuses'. In her research, on the other hand, Polletta shows how *spontaneity* figured in many stories told by students about the sit-ins. However, spontaneity did not mean unplanned, but 'denoted independence from adult leadership, urgency, local initiative, and action by moral imperative rather than bureaucratic planning' (Polletta 1998b: 138).

Importantly, Polletta distinguishes 'narrative' from collective action 'frames'. According to framing theorists, frames are crucial recruiting devices because they provide clearly articulated explanations of a problem needing a remedy, a means of solving a problem, and a justification for action. In other terms, '[f]rames motivate participation by persuasively distinguishing insurgents ("us") from antagonists and irrelevant others ("them"), and by clearly representing the possibility, necessity, and efficacy of collective action by deliberate actors' (Polletta 1998b: 140). By contrast, because it relies on emplotment rather than explanation, narrative 'engages potential activists precisely by its *ambiguity* about the causes of collective action' (Polletta 1998b: 139, original emphasis).

That is not to say narrative plays any less of a role in collective action. For instance, students' stories and characterization of the 1960 sit-ins as spontaneous indicated 'a break with adult gradualism, a moral rather than political strategy, a joy in action' (conveying a sense of fun), and 'motivated students to engage in time-consuming and dangerous activism' (Polletta 2002: 42). In this way, students were 'constituting an action-compelling collective identity as they narrated it' (Polletta 2002: 32); thus providing some insight into 'the interpretative processes [. . .] occurring *during* initial episodes of collective action' (Polletta 1998b: 138, original emphasis).

Therefore, Polletta (2002: 32, emphasis added) argues, narrative analysis exposes a gap in framing theories of social movements, that is, 'their neglect of the discursive processes that occur *before* formal movement organizations with clear recruitment objectives have been established'. It also demonstrates their neglect of emotions in social protest (Polletta 2002: 32). However, during the student sit-ins, spontaneity also became an 'organizational commitment' that both animated and constrained strategic action (Polletta 2002: 43). Hence, Polletta (2002: 37) argues, narrative analysis of the student sit-in shows how spontaneity was instrumental *and* expressive, thus challenging the 'widespread assumption that passion and rationality are opposed', which 'is a cultural belief that activists have to work with and around'. It will be recalled that, in Chapter 4, similar issues about the potential coexistence of instrumental and expression elements within a single movement were raised in respect of the organizational form of women's movements (see Box 4.2).

BOX 5.4 EMOTIONS IN SOCIAL MOVEMENT ORGANIZATIONS

It is worth noting that while the 'emotional turn' in social movement studies emerged partly as a reaction against the overly rationalistic approach of resource mobilization theory, emotions are nonetheless evident in 'social movement organizations', which, as discussed in Chapter 3, is a key concept of resource mobilization theory. For instance, Rodgers (2010) has shown how paid activists at the human rights organization Amnesty International struggle with the emotional components of their work, and that this has implications not only for the quality of their working lives, but also for the stability of such organizations, as well as the maintenance of social movements generally.

An ethos of selflessness is engrained in the organizational culture of human rights organizations like Amnesty. Although this motivates potential recruits to become involved in activism, it also tends to foster a culture of overwork, where employees feel morally obliged to put the needs of victims above their own. According to Rodgers, this high expenditure of emotional energy is unsustainable in the long run. Thus, it has implications for professional social movement organizations such as Amnesty, in that professionally trained and skilled activists leave after finding better paid work in less stressful environments.[1] By contrast, in her study of militant street AIDS activists, Gould (2002) shows how the 'emotion work' of social movements is vital to both their development and persistence over time.

MUSIC AND PROTEST

Another key feature of the emotional and hence cultural life of social movements involves 'rituals, songs, folktales, heroes, denunciation of enemies, and so on' (Goodwin et al. 2001: 18). Notwithstanding that, Goodwin et al. argue, most discussion of solidarity building in social movement studies has focused on the role of shared rhetoric and beliefs, neglecting the emotions that accompany these. Collective emotions, they say, are linked to the *pleasures of protest*, the most obvious of which are the pleasures associated with being with like-minded people; pleasures, that is, arising 'from the joys of collective activities, such as losing oneself in collective motion or song' (Goodwin et al. 2001: 20). This point is reiterated by Johnston (2009: 17), who says it would be a mistake to see music as *only* a social movement artifact, or *just* (another) resource to build solidarity. Following Eyerman and Jamison's (1998: 162) view on the subject, Johnston says:

> . . . music not only can function as a resource to build collective identity, or to pass information, or preserve a tradition, but can also be integral in the unfolding performance of the movement itself, constituting it by the way songs bring people to participation, by the meaning the songs come to assume, and by the meaning the opponents come to attribute to it.
>
> (Johnston 2009: 17)

Much in the same way as we saw earlier how past narratives impact upon future collective action and can perform an abeyance function, Eyerman and Jamison (1998: 2) argue that music in social movements may act as a means of 'mobilizing traditions', which create in participants feelings of connectivity to historic movements, since they 'are made and remade, and after the movements fade away as political forces, the music remains as a memory and as a potential way to inspire new waves of mobilization'. For example, traditional Negro spirituals and slave songs served as cultural resources during the 1960s struggle for civil rights (Eyerman and Jamison 1998: 45).

The role of ritual is also important here. In particular, music 'embodies tradition through the ritual of performance. It can empower, help create a collective identity and a sense of movement in an emotional and almost physical sense' (Eyerman and Jamison 1998: 35). Collective singing rituals, whether that be singing a song like 'We Shall Overcome' at a mass demonstration or the 'International' at a union gathering, not only remind participants of their place in the long-standing traditions of the movement, but they 'can also capture, in a brief, transient moment, a glimpse of, and a feeling for, a spiritual bonding which is both rational and emotive at one and the same time' (Eyerman and Jamison 1998: 36).

From this, it should be apparent that, to Eyerman and Jamison, the study of music and social movements is inextricably linked to some of the other features we have identified in this chapter as being key components of social movements and culture, and, in particular, the parts played by emotions and narrative or storytelling in collective action. In their earlier work, Eyerman and Jamison (1991) conceive of social movements as being involved in 'cognitive praxis', namely that as bearers of new ideas involved in knowledge-producing activities, they might, among other things, affect scientific research programs, professional intellectual identities, and technological development trajectories. In this way, the measure of a successful movement can be observed by looking at how influential it is 'in spreading its knowledge interests or diffusing its consciousness' (Eyerman and Jamison 1991: 3–4). Accordingly, as shown earlier in the chapter, social movement outcomes can be assessed in terms other than concrete policy achievements. We also looked at something similar in Chapter 4, when we discussed how social welfare movements can be concerned with the twin goals of redistribution *and* recognition (Martin 2001).

Eyerman and Jamison (1998: 7) apply their cognitive approach to social movements 'to consider musical expression in social movements as a kind of cognitive praxis'. Therefore, like others who argue social movement activity should not be reduced to politics (see Chapter 4),

Music as Cognitive praxis

Eyerman and Jamison (1998: 24) show how, as cognitive praxis, 'music and other forms of cultural activity contribute to the ideas that movements offer and create in opposition to the existing social and cultural order'. For instance, social movements can impact significantly on musical taste and popular culture, as happened during the 1960s when 'American-inspired rock music became a major source of knowledge about the world and their place in it for millions of youth around the globe' (Eyerman and Jamison 1998: 24; see also Friedman 2013).

BOX 5.5 PUSSY RIOT AND THE SUCCESSFUL DIFFUSION OF FEMINIST IDEAS

The case of Russian feminist punk band Pussy Riot provides a recent example of the operation of cognitive praxis in music and protest. After performing a 'punk prayer' in the Cathedral of Christ the Saviour in Moscow in February 2012, three members of the band were convicted for 'hooliganism motivated by religious hatred' and sentenced to two years in a Russian penal colony (Seal 2013: 293). Pussy Riot's members are expressly feminist protestors who frame Vladimir Putin's authoritarianism in terms of patriarchal oppression. Their songs include, 'Death to Prison, Freedom to Protest', which invites 'LGBT, feminists, defend the

© ZUMA Press, Inc./Alamy

Figure 5.2 Russia's punk band Pussy Riot conducting an anti-Putin action in front of the Kremlin in central Moscow, 20 January 2012

nation!', and 'Kropotkin-Vodka' that demands 'The fucking end to sexist Putinists!'.

Lizzie Seal uses the example of Pussy Riot to confound Alison Young's (1990) prediction that feminist political dissent will always be undermined and represented negatively in the news media. Young examined press discourses of women peace protestors at Greenham Common in the 1980s to show how their visibly public and apparently unruly actions and 'disrupted femininity' led to portrayals of them as wild and deviant, and thus in violation of dominant norms about womanhood as passive and private. By contrast, Seal shows how media coverage on news websites about Pussy Riot has, on balance, been positive and supportive.

She says this largely has to do with the post-Cold War context within which Pussy Riot's dissent has taken place. Hence, their feminism has gained acceptance as it chimes with a post-Cold War narrative about the progressive nature of Western values such as freedom of speech and freedom of expression, as well as a human rights discourse, which are counterposed to the old-fashioned repression and authoritarianism of Russia. While she acknowledges women in the West do continue to be stereotyped and represented negatively in terms of their femininity, Seal (2013: 298) says this endorsement of Pussy Riot's feminism 'can perhaps be explained by the incorporation of elements of feminism and post-feminism into the discourse of the Western news media in the two decades since Young published her study'. This argument then supports Eyerman and Jamison's cognitive approach to social movements, as it appears to indicate that since Young's study, the women's movement has succeeded in diffusing its consciousness, ideas, and knowledge interests.

PERFORMING PROTEST

As well as providing an example of the cognitive praxis of feminism and the women's movement, the case of Pussy Riot (Box 5.5) highlights the role of performance, art, and theatre, which are also aspects of the cultural dimension of protest and social movements (Johnston 2009: 4). Seal (2013: 295) shows how Pussy Riot's use of style, imagery, and symbolic meaning – young women evoking the Virgin Mary in church to save Russia from Putin – 'intentionally mobilized religious, political, and gender-based meanings to challenge social and political boundaries'. Accordingly, she states, their protest can be seen as 'carnivalesque',[2] in that it turns the world upside down: 'young women occupying sacred space that is symbolic of patriarchal religious power and authority' (Seal 2013: 295).

Following that analysis, the material presented in this section of the chapter examines performative approaches to the cultural life of social movements (Johnston 2009: 8), which we have already considered in passing in earlier parts of the book. In Chapter 2, for instance, we saw how Benford and Hunt (1992) have developed a 'dramaturgical' perspective to make sense of collective actors employing various dramatic techniques (i.e., scripting, staging, performing, interpreting) to define, communicate and challenge existing power relations (Box 2.5). And, in Chapter 4, we saw how the European precarity movement's use of performance, street parades, festivals, visual images, and counterimages on posters, along with its use of the colour pink to express affinity with queer politics and global justice protests, have been explained in terms of a frame emphasizing 'playful, ludic and carnivalesque forms of protest [which] valorizes the creative and expressive over the instrumental and rational, and utilizes a variety of performative repertoires' (Chesters and Welch 2004: 328; see also Roberts 2008).

Graham St John (2008: 168) has talked of similar events in terms of 'protestival', which is a polyvalent tactic involving the festal, mobilized by the alter-globalization movement; 'a creative response to the traditional political rituals of the left', building upon the meta-political tactic of new social movements by rendering power visible and posing symbolic challenges. St John argues that while new social movement theory has recognized the significance of cultural politics, new approaches are needed to understand the festal and carnivalesque character of contemporary activism, and especially transnational activism. Although St John proposes no way to fill the lacuna he identifies, elsewhere it has been suggested one fruitful line of inquiry would be to look at the carnivalesque protest tactics adopted by the European precarity movement (Martin 2014: 93).

Another case could be the public demonstrations in 2010 by Thailand's Red Shirts who emerged out of support for deposed Thai prime minister, Thaksin Shinawatra, and stood in opposition to the Yellow Shirts, who, being loyal to the king, wore the colour yellow because it is the colour used to celebrate the king's birthday. The Red Shirts wore the colour red to distinguish themselves from the Yellow Shirts, as well as 'to hint at their relatively poor support' (Forsyth 2010: 464). Their protests were also full of imagery and symbolism. Along with the vivid colours of their red shirts, protestors donated blood, which they then poured under the gates of Parliament House; an act portraying them as powerless peasants pitted against an entrenched Bangkok elite.

Women's grassroots activism in Peru is another example of the performance of protest, whereby women from Peru's shantytowns participated in street parades (pasacalle) and creative demonstrations in opposition to the repressive regime of President Fujimori, who in 1990 introduced a severe structural adjustment program – including reduced state spending – which led to new forms of poverty.

For Moser (2003: 181), the most fundamental aspect of the impact on these theatrical performances was 'the symbolic potency of making one's voice heard in a public space'. The opportunity for women to participate in the public sphere and voice their opinions was especially significant given the marginal status of women in public debate and the machismo culture of Peruvian society (Moser 2003: 182). For instance, one participant said, '[b]eing in the *pasacalle* was one of the only times I have walked through the town' (Moser 2003: 184).

The happiness and positivity generated during the theatrical protest performances stood in stark contrast to mainstream protests in Peru, which are characterized by marching, angry chants, and sometimes an aggressive police response (Moser 2003: 185). The creative protests provided safety in numbers whereby 'acting and the use of puppets effectively creates a shield from what is said, deflecting responsibility away from the individual' (Moser 2003: 185). Importantly, however, carnivalesque inversion (discussed earlier) was evident within the *pasacalle* performance, which contained a potent role reversal:

> Women actors take on the role of 'the oppressors' [. . .] and portray them as evil suit-wearers. The fact that they do so from the dominating and exaggerated height of stilts is also symbolic. Even more importantly, they depict them as fighting with the women, clutching their pots and babies, and *losing* the battle against them.
>
> (Moser 2003: 184, original emphasis)

While Moser (2003: 188) says the performative protest of women from Peru's shantytowns did not bring about the downfall of the Fujimori administration, it did make 'a contribution to the public dissent of civil society'. This raises the issue of the efficacy of performance in protest. Is it enough, as 'new' social movement theorists believe, to pose symbolic challenges to the established order, or does 'real' change entail transformation of that order or, at least, the insertion of movement demands into political agendas and government policy? As we saw earlier in the chapter, social movement outcomes can include 'cultural effects', such as the impact of influential stories (Meyer 2009), and are, therefore, not limited to specific policy outcomes. Indeed, as we have seen in the book so far, the issue of outcomes – including the unintended consequences of collective action – pervades social movement studies and is one that, in many ways, lies at the heart of protest and activism. It is also an issue we will revisit shortly when we look briefly at subcultures and social movements.

For the time being, however, it is worthy of noting that while examples of the performative nature of contemporary collective action repertoires show there is a growing tendency for social movements and protest events to incorporate music, dance, theatre, play, puppetry, and other festive, creative, and expressive elements into their repertoires of contention (Sharpe 2008: 228), equally, festivals themselves also involve radical and/or political elements, although many nowadays have become commercialized (Anderton 2008; Cummings 2008).[3] The Hillside Festival in Ontario, Canada, is an example of a festival, which, rather than simply opposing and critiquing existing social and political relations and institutions, *enacts* its politics by prefiguring a desired society and way of life, thus inspiring attendees to adopt alternative practices that lead to personal transformation (Sharpe 2008). This is very much a post-material conception of festivals similar to Melucci's (1989: 60) view of social movements as networks submerged in everyday life, or as 'cultural laboratories' involved in the formation of new collective identities (see Chapter 4). Likewise, Purdue et al. (1997: 647) consider festivals part of 'do-it-yourself' (DIY) culture, which they define as self-organizing networks with overlapping memberships and values that challenge the symbolic codes of mainstream society.

BOX 5.6 SYDNEY MARDI GRAS: GAYTMs

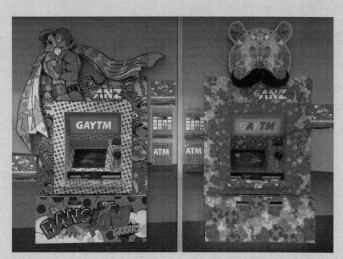

© Greg Martin

Figure 5.3 GAYTMs: Sydney Mardi Gras

Each year, the Australian city of Sydney is home to the Gay and Lesbian Mardi Gras, which is a month-long festival culminating in a street party (see: www.

mardigras.org.au). The photo in Figure 5.3 was taken during the 2015 Mardi Gras when the ANZ bank was the event's 'principal partner'. On the one hand, the expressive and creative 'queering' of automated teller machines (ATMs) could be read as playful, ludic, and carnivalesque. On the other hand, it could be seen as an example of the corporatization of 'protestivals'.

SUBCULTURES AND SOCIAL MOVEMENTS

Returning a last time to the example of Pussy Riot, Seal (2013: 295) argues that unlike subcultures, which are the traditional object of study for some cultural criminologists, Pussy Riot 'actively sought to be categorized as criminal by staging a challenging political protest, and their style was deliberately politicized as feminist and in opposition to the government'. Moreover, their use of symbolic meaning, style, imagery, and carnivalesque inversion poses a challenge to established social and political boundaries. This raises an important point to do with the intersection of culture and politics.

We have already considered one of the pertinent issues here when we looked previously at the commerciality versus radicalism of festivals. For Eyerman and Jamison (1998: 166), punk – which would include bands like Pussy Riot – cannot be equated with the social and political challenges posed by protest movements because 'punk music was from the very beginning commercial and the punk "style" began as a fashion'. However, Moore and Roberts (2009: 288) argue that 'punk was never entirely commercial nor simply a style or fashion'. Punk politics consisted of a largely defensive and reactive mobilization in a political context when the Right had gone on the offensive against the accomplishments of the civil rights, peace, and women's movements. The formation of Rock Against Race in 1976, for instance, provided a platform to communicate anti-racist ideals to a mass audience.

Synthesizing social movement theory and cultural studies also raises questions to do with the efficacy of cultural forms of politics. This notion was central to the research of Birmingham's Centre for Contemporary Cultural Studies during the 1970s. They saw working-class youth subcultures as offering symbolic solutions to concrete problems associated with transformations adversely affecting the cohesion of working-class culture and communities in post-war Britain, such as reconstruction and rehousing/resettlement projects. However, rather than offering 'real' solutions to these specific problems, as well as the general problem of being in a subordinate structural location, working-class youth subcultures offered only symbolic solutions, which were apparent in their 'style':

> 'The mod style, for example, was an attempt to realize, although in an imaginary way, the conditions of existence of socially mobile white collar workers; the dress and music of mods reflected hedonistic images of the affluent consumer'.
>
> (Martin 2013: 1288)

Not only did working-class youth subcultures lack concrete solutions to real problems, such as unemployment, low pay, loss of skill, and educational disadvantage, they actually tended to 'reproduce the gaps and discrepancies between real negotiations and symbolically displaced "resolutions"' (Clarke et al. 1976: 47). Moreover, while working-class subcultures (and middle-class countercultures) lived out important critiques of capitalism and modern institutions, those were only symbolic and confined to the level of culture.

In his classic study of motorbike boys and the hippies, Paul Willis showed how these two groups were unable to enter the arena of 'proper politics', or challenge the larger world of political and social institutions that constituted 'the material base for their experience of the classes from which they came' (Willis 1978: 176). To Willis, that signaled the 'tragic limit' of these cultures, which raised, more generally, 'the whole question of the status and viability of cultural politics and of a struggle waged exclusively at the level of lifestyle' (Willis 1978: 175). In fact, Willis argued, the motorbike boys and hippies were premature post-revolutionary cultural responses to pre-revolutionary conditions:

> It is almost that the cultures, in their silent way, lived as if the basic structures were changed – enjoying that in imagination while making no attempt to bring it about in reality. It is this prolepsis which is often the motor for cultural politics – and also its final tragic limit.
>
> (Willis 1978: 177)

In many respects, this analysis of subcultures echoes Melucci's view of social movements as posing 'symbolic challenges' to dominant cultural codes (see Chapter 4). However, Melucci would regard Willis' analysis as politically reductivist because it appears to measure efficacy solely by reference to impact upon the political system. It therefore denies the messages social movements and oppositional subcultures are able to communicate to the rest of society, which, as we have seen throughout this chapter, they can do by challenging and changing culturally engrained values, ideas, attitudes, knowledge, and so on, which are just as much markers of movement success as the attainment of concrete political, legal, or policy goals.

CONCLUSION

The material covered in this chapter augments some of the work around social movements and culture that we encountered in Chapter 4. Following the 'cultural turn' in social movement studies, scholars have become increasingly interested in an array of cultural activity associated with social protest, including, as we have seen, the role of passion and emotions, stories and narrative, music, and other forms of performativity in collective action. Much of this work has developed out of a critique of the political process and resource mobilization perspectives, which, it is argued, offer overly rationalistic and instrumental approaches to understanding social movements. Moreover, while the framing perspective has attempted to incorporate a concern for cultural processes in studies of protest, it, too, has been criticized for emphasizing rationality and cognition to the neglect of affect and emotion. In the next chapter, we continue to explore some of the issues discussed in this chapter, as well as in the book so far, when we turn to look at the relationship between social movements and religious movements, which is something that has tended to be of only passing interest to social movement scholars, or incidental to other areas of concern.

SUGGESTED READINGS

The following texts and resources can be used to explore issues raised in this chapter.

Books

Baumgarten, B., Daphi, P., and Ullrich, P. (eds.) (2014) *Conceptualizing Culture in Social Movement Research*. Houndmills: Palgrave Macmillan.

Davis, J. E. (ed.) (2002a) *Stories of Change: Narrative and Social Movements*. Albany, NY: State University of New York Press.

Eyerman, R. and Jamison, A. (1998) *Music and Social Movements: Mobilizing Traditions in the Twentieth Century*. Cambridge: Cambridge University Press.

Goodwin, J., Jasper, J. M., and Polletta, F. (eds.) (2001) *Passionate Politics: Emotions and Social Movements*. Chicago: University of Chicago Press.

Johnston, H. (ed.) (2009) *Culture, Social Movements and Protest*. Farnham: Ashgate.

Johnston, H. and Klandermans, B. (eds.) (1995) *Social Movements and Culture*. London: UCL Press.

Williams, R. H. (2004) 'The Cultural Contexts of Collective Action: Constraints, Opportunities, and the Symbolic Life of Social Movements' in D. A. Snow, S. A. Soule, and H. Kriesi (eds.) *The Blackwell Companion to Social Movements*. Oxford: Blackwell Publishing, pp. 91=115.

Journals

Goodwin, J., Jasper, J. M., and Polletta, F. (2000) 'The Return of the Repressed: The Fall and Rise of Emotions in Social Movement Theory' *Mobilization* 5(1): 65–83.

This article was a forerunner to the publication of the 2001 book, *Passionate Politics: Emotions and Social Movements*, by the same authors. It provides a useful survey of the various ways emotions have been treated over time, including theories of collective behaviour, resource mobilization, political process, framing, and new social movements. Another helpful source is the special issue of *Mobilization* 7(2) (2002), which is dedicated to 'Emotions and Contentious Politics'. The following journal article looks more generally at the cultural aspects of social movements:

Hart, S. (1996) 'The Cultural Dimension of Social Movements: A Theoretical Reassessment and Literature Review' *Sociology of Religion* 57(1): 87–100.

▌NOTES

1   Although Rodger's (2010) study forms part of the wider backlash against rationalistic approaches to studying social movements, it is also reminiscent of work in the sociology of organizations and critical management studies, which takes issue with the conception of organizations as hierarchically ordered, rational bureaucracies. It has been argued that such a view forgets that informal structures, emotions, and symbolism are important aspects of organizational cultures (Albrow 1992; Parker 2000).

2   The notion of 'carnivalesque' is adapted from Mikhail Bakhtin's (1968) conception of the medieval carnival as representing a topsy-turvy world. It was a time and place where the dominant authority structures could be challenged, reversed, or overturned. But, importantly, the carnivalesque constituted a kind of *sanctioned deviance* where acts of transgression were temporarily permitted by the ruling class. Accordingly, 'the medieval carnival can be regarded as a kind of societal "safety valve": the peasantry were permitted to let loose for a limited period of time, allowing tensions and contradictions in society to be raised and released, while the status quo remained protected' (Anderton 2008: 41).

3   The commercialization of festivals is a process paralleling the co-optation of social movements by actors in the political system, which can result in the dilution or compromise of a movement's original (radical) goals. Similarly, the hijacking of festivals by corporate entities and commercial interests is regarded as a betrayal of their originally intended spirit.

CHAPTER 6

Religious movements and social movements

▌INTRODUCTION

In various parts of the book so far we have seen how religion has figured in studies of social movements. In Chapter 2, we saw how early theorists of collective behaviour included religious movements in their taxonomies and conceptual frameworks, although they tended to regard these movements as *expressive* or *value-oriented* and, hence, less significant than social movements striving for purposive social change. Also in Chapter 2, we considered briefly how Nazism has been described as a 'political religion' (Evans 2007), which, we might add, could be equivalent to 'civil religion' (Bellah 1970), in that it performs the same social function as religion (i.e., promoting social cohesion), albeit with a secular content. And, in Chapter 4, we saw how the precarity movement has utilized religious imagery, inventing its own saint, San Precario, to protect all precarious workers (see Figure 4.2.2).

While discussion of religious movements has been largely tangential up to now, the main focus of this chapter is on the relationship between social movements and religious movements. The chapter begins by considering why there has been relatively little cross-fertilization of ideas between the two fields of study, noting that most resistance has come from Marxist-influenced quarters of social movement theory, which view religion as regressive, reactionary, and conservative and, accordingly, see religious movements as retreatist or inward-looking, rather than progressive or emancipatory.

More recently, however, and especially with the advent of new social movement theory, which we looked at in Chapter 4, scholars have tried to reconcile the two fields, treating religious movements *as* social movements, or else acknowledging the religious qualities of some social movements. Indeed, if we accept the functionalist argument underpinning the idea that secular forms of civic religion bind people together in ways similar to traditional religion, we ought not be surprised by observations pointing to the quasi-religious nature of contemporary new social movements, which, like new religious movements, are searching for meaning, spirituality, and alternative conceptions of the sacred. Thus, some of the material contained in this chapter relates to developments associated with what we have previously identified as the 'cultural turn' in social movement research, which, as noted later, has engendered interest not only in culture and identity, but also in spirituality and the sacred, as well as other religious-like qualities of social movements.

RELIGIOUS MOVEMENTS AND SOCIAL MOVEMENTS: NEVER THE TWAIN SHALL MEET?

There has been a long-term estrangement between the sociology of religion and the study of social movements. Historical factors for this estrangement, which we considered in Chapter 2, have included the equation of religious sentiments with intolerance and fanaticism (Le Bon 1960 [1895]), as well as rigid conceptual distinctions between religious movements and political movements evident, for example, in the work of Blumer (1951: 216), for whom 'the latter sought to effect a political revolution as well as a change in ideology while the former were "expressive movements" whose members were unable to release their tension in the direction of some actual change' (Hannigan 1991: 313). When social movement theorists have included religious movements in their texts, it has usually been as illustrations of charismatic leadership, deviant systems of belief, relative deprivation, or conversion processes (Hannigan 1991: 314).

More recently, social movement scholars have disregarded religion and religious movements because just as they have been inclined to reduce collective action to organized (state) politics (see Chapter 4), so they tend to reduce religion to organized religion or 'religious organizations' (Diani 1992: 13–14). In this way, they have ignored the multiple definitions of religion and meanings of religious practice beyond church-oriented religion, such as the various contemporary forms of 'believing without belonging', which provide a counterpoint to the secularization thesis, where secularization is measured strictly by declining church attendance (Davie 1994). Having said that, some social movement research does acknowledge the important part religion and religious organizations can play in successful mobilizations. The most prominent example here is the role of black churches in the US civil rights movement, which was discussed in Chapter 3. It will be recalled that, according to McAdam (1982), the relative success of the US civil rights movement depended upon the prevailing 'political opportunity structure', that is, the constraints of the political, legal, and economic context, and the opportunities afforded the movement within that context, including the presence of preexisting networks, such as those provided by the black churches. However, as this political process model is founded on the assumptions of resource mobilization theory, religion is seen as having no inherent value; rather, 'it is conceptualized as but another movement "resource"' (Hannigan 1991: 315).

Nonetheless, the idea that religious movements might be affected by political opportunities has been applied to a variety of religiously motivated protests in the former Soviet Union and Latin America, to the Falun Gong movement in China, and Islamist movements in the Middle East and North Africa (Beckford 2003: 174). Moreover, sociologists of religion have used a similar logic to the political process approach, proposing that 'religious movements are expected to flourish in circumstances where formerly, actual or would-be monopoly religions are weak and where political and legal constraints on religious activity are also weak' (Beckford 2003: 167).

Another reason social movement theorists have tended to ignore religion and not taken religious movements seriously is born of an ideological bias, based in Marxism, which, to quote Marx himself, regards religion as 'the opium of the people' (Hannigan 1991: 317). This, in turn, has caused social movement thinkers to regard religion as a dogmatic, conservative, and reactionary social institution rather than as a potentially progressive force for change in society (Beckford 1989: 143–162). Moreover, even when religion offers radical alternatives, it is ultimately seen to do so in a manner and form that is retreatist, inward-looking, or 'world-rejecting' (Wallis 1984). On this view, religion has little or no emancipatory function (beyond individual salvation or enlightenment, that is).

However, Hannigan (1991: 318) says that, generally speaking, the ideological critique of religious movements 'does not hold up very well', for, '[w]hile religious experience and political action can both be interpreted as differential responses to situations of economic and social discontent, there is little empirical evidence to show that choosing one form necessarily precludes choosing the other'. Hence, expressive religious belief and radical social action are not necessarily incompatible. Indeed, for some members of religious movements, 'inner transformation is compatible with a more responsible participation in social life' (Diani 1993: 125). For instance, the radical personal transformation of 'born again' Christians can translate into radical social action on ostensibly nonreligious issues, although this can assume a conservative expression, as in pro-life activism against abortion. Regardless of the radical/progressive or conservative/reactionary nature of the activism, it remains the case that 'religious ideologies can be powerful vehicles for articulating "injustice frames" that diagnose social problems' (Williams 2000: 85).

Accordingly, religion and religious movements can have a significant role in public life and can contribute to the vitality of civil society, which in itself is nothing new, since religious communities and organizations have historically been seed beds for movements aimed at political reform and social justice, including mobilization around abolitionism, temperance, and disarmament (Williams 2000: 2–3; McCammon and Campbell 2002). Furthermore, some religious movements can be politically revolutionary, as demonstrated by Shi'ite Muslim fundamentalism in Iran (Hannigan 1991: 318; Kurzman 1998: 36–39), which provided the impetus for the Iranian Revolution of 1977–1979, wherein the 'mosque network' constituted a key resource (Kurzman 1994), equivalent to the role played by black churches in the US civil rights movement (see Chapter 3). The Iranian Revolution is but one example of 'Islamic activism' or 'the mobilization of contention to support Muslim causes' (Wiktorowicz 2004: 2). Indeed, Wiktorowicz (2004: 4–5) argues that:

> . . . [g]iven the variety of collective actors that operate in the name of 'Islam' (prayer groups, terrorists, propagation movements, study circles, political parties, nongovernmental organizations, cultural societies, etc.), one might even make a strong claim that Islamic activism is one of the most common examples of activism in the world.

BOX 6.1 RELIGIOUS PROTEST REPERTOIRES

One way social movements can resemble religious movements is via their adoption of what we might term 'religious protest repertoires'. This is a variant of the concept 'repertoires of contention', which, as we saw in

Chapter 3, refers to 'the tactics groups employ in their struggles with one another' (McAdam 1995: 235). An example here would be Greenpeace's early direct actions that were rooted in the Quaker idea of 'bearing witness', which 'is supposed to change the observer and increase their level of activism, compassion, anger, whatever it is' (Dale 1996: 17).

Although the act of bearing witness does not necessarily intend to affect directly any political or policy change, it can constitute a 'symbolic challenge' (Melucci 1984; 1985). Hence, in Chapter 5 we saw how the creative protest of women's grassroots groups in Peru contributed to dissent in civil society about the corrupt and repressive regime of Prime Minister Fujimori. While the radical street performance of the women did not lead to Fujimori's demise, Moser (2003: 187) says that was not the point; what they actually did was 'bear witness' to the government's corruption and, as such, their protests posed a symbolic challenge to the incumbent regime.

As an act of bearing witness, the performative protest of Peru's women 'creates a connection between knowledge and responsibility for the audience: their awareness of the issue means that they may choose to act or not, but that they cannot turn away in ignorance' (Moser 2003: 188). Moser (2003: 188) goes on to note that while bearing witness is rooted in the Quaker tradition, 'it also has an established presence in the political context of Latin America'. The paradigmatic example here being the *Madres de la Plaza de Mayo* (Figure 6.1), who are the group of mothers of the disappeared that, since the late 1970s

. . . have taken over the main public square in Argentina every Thursday afternoon, to walk slowly around the perimeter, dressed in white headscarves and holding pictures of their missing relatives in a courageous act of defiance which they explicitly regard as 'bearing witness' to state oppression.

(Moser 2003: 188)

The concept of repertoire of contention has also been applied to Islamic activism (mentioned earlier) and, in particular, the various protest events that emerged in opposition to the US-led invasion of Afghanistan following the terror attacks of 11 September 2001. Along with marches and rallies, protestors used other 'tools of dissent', including petitions directed at US representatives as well as Muslim governments, the unveiling of banners in both indigenous languages (to capture local audiences) and English (to capture global audiences), and symbolic props and actions, especially religious idioms and the burning of American flags and effigies of US President George W. Bush (Wiktorowicz 2004: 2). As we will see in Chapter 8, the use of new forms of social media during the Arab Spring can be seen to have added to the protest

© imageBROKER/Alamy

Figure 6.1 *Madres de la Plaza de Mayo* during Thursday demonstrations, Plaza de Mayo, Buenos Aires, Argentina, South America

repertoire of Islamic activism, although new media were also central to earlier anti-war protests post-9/11 (Carty and Onyett 2006; Gillan et al. 2008).

David Snow (2004: 18) has pointed out that scholars have tended to ignore the social movement activity of religious movements because 'they typically are only indirectly and secondarily politically-oriented, and therefore do not fit neatly under the contentious politics umbrella'. To compensate for this shortfall, Snow (2004: 19) says, 'we need to broaden our conceptualization of movements to include collective challenges to systems and structures of authority beyond the government and state', including movements that challenge authorities indirectly 'by exiting the system and thus the bailiwick of the authority, as in the case of communal movements and other-worldly religious "cults"'.

This relates to what Beckford (2003: 175) says about religious movements illustrating 'some of the interesting complexities and ambiguities concerning the mapping of public and private spheres of social life in modernity'. Paradoxically, he states, they 'press for the extension or defence of free, public space *and*, in some cases, make use of it in order to create inward-looking communities that appear to isolate their members from public life' (Beckford 2003: 175, original emphasis). However, the more outward-looking they are, the more likely religious movements contribute to strengthening civil society:

> . . . movements such as Scientology, the Unificationists and some of the New Religions of Japan have repeatedly offered to serve the interests of wider society by providing drug rehabilitation programs, schemes to reduce levels of crime and environmental pollution, and support for human rights campaigns.
>
> (Beckford 2003: 175)

Just as it is for social movements, establishing and retaining autonomy is an ongoing dilemma for religious movements and organizations. Fitzgerald (2009) has explored some consequences of 'cooperative collective action' by looking at the impact of government funding on religious identity and autonomy in faith-based community development organizations in the United States. He shows how while partnering with government agencies in the creation of community development and social services provision is key to revitalizing some neighbourhoods, it also has its dangers. For instance, like all not-for-profit organizations, faith-based organizations run the risk of becoming dependent on state resources, which may have negative organizational consequences. In one instance, Fitzgerald (2009: 194) found the organization 'was encouraged to grow at a faster rate than initially planned after receiving a government contract', and '[w]hen the contract was not renewed, the organization was forced to downsize rapidly and lay off nearly half of its staff'.

Ricardo Blaug (2002: 112–113) notes a similar process in the context of British politics, which, he says, has become wholly undemocratic, as it has moved away from deliberative participation towards 'engineered democracy' whereby grassroots and self-help groups are subject to a process of colonization, being offered resources with strings attached and threatened constantly by co-optation. One consequence of this development is that organizations with once-radical, nonhierarchical structures become institutionalized and instrumental forms subject to bureaucratic procedures.

Another tension can arise between partnering with the state *and* exercising a prophetic voice against injustice, such that, 'it is difficult (and perhaps unwise) to publicly challenge or criticize the state when the state is your partner' (Fitzgerald 2009: 194). Arguably, it is easier to challenge the state or government from a position of power and authority, which raises interesting questions about the relationship between religion, church, and state. And we will look at some of those issues later when we consider the Catholic Church's espousal of liberation theology in Latin America (see Box 6.2), the Church of England's political interventions during the Thatcher era in Britain, and, more recently, the churches' support for the Occupy movement.

RECONCILING NEW RELIGIOUS MOVEMENTS AND NEW SOCIAL MOVEMENTS

Studies that recognize 'the disruptive, defiant and unruly face of religion' (Smith 1996: 1) suggest it is not sufficient to treat religious movements as clearly retreatist or purely cultural (Hannigan 1991: 318). Furthermore, researchers who have explored the similarities and differences between new religious movements and new social movements argue that even though the former, like the latter, may not strive to achieve any political or policy objectives, they nevertheless can offer important and meaningful contributions to transforming social institutions and cultural values. These arguments relate to the efficacy of cultural politics and symbolic challenges to dominant codes that are posed by some forms of contemporary protest, including new social movements, which was discussed in Chapters 4 and 5.

Regardless of the apparent similarities that exist between social and religious movements, there has been an impasse between social movements studies and the study of religious movements, which, with a few exceptions, has prohibited the transference of ideas between the two fields. In America, that has largely been a result of sociologists of religion choosing to 'embrace the homegrown "resource mobilization" paradigm' (Hannigan 1993: 3; see also Hannigan 1990: 255). Given this perspective regards social movements as 'rational, strategically calculating, politically instrumental phenomena', it is hardly surprising, says Smith (1996: 3), that 'in the move to sweep irrationality and emotion out of social movement theory, religion – bearing all of those associations – was also swept away with the classical theories'.

On the other hand, European social movement theorists have displayed the kind of ideological opposition to religion that was discussed earlier, whereby religion is seen to reflect dominant class interests, and is therefore conservative and reactionary, 'and religious movements are regarded as withdrawals from rather than encounters with social change' (Hannigan 1993: 3). However, with the advent of new social movements and new religious movements, a constructive conversation began to take place between scholars from their respective fields.

In the sociology of religion, Barbara Hargrove (1988: 45) applied Wallace's (1956) conception of 'revitalization movements' to what she termed 'new mazeways' that could give rise to a 'larger vision of global responsibility and economic thinking'. These included:

> . . . the indigenous spirituality of Native Americans, the 'recovery by women's groups of ancient understandings of human relations to one another and to the earth', liberation theology, and the world view of the ecology movement 'where concerned persons are fighting for the preservation of a balance of nature that the rush towards development has upset'.
>
> (Hannigan 1991: 321, quoting Hargrove 1988: 45–46)

Like new social movements (Hannigan 1990: 252), these new religious formations contained high concentrations of the 'new middle classes' (managers, professionals, etc.), thus gainsaying another ideological bias in the study of religious movements, which sees them as the religion of the oppressed and lower orders (Hannigan 1991: 318, 321).

BOX 6.2 LIBERATION THEOLOGY

At a conference in Medellín, Colombia, in 1968, Latin American Catholic bishops declared the right of the poor to seek justice and challenge unjust military regimes. Soon after, the popular church began to articulate beliefs that effectively reversed traditional biblical teachings. These biblical beliefs of the poor became known as 'liberation theology', the central tenets of which constituted a radical challenge to established beliefs insofar as they assigned different meanings to orthodox Christian teachings. First, liberation theology was premised on the view that rather than being time neutral and culturally neutral, theology must be contextual: it 'must be culturally relevant and cannot be separated from its socio-economic and political contexts' (Erickson Nepstad 1996: 110).

Second, while God loves both rich and poor, God has a preference for the poor. Moreover, sin is not understood in terms of personal and individual wrongdoing, but is equated with capitalism and the exploitation of the poor by the rich, who have also used religion as an ideological means of justifying the status quo (see Box 6.4). Third, in a reversal of the traditional view of salvation as a personal reward given a Christian in the afterlife, liberation theology maintains God's kingdom is 'an ambition for a just society in this lifetime' (Erickson Nepstad 1996: 111).[1] This utopian vision aims to reverse social inequality and injustice in the present, where, it is believed, God's kingdom can be established with the abolition of classes, private property, and ruling elites. Accordingly:

> The salvation message is changed to mean a human liberation in the present, instigated by popular church adherents. This transformed understanding of salvation means that the Christian mission no longer consists only of proselytizing souls, but also of establishing social justice.
>
> (Erickson Nepstad 1996: 111)

In a development paralleling the key role of black churches in the US civil rights movement (see Chapter 3), the popular Central American church has provided the necessary resources and organizational structure to enable the expression of people's aspirations for revolutionary change (Erickson Nepstad 1996: 110; see also Kurzman 1998). Moreover, the strong political language and abiding concern for a just social order voiced by liberationists has resonated at the highest levels of Church governance, which Hewitt (1993: 75) sees as 'an important development, given that it is precisely here that the resources and the power of the Church can be most effectively marshaled to effect real change'. This has been most evident in Brazil, 'where the Church has developed a reputation as one of the most progressive within world Catholicism in implementing the "preferential option for the poor"' (Hewitt 1993: 74).

Similarly, the Canadian Church has long spoken out against social injustice and been a defender of the downtrodden. As in Brazil, the United Church of Canada has institutionalized its social justice concerns, at one time identifying the following three programs or priority areas: (i) faith and justice; (ii) regional inequality, native people, and urban poverty; and (iii) justice in the Third World, including issues of human rights, world peace, and environmental protection (Hewitt 1993: 83–84). Furthermore, as in Brazil, there has been an emphasis in Canada on grassroots organizations, or 'base ecclesial communities', such as parish and local community groups, which 'are seen as playing a vital role in the fight for social transformation by denouncing injustices' (Hewitt 1993: 84).

By contrast, the Catholic Church in the United States has been a less vociferous critic of social injustice and defender of the poor. Although, like Canada, the United States differs from Brazil since it is a developed country and major industrial power, that is not to say the US Church operates in a society without social problems. Nonetheless, rather than addressing the structural causes of social ills, it has been observed that the response of the Church in the United States has been 'a mere reflection of the dominant liberal tradition in America insofar as it advocates a piecemeal or individualistic approach to the solution of social problems' (Hewitt 1993: 80). Accordingly, bishops there 'have directed their pastoral on the economy to those in authority in America, not to the grassroots in the first instance, as the "option for the poor" would seem to dictate' (Hewitt 1993: 80–81). Moreover, in concrete undertakings, US bishops have adopted a similarly circumscribed approach, focusing on education, 'with little or no emphasis on organizing active opposition to particular forms of injustice' (Hewitt 1993: 81).

Hannigan (1990, 1991, 1993) has attempted to reconcile the study of new social movements and new religious movements by proposing a synthetic approach to religious movements and change that applies the framework of new social movement theory to the sociology of religion. For instance, he recommends eliminating the analytical distinction between religious movements and social movements. If we accept Turner and Killian's (1988: 237) argument that every social movement is ultimately a 'moral crusade' (cp. Eder 1985) and the classical view of Emile Durkheim (1965 [1912]) that religion and morality are different sides of the same coin, we can set aside any ideological opposition to the study of religion and religious movements, recognizing that 'religious and nonreligious social movements are thus potentially cut from the same cloth' (Hannigan 1991: 327). According to Hannigan (1991: 326), this provides 'a deeper rationale for treating religious and social movements in the same terms beyond simply observing that segments of the new social movements appear to have spiritual or theological themes'.

Documenting the religious or spiritual dimensions of new social movements is precisely what James Beckford (1989, 2003) has done. Beginning his analysis with a critique of those European scholars (i.e., Habermas, Offe, and Touraine) who have taken ideological exception to religion and religious movements, Beckford draws attention to the religious quality of new social movements. As suggested earlier, many of the problems flowing from this ideological opposition to religious movements derive from the fact that, like some sociologists of religion (Hannigan 1990: 255), social movement scholars tend to have a limited conception of religion, which they equate with formal religious organization, such as churchgoing. Significantly, there are echoes here of new social movement theorists' critique of resource mobilization theory for focusing exclusively on social movement organizations, which Melucci (1989: 44) sees as symptomatic of a 'myopia of the visible' prevalent in studies of collective action and mass mobilization.

Notwithstanding the fact that, as discussed earlier, many quasi-Marxist theorists of new social movements are ideologically opposed to religion,

Beckford shows how, interestingly, there are religion-like elements in their work (Beckford 2003: 161–165). For instance, Habermas (1987: 393) differentiates the 'emancipatory potentials' of anti-nuclear movements, feminism, and peace movements, among others, from 'potentials for resistance and withdrawal' evident in some youth sects and in religious fundamentalism. Because they are capable of 'conquering new territory', Habermas (1987: 393) classifies the former as 'offensive movements', while the latter 'have a more defensive character'. Nevertheless, Beckford (1989: 151–152) shows how Habermas has some:

> . . . guarded support for a humanistic kind of religion which might have emancipatory effects [. . .] if it served as a vehicle of critical self-reflection and if, as a result of the process of secularization, it became separated from dominant interests.

By highlighting the themes and values of new social movements as 'autonomy and identity [. . .] and opposition to manipulation, control, dependence, bureaucratization, regulation, etc.' (Offe 1985: 829), Beckford (1989: 156) shows how Claus Offe impliedly points to the religious quality of new social movements 'insofar as they have to do with the values that are considered ultimately important for human life and which transcend particular social arrangements'. Touraine also 'appears to touch indirectly on matters of religion' (Beckford 1989: 157). Indeed, as we saw in Chapter 4, Touraine's 'mission' could be described as discovering *the* social movement of post-industrial society. To Beckford, this project chimes with the general objectives of many religious movements:

> . . . some broad religious movements exhibit precisely the kind of traits which, for Touraine, constitute *the* social movement: a strong sense of distinctive identity for participants, a clear idea of their opponents and a sharp awareness of what is at stake in the movement's struggle against its opponents.
>
> (Beckford 1989: 160–161, original emphasis)

Furthermore, for Beckford (1989: 161), 'in view of their all-encompassing diagnoses of problems and prescriptions for remedies', some religious movements could be exemplars of Touraine's notion of social movement. In fact, he states, 'it seems almost perverse and arbitrary for Touraine to deny that such movements as Christian evangelicalism, liberation theology, or Islamic fundamentalism could qualify as social movements' (Beckford 1989: 161). Presumably, however, they do not qualify as social movements because they are not self-directing and, therefore, in Touraine's opinion, '[e]ven if they intend to create a new form of society, it would not amount to a truly autonomous creation' (Beckford 1989: 161).

Elsewhere in this chapter the social movement-like qualities of both liberation theology and conservative forms of Christianity are considered. For now, we will note one study of 'Islamic activism' (Wiktorowicz 2004) that does indeed attempt to show how some of the central features of new social movements (e.g., autonomy, loose network of associations, adherence to post-material values) characterize both moderate and radical Islamic movements (Sutton and Vertigans 2006). On the other hand, it has been suggested that the international growth of Islamic terrorism after the terror attacks of 11 September 2001 has given rise to a global 'anti-movement', which is defined as 'a distorted, inverse image of a social movement' (Wieviorka 2005: 15).

Although Beckford is able to see some religious-like qualities in the new social movement theories of Habermas, Offe, and Touraine, for him, the strongest case for the view that new social movements have a religious quality is presented by Alberto Melucci. For example, Melucci (1985: 801) proposes that contemporary new social movements have a *prophetic* function, since '[t]hey practice in the present the change they are struggling for'. In this way, as we saw in Chapter 4, contemporary collective actors resemble nomads dwelling in the present (Melucci 1989: 55). Furthermore, and unlike collective behaviour theorists of the past, Melucci does not categorically distinguish new religious movements and new social movements since he 'accepts the sacred can serve as the basis for an appeal to a different, alternative social order' (Beckford 2003: 162). A similar point is made by Hannigan (1990: 255) who says that the 'holistic' ethics and imagery of both contemporary new religious movements and new social movements 'constitutes a new and distinctive conceptualization of the sacred'.

The religious quality of new social movements is particularly evident in environmentalism and feminism. Mario Diani (1993: 125) has shown how both adherents of neo-oriental religious groups and ecological activists in Italy articulate similar critiques of modern society (which we will see later is also something common to religious fundamentalist movements) that are based on a 'version of individual freedom which is not indifferent to social problems but rather aims at a balanced growth of both the private and the public sphere'. Similarly, Hannigan (1990: 253) shows how the holistic worldview of 'New Age' spirituality is evident in segments of new social movements (see also Box 6.3). For instance, 'deep ecology', which 'is an ecophilosophy that stresses the fundamental interrelatedness and value of all living things' (Hannigan 1993: 14), suggests 'a kind of mystic religiosity based on nature worship' (Hannigan 1990: 253).

▋BOX 6.3 RELIGIOUS 'LIFESTYLE MOVEMENTS'

Kemp (2001: 37) has argued that a Christian form of New Age spirituality, dubbed 'Christaquarianism', should be referred to as a 'new socio-religious movement [. . .] to emphasize the wider cultural base and similarity to the new social movements'. On the other hand, Shimazono (1999) has said it is more apt to refer to what is commonly called the New Age Movement as the 'New Spirituality Movements and Culture'. The fact that many adherents have individualistic inclinations and are reluctant to take part in collective actions suggests classification as a 'culture' rather than a 'movement', where 'culture' means 'aspects of the production or consumption of culture, rather than active individual practices' (Shimazono 1999: 125). Another way of viewing Shimazono's observations about New Age adherents is through the lens of what Haenfler et al. (2012: 14) call 'lifestyle movements', which because they 'encourage adherents to take action in their daily lives [. . .] the vast majority of people will never engage in civil disobedience or even symbolic demonstration'.

Lifestyle movements 'consciously and actively promote a lifestyle, or way of life, as their primary means to foster social change' (Haenfler et al. 2012: 2). While some established social movements have lifestyle 'wings', such as the green living segment of the environmental movement, lifestyle movements differ significantly from overtly political movements, since they are (i) relatively individualized and private, (ii) ongoing rather than episodic, and (iii) aimed at changing cultural and economic practices rather than targeting the state (Haenfler et al. 2012: 6). Examples include the voluntary simplicity movement, which 'advocates reducing overall material consumption by fixing broken items, reusing old items, and "doing without" in order to reduce environmental burdens', and the social responsibility movement, which 'encourages participants to "vote" with their dollars, buying from socially responsible companies (and boycotting others), supporting locally owned businesses, purchasing "fair trade" products, and making socially responsible investments' (Haenfler et al. 2012: 6).

Whereas green living, voluntary simplicity, and social responsibility movements form part of the environmental and social justice movements, other lifestyle movements include religious movements or sects. Examples here are Promise Keepers (men committed to 'changing the world' by being spiritual leaders of their families), virginity pledgers (sexual abstinence aimed at both personal spiritual fulfillment and challenging 'hookup' and 'pornographic' culture), and Quiverfull (a pronatalist movement that 'trust the Lord' to determine family size), which are considered lifestyle 'wings' of the broader conservative Christian Right movement (Haenfler et al. 2012: 5, 12). Indeed, in accordance with Beckford's (2003: 165–167) treatment of religious movements *as* social movements, religious and secular movements can be seen to intersect – both now and historically – to produce hybrid movements, which focus on both contentious politics and lifestyle action (Haenfler et al. 2012: 12). For instance, Soule (2009: 12) shows how, in the United States, at least, responsible investment has its roots in Colonial America 'when certain religious groups (e.g., Quakers and Methodists) refused to invest in enterprises that benefitted the slave trade'.

Significantly, Haenfler et al. (2012: 13) argue that lifestyle movements 'may also serve as refuges in times of unfavourable political opportunity, acting as abeyance structures until opportunities improve' (see also Taylor 1989, discussed in Chapter 4). Moreover, while lifestyle movements bear a strong resemblance to new social movements, not least because they reflect the post-material values of post-industrial societies, they 'are in a sense *newer* than typically studied new social movements, that is, lifestyle movements are more individualized and more deeply infused with *personal* identity work' (Haenfler et al. 2012: 15, original emphasis). Haenfler et al. see this as symptomatic of broader trends in contemporary societies that are individualistic and consumer oriented in nature, and which stress the importance of lifestyle in identity construction:

> ... encouraging people to individualize the self by altering daily habits (especially consumption). Just as people 'shop' for and attempt to personalize their style, hobbies, and religious/spiritual identities, so too do they customize their involvement in social change.
>
> (Haenfler et al. 2012: 15)

Feminism also has a religious side. For instance, 'spiritual feminism' emphasizes 'holistic thought' and 'interconnectedness' (Hannigan 1990: 253), as does 'ecofeminism', which 'equates the suppression and domination of nature with the domination of women and encourages a more spiritual approach to the natural world' (Hannigan 1993: 6). Both deep ecology and ecofeminism draw sustenance from what Albanese (1990) calls 'nature religion', which acknowledges that 'the beliefs and traditions of North American indigenous peoples are important ingredients in the ideologies of radical environmentalists' (Hannigan 1993: 7).

Given the multiple examples provided here, and notwithstanding the ideological bias of many European new social movement theorists, it is something of a surprise that religion has been a neglected area of social movement studies. Indeed, as Beckford (2003: 165, 171) notes, following

Calhoun (1999: 237), this is even more surprising given the 'cultural turn' seemed to foster greater interest not only in culture and identity, but also in the spiritual, sacred, and other religious-like aspects of social movements (see also Hart 1996; Williams 2004: 106–108; 2006: 84–85). Arguably the most likely and possibly most fruitful area for synthetic research in this area relates to the struggle of religious movements for 'free space' and 'identity spaces' (Beckford 2003: 172), which can be regarded as similar to the struggle of new social movements for autonomy.

FREE SPACE AND AUTONOMY

In Chapter 4, we saw how Melucci (1985: 815) argues that contemporary social movements seek to establish an intermediate public space, between state and civil society, in which they strive to maintain their autonomy. Similarly, Touraine proposes *the* new social movement of a programmed society will seek 'self-management' against technocratic encroachment into more and more areas of social life. Likewise, for Habermas (1987: 395), '[t]he new conflicts arise along the seam between system and life–world', to resist the 'colonization' of the latter by the former. Religious movements similarly 'are contending for the possibilities of creating and exploiting free space' (Beckford 2003: 175), which they use for religious experimentation.

There are clear similarities here between Melucci's characterization of the submerged networks of contemporary movements that act as 'cultural laboratories' (Melucci 1989: 60), experimenting in alternative forms of socialization (Melucci 1984: 829; 1985: 789) and cultural innovation, and which enable individuals to experience new cultural models and codes (Melucci 1984: 829; 1989: 60), and Beckford's (2003: 172) depiction of religious movements as 'quasi-laboratories in which profound social and cultural experiments can be relatively easily observed [. . .] whereby religious movements construct distinctive codes of meaning and modify them over time, often in conflict with the rest of society'. Yet, Beckford (2003: 172) goes on, 'religious movements are rarely free to construct their cultural codes in complete independence from existing codes and social structural constraints'.

Indeed, the availability of free space for religious experimentation often depends upon wider structures of opportunity, including political opportunities, which, in turn, affect the varying degrees of success of religious movements (Beckford 2003: 172–173). That means religious movements 'often develop a form of intense, inward-looking solidarity that is articulated and celebrated through controversies and conflicts with external agencies' (Beckford 2003: 172), often with lethal consequences. Examples here include the cases of the People's Temple of the Disciples of Christ, which involved the mass suicide and killing of 920 people in Guyana in 1978, and the Branch Davidians, whose fifty-one-day siege of their property, the Mount Carmel Center, in Waco, Texas, in 1993, ended in the death of eighty-three Branch members and four federal law enforcement agents.

The *relative autonomy* of religious movements, then, leads to a paradoxical situation whereby they press for the extension or defence of free, public space, while simultaneously forming insular, inward-looking communities isolated from public life (Beckford 2003: 175). Hence, their contribution to civil society is likely to be minimal; although one may expect that to differ if they were to adopt a 'world-affirming' or 'world-accommodating' orientation (Wallis 1984). Indeed, as we saw in Chapter 4, a similar criticism has been leveled at the autonomy-seeking new social movements that do not have political, legal, or policy objectives, and thus do not connect their demands to 'institutionally imminent possibilities' (Giddens 1991a: 155). Equally, however, as we saw earlier when we looked at Fitzgerald's (2009) study of US faith-based community development organizations, being too closely connected to the state and government agencies can compromise movement goals and values. Nevertheless, research into labour struggles in the United States during the early twentieth century indicates some of the ways in which autonomous religious institutions can foster activism.

Billings (1990) shows how religion had a significant influence on strikes that occurred in Appalachian coal mining towns between 1928 and 1931. Since coal operators built and supported local churches and encouraged ministers to denounce unions as an atheistic menace, Billings notes how during the strikes most ministers aligned themselves with management. However, most Appalachian coal miners did not heed the conservative teachings of their pastors. In fact, many openly denounced the ministers for siding with management, and up to 90 percent stopped attending company-supported churches. Instead, miners held their own alternative church services, and some militant miners even emerged as lay preachers:

> These 'miner-ministers' used this free space to promote a religious culture of resistance that fostered an insurgent mindset and a willingness to strike for union recognition. Moreover, these alternative religious services provided a context where biblical teachings were given new meaning, granting religious legitimacy to labour struggles. For instance, miners altered lyrics of traditional hymns to link faith with union activism.
>
> (Erickson Nepstad and Williams 2007: 425)

Billings argues that the oppositional religious culture fostered by the miners' services functioned as a *free space* that aided labour activism in three important ways:

> First, it provided a context where an oppositional religious culture and critical consciousness was cultivated. Second, the pro-union rituals and music in these alternative services helped sustain this insurgent mindset and reinforce union commitment among the miners [. . .] Finally, these autonomous religious groups provided a context for the emergence of indigenous leaders who were known and trusted by their co-workers.
>
> (Erickson Nepstad and Williams 2007: 425–426)

BOX 6.4 RELIGION: IDEOLOGY OR OPPOSITION?

In Chapter 5, we saw how music and song can play important roles in social movement activism. Similarly, Billings (1990) shows how, during their labour struggles, Appalachian coal miners altered the lyrics of traditional hymns to link faith with unionism, which included changing the words of one hymn as follows: 'When you hear of a thing that's called union / You know that they're happy and free / For Christ has a union in heaven / How beautiful a union must be' (Corbin 1981: 164). Previously in this chapter it was noted that some social movement scholars aligning themselves with the conventional Marxist view of religion as an opiate of the masses contest the idea of religion as opposition, seeing it instead as an instrument of domination used by the ruling class to justify the status quo.

The notion that class division is somehow preordained was clearly evident in the text of the now-oft omitted verse from the famous Anglican hymn, *All Things Bright and Beautiful*, written in England in 1848 by Cecil F. Alexander, which reads: 'The rich man in his castle / The poor man at his gate / God made them, high or lowly / And order'd their estate'. From a Marxist perspective, this provides a stark illustration of the use of religion as ideology, which functions to create a 'false consciousness' among the subordinate classes, who, by being promised emancipation (or salvation) in the afterlife, are encouraged to be satisfied with their lot, or resigned to their fate on earth, and are, therefore, less likely to revolt or question and challenge the existing order.

Despite the fact that from a Marxist perspective religion is regarded as a conservative social institution, Marxist analyses have nevertheless formed the bases for religious radicalism. For instance, a Marxist analysis was key to the thinking in Latin America of liberation theologians who, as we saw earlier, aim to establish God's kingdom in this lifetime by reversing social inequities and injustices on earth that stem from social class divisions and private property ownership. However, as revolutionary ideologies waned throughout the world in the 1970s, liberation theology downplayed its radical Marxist rhetoric. And although after his investiture in 1978 Pope John Paul II committed the Catholic Church to adopt a strong stance on alleviating poverty and inequality, the Vatican simultaneously attacked liberation theology's uncritical use of Marxism (McGovern 1989: 51), which it saw as incompatible with Christian conceptions of humanity and society (Kurzman 1998: 35).

The Church's critique of brutal regimes that 'were legitimated with the rhetoric of a perverted Marxism' (Barker 1986: 58) was particularly evident in Poland where, it has been argued, both the Catholic Church and Pope John Paul II were influential in giving birth to the Solidarity movement against communism in the early 1980s. Hence, the moral leadership of the Pope – who was himself a Pole – as well as the Church's instruction on issues of human rights from the 1960s onwards, had the effect of encouraging the working class to challenge the vanguard claims of Marxist-Leninism by shifting their attention from economic issues to a higher plane concerned with human rights and political participation (Osa 1996: 69).

STORIES, NARRATIVE, AND EMOTION IN RELIGIOUS SOCIAL MOVEMENTS

As we saw earlier when we looked at the study of Billings (1990), pro-union rituals and music performed in alternative church services proved very significant in the labour struggles of Appalachian coal miners during the early twentieth century. This example not only shows how religion might serve some wider political and potentially emancipatory purpose, but also highlights the important role culture can play in both social and religious movements. And just as the cultural life of social movements is not limited to music – but also includes, as we saw in Chapter 5, stories, narrative, and emotion – this is no less the case with religious movements, nor indeed social movements with religious dimensions, or what we might call 'religious social movements'.

An example of how emotion and religion can intersect is provided by Erickson Nepstad and Smith (2001), who show how, during the 1980s, moral outrage was a driving force in the Central American peace movement, which was responding to civil wars in Nicaragua, El Salvador, and Guatemala. Thousands of North Americans protested US political and military involvement in these countries and stood in solidarity with the poor of Central America in their struggle for social justice. And religion was a key factor contributing to the generation of moral outrage.

Erickson Nepstad and Smith (2001: 166) show how US Christians and Jews were particularly 'subjectively engageable' on account of the fact that, first, 'many embraced social teachings that emphasize peace, justice, and political engagement as essential expressions of religious commitment', and, second, 'their common collective identity as people of faith took greater precedence over their identity as Americans'. Moreover, church connections and a sense of having a shared identity also transcended national differences, which, for instance, 'enabled Nicaraguans to feel solidarity and empathy with US Christians, when they might have otherwise felt anger or enmity since the US was the source of much of their suffering' (Erickson Nepstad and Smith 2001: 168). Crucial to the development of a transnational Christian identity was the direct interpersonal encounters North American people of faith had with Central American refugees and asylum seekers whose 'stories moved North Americans both emotionally and politically' (Erickson Nepstad and Smith 2001: 162).

Similarly, a narrative approach has been used to develop a general theory of fundamentalism to show how, despite their differences, religious fundamentalist movements all share a common story of how history has gone awry, which constitutes what Yates and Hunter (2002) term a 'world-historical narrative' of fundamentalism at odds with the progression of modernity. Examining specific fundamentalist 'movement narratives' (Benford 2002) from a variety of the world's major religions (i.e., Protestant-Christian, Jewish, Islamic, and Hindu), they show how the world-historical narrative unfolds in three steps:

> It begins with the deep and worrisome belief that history has gone awry, demonstrates that what 'went wrong' with history is modernity in its various guises, and leads to the inescapable conclusion that the calling of the fundamentalist is to make history 'right' again.
> (Yates and Hunter 2002: 130)

In the narrative of Islamic fundamentalism, for example, history began to go awry when during the eighteenth century, European powers established direct economic, political, and military control over Islamic countries, which subjugated Islamic culture and ideals to Western rationalism, secularism, and pluralism. Moreover, when colonial rule ended, 'many postcolonial governments were transitioned to a Westernized Muslim administration that continued to embrace modern European modes of thought and rule and promised increased economic and social prosperity' (Yates and Hunter 2... fundamentalists, however, the accommodation of mode... values resulted in moral and political decay.

Modernity in the form of Westernization, or 'Westoxificatio... has been called, heralded a crisis for many Islamic fundamenta... some of whom characterize 'the unique destructive force of moder... nity as an unstoppable monstrous "machine"' (Yates and Hunter 2002: 136). The solution of Islamic fundamentalists:

> . . . to the insidiousness of modernity [. . .] is to return to strict adherence to Islam in every sphere of life [. . .] Like the earliest (pro-tofundamentalists') reactions against the internal 'deterioration' of Islam in the eighteenth and nineteenth centuries, twentieth-century fundamentalist movements all share the common passion to recover the classical experience of Islam, 'a history without deviation', and the original meaning of the Islamic message, 'a faith without distortion'. The fundamentalist solution demands nothing less than the establishment of a totally Islamic social and political order.
>
> (Yates and Hunter 2002: 136)

The first step toward establishing the new Islamic order is internal reform, which requires that, among other things, fundamentalists rid themselves of 'compromised' elites who embrace secular attitudes and values, having been educated in the West. Beyond internal reform, 'the establishment of a new Islamic order also requires active resistance to the external influence of pagan societies', and nowhere has this shift from passive to active faith been more pronounced than in contemporary Iran (Yates and Hunter 2002: 138). Here, the traditional religious scholars, or *ulama*, weaved together selective moments in Persian history into a 'militant theocratic and messianic movement narrative', which 'created the religious legitimation for a revolutionary resistance in what was the most modernizing society in the Middle East' (Yates and Hunter 2002: 138). Against that background, and using highly emotive rhetoric, the Ayatollah Khomeini condemned all foreign powers, but especially Western powers, as inherently satanic, corrupt, and evil, which accordingly need to be fought, rooted out, and, ultimately, overthrown (Khomeini 1980: 5).

Rhetoric and emotion are also used by Christian fundamentalists, who frequently see themselves as involved in a Manichean battle, or 'culture war', against liberal, secularizing forces in contemporary society. In her study of battles over the issue of homosexuality that occurred in numerous small communities in the US state of Oregon during the 1990s, Arlene Stein (2001: 117) depicts the Oregon Citizens Alliance g part of the conservative Christian Right in the United she says, is itself a 'moral movement'. Drawing on inter- ducted with Christian conservative activists, Stein (2001: how the OCA is a movement with 'profound emotional she shows how the 'emotion of shame' figured promi- narratives of the religious conservatives she interviewed 118), whereby, for instance, shame is linked to sexual call up emotions (Stein 2001: 128). Moreover, 'shameful in 2001: 119) are mobilized for political ends, confirming Jasper's (1998: 215) view that social movements combine strategic purpose and emotion (see Chapter 5). However, Stein (2001: 127) argues, the OCA campaigns to amend local charters in rural parts of Oregon 'were largely symbolic', since 'the vast majority of these localities had never considered passing any such gay rights ordinances, or if they had done so they would have a negligible effect'. To Stein (2001: 127), then, '[t]hese campaigns were much more about consolidating a religious right collective identity than about affecting public policy'.

RELIGION AND POLITICS

Previously, we have seen how social movement scholars have largely avoided looking at religious movements because, it is believed, they tend to be retreatist, reactionary, or conservative. According to this view, religious movements have little or no emancipatory potential, nor are they capable of contributing positively to social change. Indeed, Stein's (2001) study underscores that very point, as do the examples of religious movements, discussed earlier, which are lifestyle 'wings' of the wider conservative Christian movement, such as groups like Quiverfall and Promise Keepers (Haenfler et al. 2012).

However, just as religious movements can be conservative or reactionary, so, too, can social movements. This sometimes assumes the form of countermovement opposition to social movements, such as in the case of pro-life (anti-abortion) activism against the pro-choice (abortion rights) movement, although this example also highlights the fact that, as we have seen throughout this chapter, social movements (and countermovements) may contain religious elements or have religious qualities. Hence, the pro-life movement began almost entirely as a Catholic movement, but it took on a new dimension with the rise of right-wing movements like the Moral Majority and Christian Coalition, which drew strength from white Southern evangelicals (Kniss and Burns 2004: 703). Things get even more complicated when we consider the prospect that some conservative religious movements might have progressive outlooks. For example, Andrea Smith (2008) has uncovered some 'unlikely alliances' between Christian Right activists and progressive groups, including coalitions to do with prison reform, and potential alignments on abortion and Native American women.

These examples not only confound the narrow view of religion as having limited, if any, progressive or emancipatory potential, but they also raise important questions about the relationship between religion and politics, which is a key dynamic lying at the heart of many issues considered in this chapter. Indeed, in Box 6.2, we saw how the Catholic Church in the United States has been less inclined to engage in liberationist projects than its counterparts in Brazil and Canada. This is especially interesting given the formal separation of church and state in the United States under the First Amendment to the Constitution, which, in theory, at least, gives religious organizations carte blanche to criticize governments and politicians. Alternatively, it may be that the church-state separation is the cause of the Church's relative inaction. That is, the Church does not feel the need to intervene in matters beyond its religious remit.

Nevertheless, the fact remains that the nature of the US church-state relationship guarantees American churches a great deal of autonomy, which, according to Kniss and Burns (2004: 710), also 'may help explain the apparent paradox that religious affiliation does not predict political affiliations well'. Thus, they say:

> . . . while most American social movements have had a strong religious component, most religious adherents in the US typically do not connect their religion with political causes and, even when they do, they may find that the right-wing version of religion they favour is opposed by a leftist sitting in the next pew.
> (Kniss and Burns 2004: 704)

However, although church autonomy is particularly strong in the American context and has led to significant political interventions, such as the involvement of US churches in the Central America peace movement of the 1980s (discussed earlier), churches have also played a key role in opposing repressive regimes, as well as advocating for human rights in other parts of the world, including, as we have seen, in Poland and Latin America.

In Britain, unlike in the United States, church and state are, to some extent, constitutionally entwined. The Church of England is the officially established Christian church in England, for instance. And, even though it is not expressed in terms of liberation theology, the Church of England has on occasion been a vocal opponent of British governments and their policies. A prominent example was the Archbishop of Canterbury's Commission on Urban Priority Areas, which was established in 1983 and yielded the report, *Faith in the City*, which was published in 1985 (Davie 1994: 151–154). Among other things, the report contained a devastating critique of Thatcherite policies, which it saw as the cause of growing spiritual and economic poverty in Britain's inner cities. A more recent example is the extensive involvement of churches in the Jubilee 2000 campaign for the cancellation of Third World debt (Staggenborg 2011: 160).

BOX 6.5 JUBILEE 2000

The Great Jubilee of 2000 was a major celebration in the Roman Catholic Church, involving several events, held between 24 December 1999 (Christmas Eve) and 6 January 2001 (Epiphany). It was commemorated by the building of numerous memorials, including the one depicted in Figure 6.2.

© Irene Abdou/Alamy

Figure 6.2 The Memorial of the Great Jubilee of 2000 is one of several monuments on the beach of Ouidah, Benin, West Africa

Beyond the Catholic Church, activists took the opportunity provided by the Great Jubilee celebrations to shed light on various social issues. With particular reference to the forgiveness of debts that biblical Jubilees entail, activists, including high-profile figures, such as Bono, Bob Geldof, and Muhammad Ali, supported the Jubilee 2000 campaign that aimed to highlight the struggle of developing nations faced with insurmountable foreign debt. Pope John Paul II gave his blessing to the campaign, which called for governments and international banks to cancel Third World debts in the year 2000.

Perhaps, unlike churches and other religious organizations in the United States, where, as we have seen, church and state are formally separated, the established Church in Britain feels that *because of* its inextricable link to the state, it is incumbent upon it to speak out and act when it perceives injustices promulgated by government policies. In such circumstances, the Church may become the state's conscience and society's moral compass. More recently, and particularly in the wake of the austerity packages that were introduced across Europe from 2008, religious leaders on both sides of the Atlantic and across denominational divides have spoken out forcefully in condemnation at growing social inequality and the rampant greed of consumerism. For instance, Pope Francis has not only shown 'intense empathy for the poor, unemployed and struggling migrants', but has also set out 'to cleanse his Church of luxury', making him, according to one commentator, 'truly the Austerity Pope for this new age of austerity' (Kneale 2013: 23). Moreover:

> Rowan Williams, the Archbishop of Canterbury, in a sermon commemorating the Golden Jubilee in the United Kingdom, criticised the culture of greed, hostility to strangers and lack of responsibility to society. There has also been support for Occupy Wall Street from the Churches, which have also criticized the irresponsibility of a greedy society.
>
> (Turner 2013: 148–149)

To Bryan Turner (2013: 80, 149), this suggests there is a significant 'legitimacy deficit' in modern societies. Moreover, while these developments have, in part, given rise to waves of protest against social inequality, injustice, and exploitation, they are also a root cause of modern populism in the form of the Tea Party movement, which shares mobilizing structures with centre-right predecessor movements, including the Christian Right, but is distinct from the Christian Right, which focuses on social issues, while the Tea Party movement's focus is fiscal. It has also been observed that the Tea Party movement 'does not share the Christian Right's built-in hindrance to growth because it does not proffer theological tenets that anti-tax, anti-government folks might find off-putting' (Boykoff and Laschever 2011: 344).

CONCLUSION

Towards the beginning of this chapter, we saw how there has been an impasse between the study of religious movements and social movement studies, which has tended generally to preclude crossover between the two fields. Generally speaking, it has been social movement scholars who have resisted studying religious movements, which, as we have seen, is an attitude based in the Marxist view of religion as the opium of the masses. And, in this respect, religion has been regarded as negative – or otherwise ancillary to the purposive action of social movements – in much the same way as emotions were viewed as negative in the early theories of social movements and collective behaviour, discussed in Chapter 2.

However, what our explorations in this chapter have shown us is that religion, religious movements, and religious organizations are not always necessarily conservative, reactionary, and inward looking, but, on the contrary, they may actually provide valuable insights and contribute positively to civil society, public debate, and politics. In this way, then, there is an argument for *bringing religion back into* social movement research, which parallels the argument of those who, as discussed in Chapter 5, posit the value of bringing emotions back into social movement studies.

SUGGESTED READINGS

The following texts and resources can be used to explore issues raised in this chapter.

Books

Beckford, J. A. (1989) *Religion and Advanced Industrial Society*. London: Unwin Hyman.
Beckford, J. A. (2003) *Social Theory and Religion*. Cambridge: Cambridge University Press.

In both of these books, James Beckford engages with issues to do with the relationship between religious movements and social movements. Both books are also useful studies in the sociology of religion.

Smith, C. (ed.) (1996) *Disruptive Religion: The Force of Faith in Social Movement Activism*. New York: Routledge.

The intention of Christian Smith's edited volume is to fill the void left by scholars' neglect of the important role religion often plays in social movement activism. Accordingly, it provides a useful collection of case studies that consider the disruptive potential of religion and religious movements.

Swatos, W. H. (ed.) (1993) *A Future for Religion? New Paradigms for Analysis*. Newbury Park, CA: Sage.

This is an interesting collection of early essays that explore new research agendas for the sociology of religion in contemporary society.

Journals

Diani, M. (1993) 'Themes of Modernity in New Religious Movements and New Social Movements' *Social Science Information* 32(1): 111–131.

Hannigan, J. A. (1990) 'Apples and Oranges or Varieties of the Same Fruit? The New Religious Movements and the New Social Movements Compared' *Review of Religious Research* 31(3): 246–258.

Hannigan, J. A. (1991) 'Social Movement Theory and the Sociology of Religion: Towards a New Synthesis' *Sociological Analysis* 52(4): 311–331.

Each of these articles considers the relationship between social and religious movements.

NOTE

1   In this way, liberation theology resembles the Social Gospel movement of the early twentieth century, which sought to put into practice the sentiment, expressed in the Lord's Prayer: 'Thy kingdom come / Thy will be done / on earth, as it is in heaven'. The Social Gospel also influenced activists in the US civil rights movement of the 1960s, has inspired Christian socialists, and can be regarded as part of the ecumenical movement insofar as it has parallels in Catholicism and Judaism (White et al. 1976).

Struggles over space

6) UOC

INTRODUCTION

In Chapter 4, a principal concern of ours related to questions about the novelty of contemporary 'new' social movements, where the focus was on temporal issues and historical context. In this chapter, we will look at a rather more neglected area of social movement studies that is concerned with spatial issues and geographic context. In previous parts of the book, we have seen how various 'turns' (i.e., cultural, emotional, narrative) have influenced social movements studies. In this chapter, we consider the influence of the 'spatial' or 'geographic' turn. A fundamental premise of the chapter is that space is socially produced and infused with power relations. Space is also conceived broadly as both physical and nonphysical space, where the latter includes (geo) political space, social space, and cultural or identity space. We will see how the study of geography and social movements also requires an exploration of the related concepts of place and scale.

After examining some of the key theoretical and conceptual concerns relating to geography, space, and social movements, a series of case studies and examples is presented, including forms of resistance and retreat from urban life; immigrant struggles for recognition and citizenship rights; and indigenous peoples' struggles for land rights, spaces of autonomy, and self-government under neoliberalism. Although they raise very different (almost diametrically opposed) substantive issues, the Tea Party and Occupy are both considered social movements with spatial and geographic implications. Also considered are studies that explore the relative effectiveness of local social movements by reference to their geographically broad framing of issues. The final part of the chapter considers some of the ways states respond to social movements, which, particularly at large-scale protest events, involves the policing of space.

SPACE: THE FINAL FRONTIER?

In previous chapters, we have looked at various 'turns' (e.g., cultural, emotional, narrative) that have occurred in the human, social, and political sciences, which have had a variety of effects on social movements studies, including the expansion and enhancement of research into social movements. In this chapter, we examine another turn, variously referred to as the 'spatial turn' (Martin and Miller 2003: 143) or 'geographic turn' (Miller 2000: xii, 6, 36). As with some of the other areas we have examined, scholars working at the intersection of geography and social movements have argued that, until recently, the geographic structuring of social movements has largely been ignored. While there has been some cross-fertilization of ideas between geography and sociology, it is mostly geographers who have shown interest in social movements, rather than social movement scholars showing an interest in the spatial aspects of collective action, which, with some exceptions, has resulted in a 'dearth of geographic analysis in the social movements literature' (Miller 2000: 7), and, consequently, 'the aspatiality of most social movement research' (Miller 2000: 5). Martin and Miller (2003: 145) argue that in order to further our understanding of the geographic analysis of social movements, we must look at the key concepts of *space*, *place*, and *scale*, which they relate to Henri Lefebvre's (1991 [1974]) idea of space as socially produced.

The debate about the novelty of new social movements, discussed in Chapter 4, indicates that within social movement studies there has been a recognition of the need to pay attention to context, although that has tended to be limited to historical context (Miller 2000: 4). However, just as time is important, so, too, is space (Martin and Miller 2003: 145). Lefebvre's ideas about the production of space are fundamental to the social theory of geography. Lefebvre (1979: 241) distinguishes between *abstract space* and *social space*, where the former refers to 'the externalization of economic and political practices originating with the capitalist class and the state', and the latter (also called *concrete space*) relates to 'the space of use values produced by the complex interaction of all classes in the pursuit of everyday life'.

It has been observed that this distinction has strong parallels to Habermas' differentiation of system and lifeworld (see Chapter 4). However, while Habermas neglects space and is generally insensitive to spatial differentiation, Lefebvre 'provides a nuanced account of spatial practices affecting "the colonization of everyday life [through] the superimposition and hyperextension of abstract space"' (Miller 2000: 13, quoting Gregory 1994: 403). Moreover, as David Harvey (1990: 218) observes, spatial and temporal practices 'are so closely implicated in processes of reproduction and transformation of social relations' that '[t]he history of social change is in part captured by the history of the conceptions of space and time, and the ideological uses to which those conceptions might be put'. While Lefebvre's notions of space help clarify relationships between social life and spatiality, Martin and Miller (2003: 147) contend it is nonetheless useful to supplement them with the two additional concepts of *place* and *scale*. For them:

> Understanding the dynamics of 'place' is crucial to the analysis of social movement mobilization, not only because it directs us to geographically specific social relations, but because place can be a powerful basis for collective identity construction – a crucial component of virtually all forms of collective action.
>
> (Miller 2000: 14)

We will look in more detail at the significance of place and the related experiential concept, 'sense of place', shortly, when we consider some of the ways geographic research might help further our understanding of movement mobilization and theories of social movements. Like space and place, scale is not given, but is socially constructed. One of the most common conceptions of geographical scale 'is as jurisdictional hierarchy such as the nested relationships of city, country, state, national, and transnational governance' (Martin and Miller 2003: 148). Conceiving of scale as jurisdictional territory in this way has implications for contentious politics:

> Scale issues are clearly inherent in the strategies of social movements. Scale variations in political opportunity structures, for instance, may cause movements to emphasize decentralised struggle within local states or to focus on the central state. Likewise, contested framings of the appropriate geographic scale at which to address particular social issues may dramatically affect the legitimacy of a movement.
>
> (Miller 2000: 18)

Questions of scale will become a focus of our attention again in Chapter 9, when we look at global and transnational activism. It is worth noting, however, that we have previously considered issues of scale when, in Chapter 3, we looked at David Meyer's (2003) exploration of relations between the global and the local, in which he used the example of the New Zealand anti-nuclear movement to extend the geographical reach of the 'political opportunity structure' concept. It will be recalled that, for Meyer (2003: 19, original emphasis), 'national political opportunity structures are *nested* in a larger international environment that constrains or promotes particular kinds of opportunities for dissidents within the state'. In that chapter, too, we saw how the concept of political opportunity structure itself originated in Eisinger's (1973) geographically specific research into city riots. In the next section, we consider these ideas in greater depth, when we look at some of the ways geographic approaches might be brought to bear on major theories of social movements.

BOX 7.1 FREEGAN ANTI-CONSUMERISM: SPACES OF URBAN RESISTANCE

Since its inception, the discipline of sociology has been concerned with the various ways urban-industrial capitalism has impacted, positively and negatively, on both society and the individual. One response to the perceived ills of urban living is exit or escape, often to rural settings, as evident in the formation of communal groups, that might also comprise insular, retreatist, or otherworldly religious movements and sects (Hall 1978; Schehr 1997). Another response is to create spaces of resistance *within* urban society – a classic example here being squatter movements (see Holzner 2004; Montagna 2006; Owens 2008), of which Occupy (discussed later) is conceivably a recent manifestation. This type of internal resistance is also evident in the concerns of the 'voluntary simplicity movement', which we considered in Chapter 6. It will be recalled that the voluntary simplicity movement advocates for reducing material consumption by fixing broken items, reusing old items, and 'doing without' in order to reduce environmental burdens (Haenfler et al. 2012: 6). Allied to this movement is the freegan movement, which:

> . . . mixes urban scrounging with an oppositional politics of cultural transformation. Emerging out of an underground culture of do-it-yourself anarchist, anticapitalist, and animal rights activism that today animates many outside the American political mainstream, freegans take the do-no-harm ethics of a vegan diet into the realm of consumption and waste. As

they point out, 'Freegan is a play on the word vegan. Freegans go farther than vegans by choosing to monetarily consume nothing so as to give no economic power to the capitalist consumer machine'. Rather than shopping, and labouring to earn the money to shop, freegans 'live off the massive waste of modern capitalist society', Dumpster diving vegetables, fruit, and other necessities. In this way, they quite consciously withdraw from a global economy founded on the twin demands of alienated work and ongoing consumption, and try to invent an everyday politics of survival that can undermine these foundations one Dumpster at a time.

(Ferrell 2006: 170)

Freegans have been depicted as 'modern-day foragers' who are resistant to capitalist foodways (Gross 2009), and freeganism itself has been described as 'an anti-consumerist movement' with 'an alternative consumption strategy which involves taking goods that appear abandoned, without paying for them' (Thomas 2010: 98). That includes the controversial practice of 'Dumpster diving', which is scavenging for food and nonfood items 'for a blend of economic, political and environmental reasons' (Edwards and Mercer 2007: 282). Accordingly, freegans tend to 'know where the best dumpsters are located in cities' (Gross 2009: 68). However, it is questionable whether, given their anti-consumerist orientation, freegans can be regarded as a 'lifestyle movement' in the same way as the voluntary simplicity movement, because, for lifestyle movements, identity 'shopping' is seen as part and parcel of consumer societies (Haenfler et al. 2012: 15).

GEOGRAPHY AND SOCIAL MOVEMENT THEORY

In considering some of the ways that spatial analysis might inform social movement studies, Byron Miller argues it may be helpful, first, to consider the geographical dimensions of issues lying at the heart of resource mobilization theory. For instance, place-based communities can, in place-specific ways, affect the monitoring of individual behaviour, which, in turn, can affect the formulation of collective action strategies. Moreover, place-based identities may be formed in geographically specific ways. Miller (2000: 21) draws on Rebecca Smith's work (1984; 1985), which looks at the role of 'place identity' in neighbourhood activism in Minneapolis. Smith argues that instead of being tied to high levels of home ownership, education, and income, participation in a neighbourhood organization is tied to having a strong *sense of place*, which, she says, can be measured by boundary recognition and use of a neighbourhood name.

Miller (2000: 21) goes on to argue that, in spite of the fact that resource mobilization theory 'has been concerned with the networks, groups and structures through which social movements recruit members, accounts of how differing geographies of recruitment affect resource mobilization are relatively rare'. However, the 'geography of movement support' (Miller 2000: 21) has been considered by Harvey (1985), for instance, in his analysis of the politics of class and gender in Paris from 1850 to 1870, in which his discussions of 'the city's geography and maps of public meeting places and electoral patterns provides a clear sense of the geography of recruitment and support for the workers' movement' (Miller 2000: 21). Miller (2000: 22) also shows how in his pioneering book, *The City and the Grassroots*, Manuel Castells (1983) offers another example of place-specific recruitment, when he considers 'the role of gay bars, social gathering places, businesses, stores, and professional offices in the construction of the San Francisco gay community'. Moreover, Kriesi's (1988) study of the local mobilizing efforts of the Dutch peace movement demonstrates how 'pre-existing countercultural network structures vary among six different places, and how those place-specific differences alter recruitment' (Miller 2000: 22).

BOX 7.2 L'AFFAIRE DES SANS-PAPIERS

Given Lefebvre's notion that space is socially constituted, it should be apparent that geographical issues relating to social movements are not limited to physical space, but also concern nonphysical space, including (geo)political, cultural, and symbolic space. As we have seen, and will do throughout this chapter, physical and nonphysical space frequently entwine, and struggles relating to social identity, for instance, are often played out in physical spatial environments. Moreover, and as Miller (2000:14) shows, place can be a powerful basis for the formation of collective identities. The movement of undocumented immigrants in France provides a poignant example of how social struggles are played out in physical spaces, as well as how collective identity is constructed on the basis of place, or, as with undocumented migrants, having no place to go or call home.

In 1993, the French Interior Minister Charles Pasqua introduced legislation designed to curb immigration. The 'Pasqua laws', as they became known, prevented foreign graduates from applying for jobs with French employers, increased from one to two years the time for family reunification, and denied residency permits to foreign spouses who had been living in France illegally before getting married. The legislation also enhanced the powers of the police to enforce the deportation of foreigners, and made it harder for asylum seekers to challenge decisions to deny them visas. Importantly, these laws operated retrospectively, thus rendering illegal formerly legal noncitizens (Freedman and Tarr 2000: 37; Gueye 2006: 232).

It was against this background that the movement of the Sans-papiers (undocumented immigrants; meaning literally, 'without papers') was born in Paris. On 18 March 1996, 300 Sans-papiers occupied the Church of St Ambroise in the eleventh arrondissement of Paris. On 22 March, they were evicted by police and thereafter forced to move from place to place, residing in a gymnasium, a theatre, and then in a disused warehouse, which was owned by the Société Nationale des Chemins de Fer (the national rail workers' trade union, CFDT). Finally, on 28 June, they found temporary shelter at the Saint-Bernard Church in Paris' eighteenth arrondissement. While at Saint-Bernard, ten of the Sans-papiers started a hunger strike to draw attention to their cause. In the early morning of 26 August, more than 1,000 police officers converged on the area, surrounding Saint-Bernard, intending to forcibly remove the Sans-papiers. Television footage showed police 'breaking down the doors of a church with axes, terrifying children, separating men and women, blacks and whites, and forcing everyone into buses' (Rosello 1998: 145).

© David Firn/Alamy

Figure 7.1 A demonstration by the Sans-papiers movement in Rue Danielle Casanova, central Paris, on 19 September 2012. The Sans-papiers movement is campaigning for mass legalization of undocumented migrants living in France.

The principal demand of the Sans-papiers was papers for everyone. That is, the right for all undocumented immigrants to regularization in France, or 'the quest to be incorporated officially as members of French society' (Gueye 2006: 229). It is important to remember that for many years the Sans-papiers had been living, working, and paying taxes in France (Cissé 1997: 44). Typically, however, '[i]rregular migrants are policed as outsiders even though they are economically incorporated into political communities through informal neoliberal labour markets' (McNevin 2006: 136). In this sense, they are 'immanent outsiders' who in spite of the hostile political rhetoric leveled against them are tacitly accepted because they fulfill a vital economic function in neoliberal economies, which have a demand for cheap, flexible, and compliant labour (McNevin 2006: 140). Indeed, suffering the adverse effects of deregulated (neoliberal) labour markets is something the Sans-papiers, along with other undocumented migrants, have in common with other members of what Guy Standing (2011) calls, the 'precariat', which we discussed in Chapter 4.

Unsurprisingly, then, the struggle of the Sans-papiers went beyond the single issue of papers for all to question the status of fundamental human rights and democratic liberties in France (Cissé 1997: 40). Indeed, the populist move by the government against 'illegal immigrants' ultimately backfired, as the Sans-papiers movement gained sympathy from a large portion of the French public, especially when 'references were made to the fate of Jews at the hands of French police during the Vichy regime' (Rosello 1998: 149). Ironically, while failing to secure papers for everyone (there were deportations), and despite not being able to vote, the Sans-papiers movement did make some political gains by helping to increase the number of regularizations and changing the atmosphere in which immigration legislation was debated in the French parliament, although the Pasqua laws themselves were not repealed (Rosello 1998: 150; see also Freedman and Tarr 2000: 37).

The Sans-papiers movement was also a statement against neocolonialism, which, as we will see later, is a key grievance of indigenous peoples' movements too. The Sans-papiers were largely of African origin, but all were from former French colonies, which meant it was only natural they would migrate to France to work and live. As one migrant stated, 'It's the country we know, the one whose language we have learned, whose culture we have integrated a little' (Cissé 1997: 38). According to Sans-papiers activist and writer, Madjiguène Cissé, former French colonies have never been truly independent and continue to be subject to 'subtle forms of domination and exploitation' (Cissé 1997: 39). In particular, poor African countries suffered the adverse consequences of 'structural adjustment programs' where they are loaned money on condition the state withdraws from managing the economy, and neoliberal or free market economic policies are pursued. Consequently, developing countries amass debts they cannot realistically hope to pay back (see Box 6.5), and often money is diverted from aid and development schemes by corrupt officials who may collude with their French advisors to hold on to power (Cissé 1997: 39). Moreover, in countries such as Mali and Senegal, where many Sans-papiers originate, the rural peasant population suffers because they no longer receive government subsidies to purchase seeds, fertilizers, and arable land (Gueye 2006: 233). Thus, for Cissé (1997: 43), the fight against structural adjustment programs and the struggle of the Sans-papiers are one and the same:

> According to Cissé, France undermines African development and creates conditions that compel African immigrants to remain outside of Africa. The struggle of the Sans-papiers to remain in France is legitimized on the basis of France's own actions that deprive the African of the material conditions necessary for a life of dignity in Africa.
>
> (Gueye 2006: 236)

From a social movement perspective, the Sans-papiers are significant in a number of ways. Abdoulaye Gueye (2006: 226) says social movement scholars have neglected to study the collective action of African immigrants because, in France, at least, they are not regarded as political actors. However, that is to underestimate the effects of their mobilization, as well as to misconceive of it as political in the conventional sense. One of the demands of the Sans-papiers was essentially for the recognition of *difference*, which, as we saw in Chapter 4, is a central goal of contemporary 'new' social movements, according to thinkers like Melucci. Hence, in a plural society, argues Cissé (1997: 45), a balance needs to be struck between French society and immigrants: 'a minimum of will to integrate, a minimum of respect for our cultures of origin'. Moreover, the quest for *autonomy* (another key concept in new social movement theory) is something that is identified as important by Gueye (2006: 229), for whom collective action by African immigrants in post-colonial France, including the Sans-papiers, 'is largely a process by which they strive to earn a relative degree of self-government in their own existence'.

Resource mobilization theory is also relevant to the Sans-papiers movement. Of particular significance here is the role of preexisting networks for movement mobilization. In the case of the Sans-papiers, a crucial role was played by the more established anti-racist organization, SOS-Racisme, 'which initially had a coordinating role among the groups of protesting immigrants [but] left the leadership of the movement to representatives of the Sans-papiers themselves' (Ruggiero 2001: 85). Furthermore, according to Cissé (1997: 43), the support of trade unions was fundamental to the struggle of the Sans-papiers, not least because this association reinforced their identity as workers.

Recognizing that 'the geography of recruitment activity' is not alone in determining the resources and membership of social movement organizations, Miller (2000: 22–23) also considers the importance of framing approaches, which stress 'the ways in which issues are framed and how these frames resonate with various populations; to this there is also a geography', he argues. For instance, Cresswell's (1996) analysis of the Greenham Common women's peace camp shows how meaning is constructed and interpreted at the level of everyday life and how that has implications for the resonance of social movement frames. As we saw in Chapter 5, when we looked at Alison Young's (1990) study of the Greenham protests, news media representations of female peace activists were overwhelmingly negative (i.e., female protestors were depicted as wild and unruly), which, Young argued, was because their publicly visible dissent 'disrupted femininity' by violating dominant norms about womanhood as passive and private. Providing a geographical perspective on the female activists' protest, Miller (2000: 24) says that, for Cresswell, it 'attracted a great deal of attention in substantial measure because the women transgressed place-specific norms of appropriate behaviour'.

Not surprisingly, Cresswell (1996: 124–125) draws on the idea of 'symbolic inversion' that is central to carnival/carnivalesque forms of protest – which we also used in Chapter 5 to apply to the spatial transgression of Russian feminist punk band, Pussy Riot – to show how the behaviour of female peace activists at Greenham Common was 'out of place' (literally and metaphorically), since it 'denaturalized the dominant order [and] showed people that what seemed natural, could, in fact, be otherwise'. Hence, not only did the collective action of female peace protestors offend dominant gender norms, but, according to Miller (2000: 24), activists also 'deliberately framed their message to challenge the dominant norms of "proper" place-based behaviour'.

While the women's movement has challenged the spatial order of gender relations in numerous ways by, for example, contesting the private sphere/public sphere divide, transgressing the sociospatial norms of appropriate place-based behaviour is central to many social movements, including those relating to racial identity (see Box 7.2), which is itself spatialized when associated with terms like 'the ghetto' (Miller 2000: 35). Similarly, Marston has shown how when the exclusion of gay and lesbian groups from New York's St Patrick's Day parade was upheld by the US Supreme Court in 1995, those groups used pre-parade street protests to contest discrimination. Here, then, 'space [. . .] sits at the centre of the conflict over who gets to be Irish on St Patrick's Day in the United States' (Marston 2003: 230; see also Marston 2001).

Miller's (2000: 26) critique of the political process model is that it focuses on historical context, and when it 'does address geographic variations in political opportunity, it does so almost exclusively at [the] national level'. To Miller (2000: 25), 'political opportunities are as much geographic as they are historic'. Accordingly, the widely accepted four dimensions of political opportunity clearly exhibit geographic variation:

> Political systems are more open in particular places and at particular scales; elite alignments are rarely stable everywhere; the presence or absence of elite allies varies from place to place; the state's capacity and propensity for repression vary not only among states but also among regions and highly localized geographic areas within states.
> (Miller 2000: 25)

Miller (2000:4) illustrates the aspatiality of political process approaches by reference to Tarrow's concept of 'cycles of protest' (see Chapter 3), which calls attention to historical fluctuations in movement mobilization, understood in light of complex interactions between external political opportunity structure and internal resource mobilization. However, while Tarrow (1983) conceives of these interactions as building upon one another over time, according to Miller (2000: 4), 'there is no parallel attention to "spaces of protest" or "places of protest" that would direct the social movements scholar to look at geographic variations in resources, political opportunities, place-specific characteristics, and spatial interactions affecting social movement mobilization'.

When considering the possible implications of geographic analysis for new social movement theory, Miller notes that most conceptualizations are based broadly on Habermas' approach. As noted earlier, however, while there are parallels between Habermas' distinction between *system* and *lifeworld* and Lefebvre's differentiation of *abstract space* and *social space*, Habermas tends to be insensitive to spatiality. And because he largely ignores sociospatial relations, he 'thus underestimates spatial differentiation and many of the attendant dilemmas it poses for building a consensual basis of emancipatory politics' (Miller 2000: 32). However:

> The geographic constitution of systems and lifeworlds – or abstract spaces and social spaces, to use Lefebvre's spatial terminology – is manifest in a variety of ways. The territories that some collectivities build and defend are not just metaphorical but also real places, such as neighbourhoods, residential developments, schools, community centres, places of worship, and parks. The abstract spaces of the

economy and state include workplaces, transportation facilities, day care centres, hospitals, clinics, and other formal institutions with tangible geographic manifestations in people's lives.

(Miller 2000: 32–33)

For Miller (2000: 33), Melucci (1994: 114) is one of very few new social movement theorists who explicitly acknowledge the importance of the spatiotemporal framing of collective identity construction. Indeed, as we saw earlier, the need to consider the spatial aspects of (collective) identity formation is also something that, according to Miller (2000: 21), resource mobilization theorists ought to consider, since, he observes, '[g]eographically specific constructions of collective identity – whether place-based or not – have implications for the bases on which particular social movement organisations are built, including possible avenues for and barriers to alliance formation'.

Notwithstanding Melucci's work, it appears few new social movement theorists have explored the concrete implications of identity formation and collective mobilization by developing geographically sensitive empirical research agendas (Miller 2000: 33). However, when spatial processes have been linked to questions of identity in the geographical literature, that has demonstrated 'how common identities, experiences, understandings, and power relations are constructed in and through spaces and places of interaction' (Miller 2000: 34). In fact, according to Miller (2000: 34), there are 'innumerable examples of the ways in which sexual, gender, "racial", class, and ethnic identities are constructed through, and obtain their meaning in, space'.

Perhaps one of the most obvious ways that identity can be linked to issues of space is via the concept of autonomy, which, as we saw in Chapter 4, is crucial not only to Melucci but also to other new social movement theorists, including Habermas and Touraine. It will be recalled that Touraine (1981) wants to discover *the* new social movement of programmed society, which seeks 'self-management' against technocratic control. Similarly, Habermas (1981: 36) argues that new social movements arise at the seam between system and lifeworld to resist 'internal colonization'. Likewise, Melucci (1985: 815) observes that contemporary social movements strive to reside in a new political space – an intermediate public space – that exists beyond the state and civil society, in which movements are able to maintain their autonomy. Indeed, it has been argued that autonomy is not the sole preserve of new movements (e.g., Plotke 1990), but is something many movements seek, lest co-optation, institutionalization, or incorporation compromises their original, radical goals. And, in Chapter 6, we also saw how autonomy is important in the struggle of religious movements for 'free space' and 'identity spaces' (Beckford 2003: 172). In the following section, we will consider how, among other things, autonomy is a central theme of indigenous peoples' movements.

INDIGENOUS PEOPLES' STRUGGLES FOR IDENTITY, SPACE, AND AUTONOMY

We have already seen some of the ways indigenous peoples are connected to a variety of social movements. In Chapter 6, we saw how the Catholic Church's fight for social justice, according to the teachings of liberation theology, has, in the cases of Brazil and Canada, at least, included a search for justice for native people. Also in that chapter, we considered the impact of the spirituality of North American indigenous peoples on the emergence of environmental activism, deep ecology, and ecofeminism. In many ways, these points alert us to the fact that indigenous peoples are involved in a variety of social movements, as well as the notion that indigenous peoples themselves are concerned with a diversity of issues and are not solely focused on issues we might typically associate with them, such as struggles for land rights, cultural recognition, and self-determination. Indeed, in Chapter 6, we saw how Native American women have forged 'unlikely alliances' with Christian Right groups on matters relating to abortion (Smith 2008). Some of these ideas will recur in this part of the chapter, which is focused on exploring intersections between space, identity, and autonomy by reference to indigenous peoples' movements.

In an early effort to fuse the fields of social movement studies and critical geography, Alice Feldman (2002: 42) demonstrates the ways in which the international indigenous peoples' movement has carved out a space for itself globally. Like Miller (2000), she observes that the spatial dynamics and dimensions of social movements have largely been overlooked in the literature. Accordingly, she premises her arguments on perspectives in critical geography and geopolitics that see space as 'both a critical process and product in itself' (Feldman 2002: 43). Insofar as the incorporation of critical geography perspectives into social movement studies draws attention to the 'relationships between space, power and social transformation' (Feldman 2002: 32), it recognizes that power relations are infused in the social geographies of marginalization, which is central to many indigenous peoples' struggles. Feldman (2002: 33) illustrates this point via the work of critical geographers who see space as 'the message and medium of domination' (Keith and Pile 1993: 37), believing people 'must occupy space and have an identity that commands a recognition of that occupation' (Shapiro 1999: 161), and, consequently, regard the 'Other' spaces in which identity politics is enacted as 'strategically spacialized' (Soja and Hooper 1993: 189). Such spaces, Feldman (2002: 33) argues, 'are especially critical for those who have been silenced or marginalized', such as indigenous peoples, 'for they mark one's existence or non-existence, visibility or invisibility; one's "place", and all that springs from it'. Moreover, she shows how these perspectives are very similar to Melucci's idea, discussed earlier (and in Chapter 4), about contemporary social movements striving for the recognition of difference and formation of alternative cultural codes in autonomous public space (Feldman 2002: 33, 41–42).

During the 1970s, for instance, regional and world conferences not only provided the context for solidarity building, information sharing, and agenda setting, but they also generated formal declarations as the basis for the international indigenous peoples' movement's political and legal platform. Hence, Feldman (2002: 36) argues:

> The framing of claims and grievances in the languages of colonial subjugation and self-determination provided a language of possibility, linked to international law and steeped in a counter-colonial critique that would challenge the very foundations of colonial rule, along with the institutions and formations that have perpetuated their oppression.

Importantly, organizing processes associated with the regional and world conferences had the effect of creating a new constituency of more than 300 million people and a new world map; 'a new space of existence, *the Fourth World*' (Feldman 2002: 36). Accordingly, there emerged a constituency of indigenous peoples, who, in spite of their differences, were united by a common experience of centuries of colonial subjugation, and who created a significant imaginative space – an emotional, psychological, and intellectual space of freedom – within which 'indigenous peoples could nurture the seeds of their empowerment through self-identification and self-legitimation, regardless of the lack of official, state- or public-based recognition and in defiance of the material conditions of their oppression' (Feldman 2002: 36).

Subsequent developments included the 1993 International Year of the World's Indigenous Peoples, 'established to strengthen awareness of the problems indigenous peoples experience and the need for greater international co-operation towards their solution' (Feldman 2002: 38), and the 1994 Universal Declaration of the Rights of Indigenous

Peoples, which 'addresses three central areas of rights: cultural, land and resources, and self-determination' (Feldman 2002: 37). However, the recognition, adoption, and elaboration of international standards relating to indigenous peoples were also taken up by nongovernmental organizations and human rights groups, which linked them to larger global issues and civil society mobilizations, 'from nuclear disarmament and environmental racism, to biopiracy and intellectual property rights' (Feldman 2002: 39). Moreover, Feldman (2002: 42) argues that in contrast to top-down approaches portraying social movements as reactive to globalizing pressures, the international indigenous peoples' movement has played a very active role in what 'ultimately amounts to centuries of indigenous peoples' efforts to shape and force open international institutions and fields of mobilization'.

At a more localized level, too, indigenous peoples extend the reach of their concerns beyond claims traditionally associated with indigenous rights. While issues of identity, self-determination, resource, and land rights are frequently seen as key to indigenous peoples' struggles, Luis Angosto Ferrández (forthcoming: 6) shows how in Venezuela 'the indigenous population has shown sustained support for the ongoing socio-economic and political enfranchisement as a priority over certain notions of free determination (such as territorial and political autonomy)'. Among other things, 'enfranchisement through the materialization of socio-economic rights' requires indigenous peoples interact with the state and its agencies (Angosto Ferrández forthcoming: 6). That, in turn, has given birth to a state-sponsored indigenous movement, which is 'strongly based on an appeal to indigenous identities, but its members also build their self-identification resorting to notions of socialism and anti-imperialism' (Angosto Ferrández forthcoming: 16). The 'state-sponsored' social movement Angosto Ferrández speaks of is quite distinct from the autonomous movements envisaged by Melucci (see earlier), although as we shall see, it is not uncommon for indigenous peoples' movements to couch their claims and grievances in terms of wider issues relating to imperialism, colonialism, and capitalism. Indeed, the contention of this movement is not directed at the Venezuelan state, which it identifies as an ally. Instead, it is directed:

> . . . against imperialism, capitalism and supranational institutions that the movement members associate with such categories. The repertoire of activities of this type of collective action, including political rallies and workshops, partly runs outside conventional channels for political participation, yet it is oiled by a state agency.
>
> (Angosto Ferrández forthcoming: 17)

Given the ubiquity of neoliberal capitalism, it should be no surprise that, like other social movements (Maddison and Martin 2010), movements of indigenous peoples (and movements including indigenous peoples) have sought to resist neoliberalism. In Australia, for example, Aboriginal people have resisted neoliberal reforms that have resulted in the abolition of their national representative body, as well as amendments to legislation extinguishing 'native title' land rights (Walter 2010). However, the classic example of indigenous peoples opposing neoliberal capitalism is the Zapatistas in the Chiapas region of Mexico, who aim to fulfill the dream of land redistribution that was envisioned originally by Emiliano Zapata during the 1910 Mexican revolution.

Comprising a 'seemingly ramshackle group of students, intellectuals, radicals, and indigenous peasant rebels, the Zapatistas emerged from the jungle of the Chiapas region in 1994 within hours of the signing of the NAFTA agreement, hounding the Mexican federal forces from the region' (Tormey 2013: 130). Signed towards the end of 1993, the North American Free Trade Agreement (NAFTA) united the economies of Mexico, Canada, and the United States in a single trading bloc. As a neoliberal reform, the NAFTA had a deleterious effect on the majority of peasants and their organizations in the countryside, consisting, as it did, of the 'dismantling of government agencies, reduction of credit, the removal of guaranteed crop prices, and the opening up of cheaper imports' (Harvey 1998: 170). Functioning as a direct challenge to the NAFTA, an autonomous zone emerged in the Chiapas region, comprising some forty villages that are to this day essentially self-governing and beyond federal rule; 'an autonomous area governed by an entirely different set of principles and norms, indeed a different philosophy, to the rest of the country' (Tormey 2013: 131). This autonomous area created by the Zapatistas operates via new participatory spaces called autonomous rebel Zapatista municipalities (MAREZ) and good governance councils (JBG), both focused 'on developing health, education and justice systems, achieving the sustainable management of the territory and creating an alternative form of citizenship' (Cortez Ruiz 2010: 167).

Seen by many as the leader of the Zapatistas, the iconic figure of Subcomandante Insurgente Marcos has been pivotal in orchestrating communications with the outside world and translating the pragmatic set of principles known as 'Zapatismo', which is a mixture of poetry, philosophy, and rebel folklore (see Figure 7.2). Importantly, however,

© epa european pressphoto agency b.v./Alamy

Figure 7.2 The leader of the Zapatista Army of National Liberation (EZLN), Subcomandante Marcos (left), at the Garrucha community, in the mountainous area of Chiapas, Mexico, 17 September 2005

Marcos sees himself as a spokesperson among other spokespeople, rather than a leader, and does not regard himself as a representative of the poor and oppressed, but as a 'mirror' for oppression across the world, including the oppression of indigenous peoples. In this way, 'he is a key figure not only in the local politics of the struggles in Mexico, but in global activism generally' (Tormey 2006: 149).

In demanding cultural recognition for Indians in Mexico, it has been observed that the Zapatistas, and the global movements they inspired, resemble new social movements, where likewise 'the cultural input is distinctly high' (Wieviorka 2005: 10). Indeed, what Simon Tormey sees as arguably novel and unique about the Zapatistas is not their opposition to neoliberalism, but their desire to be free of ideology per se, which is, in a sense, wrapped up in their quest for autonomy (à la Melucci):

> To return to Marco's tale, what becomes obvious is that he saw that what the indigenous people wanted was not a new ideology, but release *from* an ideology, namely neoliberalism. The Zapatista revolt was in this sense a revolt *against* neoliberalism in the form of the NAFTA agreement, which would make the life of Mexico's poor even more miserable than it already was. Yet more than this, he began to see that the issue was not just about neoliberal ideology, but ideology more generally, even revolutionary ideology. What struck him was that the peoples of the Chiapas *already knew* how they would like to live. They simply wanted to run their own affairs rather than being pushed around by outsiders.
>
> (Tormey 2013: 132, original emphasis)

BOX 7.3 BOLIVIA'S WATER WAR

Since the 'neoliberal turn' has been a region-wide phenomenon in Latin America (Sieder 2005), it is unsurprising that opposition to it has not been limited to indigenous peoples' struggles, and has involved an array of different groups. Indeed, this is exemplified by the Zapatistas, who it has been said:

> . . . have developed a strong indigenous identity that leaves behind the old stereotypical identity of closed communities or separate ethnic groups, and instead solidifies a political identity unifying several ethnic and *mestizo* groups under an autonomous development project and their opposition to the government and neoliberalism.
>
> (Reygadas et al. 2009: 237, original emphasis)

The example of Bolivia's 'water war' provides another case in point. Fighting neoliberalism was central to protests against deregulation of the water supply in Bolivia's third largest city, Cochabamba, from 1999–2000, which also involved indigenous peoples, among others. It also relates to our theme in this chapter insofar as it entailed a spatial strategy 'involving the blocking or enhancing of access to resources [and] markets' (Martin and Miller 2003: 150). Moreover, Bolivia's water war can be seen as following in a tradition of anti-corporate activism, which we have encountered at other points in the book.

The Coordinadora por la Defensa del Agua y la Vida (Coordination for the Defense of Water and Life) was the principal social actor in the Bolivian water war. The movement was led by Oscar Olivera, a shoe factory worker and trade unionist, whose own rationale for acting, contained in the following quotation, inspired many followers: 'From my mother, the factory, the irrigators and ordinary working people, I learned that we must all be like water – transparent and in movement' (Olivera 2004: 1).

Environmental factors such as the degradation of agricultural land and droughts, combined with rapid population growth (due to rural-urban migration), meant water was a scarce resource in Cochabamba. The state agency responsible for the city's water and sewage services (SEMAPA) only provided short-term solutions to this problem, such as drilling more wells. And it was against this background that the Bolivian government sought to privatize the supply of water in the city.

In February 1999, it announced it would make investment conditions more 'flexible' for interested parties wishing to bid for the MISICUNI project – a multipurpose project to supply Cochabamba with water and surrounding agricultural areas with irrigation. The only enterprise to show any interest in the project was Aguas del Tunari, a consortium that included multinational corporations Bechtel and Abengoa. After signing a contract in June 1999, Aguas del Tunari moved into the SEMAPA offices on 1 November, pledging to improve the water supply in Cochabamba and implement the MISICUNI project. Consortium manager Geoffrey Thorpe soon announced water rate increases of approximately 35 percent for December 1999, to be paid the following month.

Meanwhile, on 29 November the Bolivian government enacted Law 2029, introducing 'a regime of concessions and licences for the supply of portable water' (Assies 2003: 17), conditions that clearly favoured large enterprises, and granted concessionaires, such as Aguas del Tunari, exclusive rights over concession areas, including Cochabamba. Subsequently, a loose coalition of different groups with little formal organization, the Coordination for the Defense of Water and Life (the Coordinadora) emerged to resist what amounted to the privatization of water.

This was a new form of organization in the history of Bolivian popular protest, which had a networklike structure and consisted of both rural and urban elements, including peasant and indigenous peoples' cooperatives, urban territorial organizations such as water committees and neighbourhood associations, workers' collectives and trade unions (although the latter played a marginal role), middle class professionals, and environmental groups. Predicting a far higher hike in water rates than Aguas del Tunari anticipated, the Coordinadora first marched into the Plaza 14 de Septiembre on 28 December 1999.

Early in January 2000, Cochabambinos began receiving water bills, some of which had increased by 150 percent. This precipitated a series of protests and battles with the authorities in the coming months: protestors marched and staged public demonstrations, threw stones and Molotov cocktails at municipal offices, organized the ceremonial burning of water bills, used roadblocks, and threatened to call a general strike. At one stage, the Coordinadora held a referendum at short notice using 150 ballots to canvass the opinion of roughly 10 percent of population of the city: 99 percent objected to the water rate increase, 96 percent believed Aguas del Tunari's contract should be annulled, and 97 percent disagreed with the privatization of water under Law 2029 (Assies 2003: 27). Police responded to the protesters by dousing them with tear gas, and, in one incident, the military cut the power supply to an area of Cochabamba where numerous radio and television stations were located, presumably to prevent the media from provoking further social unrest.

On 7 April 2000, 'an unprecedented crowd gathered in the plaza to demand a break with Aguas del Tunari and revision of Law 2029, and it was decided to continue the blockades until the demands were met' (Assies 2003: 29). Protestors expected the army to arrive, and on 8 April a 'state of siege' was declared in the city. On 9 April, the government announced the withdrawal of Aguas del Tunari. On 10 April, Oscar Olivera claimed victory before a crowd in the Plaza 14 de Septiembre after the Coordinadora signed an agreement with government officials confirming SEMAPA would resume responsibility for the water supply in Cochabamba. On 11 April, a modified law was passed by parliament, and, on 20 April, the state of siege was lifted.

Bolivia's water war is significant for a number of reasons that relate not only to our specific concerns in this chapter, but also to some of our interests in other parts of the book. As mentioned earlier, it is an example of protest against neoliberalism and anti-corporate activism, which also contained a constituent of indigenous peoples, who, along with other poor populations, often suffer disproportionately the negative effects of neoliberal government policies and corporate activity. Among other things, that is because they are less able to bear the financial costs attached to the private provision of goods and services, or because they live in areas in which corporations can accommodate their externalities: for instance, the flooding of indigenous peoples' land to make way for a hydroelectric power station – an example of 'environmental racism' experienced by indigenous peoples (Feldman 2002: 39). Indeed, the Bolivian water war also demonstrates the persistence of settler colonialism, which, as will be discussed later in the chapter, is a grievance of many indigenous peoples (Barker 2012), although this form of colonization is perpetrated not by nation-states, but by transnational corporations (with state complicity) operating under conditions of global neoliberalism.

Police dousing protestors with tear gas and the sabotaging by the military of the power supply in an area of Cochabamba with a high concentration of news media organizations provide examples of the state repression of social movements, which we examine briefly later when we look at the policing of protest, as well as in Chapter 8, when we will look at media and movements. Finally, while the modification of legislation was a key goal of the Bolivian protestors, the Coordinadora's significance and influence extended beyond that. Despite being a single-issue movement that arose at a specific point in time, innovations in its 'repertoire of contention' (see Chapter 3), such as town meetings and the referendum, promoted direct democracy by encouraging debate and participation. Consequently, other issues were taken up in the wake of the water war, including 'the revision of electricity rates and the recovery of privatized state enterprises, and an initiative was taken to organise an international conference to protest globalization' (Assies 2003: 34).

TEA PARTY, SOCIOSPATIAL STRUCTURES, AND THE GEOGRAPHY OF COLLECTIVE ACTION

Towards the end of Chapter 6 we saw how church leaders have criticized the irresponsibility of greedy consumerism and condemned growing inequality in society, and how that led to church support for the Occupy movement, which, in the case of the protest camp set up outside St Paul's Cathedral in London, culminated in the resignation of Canon Dr. Giles Fraser, who was apparently critical of police handling of the camp and refused to sanction the use of force to remove protestors (Shackle 2011). However, we also saw how these developments have produced populist responses, evident in the emergence of the Tea Party movement.

The point of convergence for the rise of Occupy and the Tea Party was the global financial crisis (GFC) of 2008 that was sparked by the recklessness of banks' predatory lending of subprime mortgages to high-risk borrowers (touched upon in Chapter 4 in the context of austerity and protest). Hence, for many, Occupy arose at 'the moment when resistance to the inequalities of capitalism finally emerged: a tipping point in which the unfairness of the bank bailouts juxtaposed against rising personal poverty' (Pickerill and Krinsky 2012: 279). At the same time, Tea Partiers saw 'their jobs vanish in front of their eyes as Wall Street [got] trillions' (Berlet 2010a). Significantly, given the focus of this chapter, it has been observed that notwithstanding the very different substantive issues they raise, analyses of both Occupy and the Tea Party movement provide useful insights into the relationship between space and social movements. Accordingly, in the next two sections of the chapter, we will consider not only the grievances of the Tea Party and Occupy, but also the spatial and geographic relevance of each movement.

The Tea Party emerged in the United States in 2009 'as a response to economic stagnation and crisis, secular challenges to traditional religious identities and the election of an African American president' (Langman 2012: 469). As a form of right-wing populism, the movement follows a long tradition of anti-establishment mobilization 'in which the "good, decent little people", the so-called "innocent victims", who distrust government, defend themselves against corrupt and evil forces from above whose policies are responsible for their pain and suffering' (Langman 2012: 470). Moreover, in contrast to indigenous peoples, discussed previously, Tea Party people 'tend to be reactionary, nativist, nationalist, and xenophobic' (Langman 2012: 470, citing Berlet 2010b). Hence, their ire is directed at:

> . . . liberal elites, big money interests, a government that served the 'big guys', and fearful that 'Obama the revolutionary' was moving their country towards socialism. They were anxious, angry and resentful, raging against federal bureaucracy, liberal government programs and policies including health care, immigration reform and labour laws, abortion, and gay marriage.
>
> (Berlet 2010b)

Tea Party activism, then, is the result of 'a complex mix of reactionary populism, anti-government rhetoric, and anger at the recent Great Recession, all focused into a sharp point by directing anger at President Obama' (Fasenfest 2012: 464). The movement also comprises some contradictory orientations. For instance, Tea Partiers are angry at 'government largesse going to the undeserved – even as they refuse to identify their own feeding at the government trough as partaking of government support', which has been observable in 'signs exhorting the government to keep its hand off Medicare, one of the biggest government programs' (Fasenfest 2012: 464) (see Figure 7.3).

It is perhaps important to note too that the original Tea Party protests of 1773 constituted some of the first anti-corporate events in American history, where anger was directed at the East India Company, which used its power as a monopoly to influence the government's introduction of the Tea Act of 1773, 'which increased taxes paid by colonists on

© Ron S. Buskirk/Alamy

Figure 7.3 Concerned citizens rally at a Tea Party political event at Farran Park in Eustis, Florida, 15 April 2009

tea, while simultaneously lowering taxes levied on the Company so it could offer its tea at far lower prices than smaller companies, thereby driving smaller companies out of business' (Soule 2009: 1).

Turning to the spatial relevance of Tea Party activism, Michael Thompson (2012) has attempted to explain the emergence of conservative movements like Tea Party by reference to the sociospatial contexts in which individuals are socialized. In particular, he wants to understand why it is that the nonurban spaces from which the Tea Party and other grassroots conservative movements emerge seem to make individuals susceptible to certain ways of thinking that lead to a more conservative ideological outlook. He argues that the characteristic spatial structure of nonurban forms of life affects a kind of 'constrained socialization', which has a strong influence on social relations and individuals' 'moral cognition', and hence forms the basis for the development of the 'conservative personality'. For Thompson (2012: 513), this 'emphasis on personality is important because', he contends, 'we need to see that there are certain social-environmental conditions that can affect the ways that individuals cognize and feel about certain moral and political themes'.

Thompson (2012: 513) calls upon social scientists interested in the genesis of conservative politics to turn their attention to the 'geographic dispersion of ideologies'. In a sense, he is trying to provide a back story to the well-established empirical data that indicates 'a strong association between national voting patterns and the urban/suburban/exurban divide, suggesting that the less "urban" an area is, the more its residents choose conservative political candidates' (Thompson 2012: 513). However, he argues 'not that voters of a particular persuasion simply move to non-urban areas, but that non-urban spaces play an active, indeed causal, role in the production and maintenance of such values' (Thompson 2012: 514). To be sure, Thompson (2012: 516) wishes to escape the crude city-suburb dichotomy, providing instead that the 'focus ought to be placed on the nature of socio-spatial form and the ways these formations can affect levels of association and degrees of homogeneity'.

For Thompson, the reason there are high concentrations of conservative voters in nonurban areas is because in those areas (which include many American suburbs) *closed* sociospatial structures predominate. In contrast to *open* sociospatial structures, which promote centripetal patterns of social interaction and heterogeneity of interaction, closed structures are defined by their centrifugal force, which disperses people and discourages interaction and dialogue, as well as by homogenous forms of interaction, which 'encourage a more limited sense of self and world thereby promoting more limited forms of moral cognition' (Thompson 2012: 518). The sociospatial distinction between open and closed structures also corresponds, respectively, to *fluid* and *dogmatic* styles of moral cognition. In the fluid form of moral cognition:

> . . . an individual is able to tolerate differing understandings and interpretations of the world. He is able to see issues from differing perspectives, is willing to depart from and critically examine his own internalized value-orientations, and is also able to consider revising his own worldviews in light of new evidence and better reasons.
>
> (Thompson 2012: 523–524)

On the other hand, an individual approaching the world with a dogmatic style of moral cognition:

> . . . is less likely to consider the ideas of others and more likely to need to assert what he believes to be true, to insist on it being taken as correct, and to see the norms that he has been socialized into as being intrinsically correct.
>
> (Thompson 2012: 524)

Thompson suggests the new grassroots conservative movements like Tea Party are an expression of dogmatic styles of moral cognition, which, he argues, is largely the product of closed sociospatial structures predominant in nonurban American life. And Tea Partiers exhibit many of the characteristics of people with a dogmatic moral cognition style, including support for the principles of economic conservatism, which forms a dimension of what they consider to be the social status quo, as well as expressing a certain kind of authoritarianism 'that "rightfully" punishes groups that do not work hard or contribute "properly" to society' (Thompson 2012: 524). Moreover, economic conservatism intersects with moral conservatism, which manifests in a defensiveness about traditional forms of community and family life. This, in turn, 'activates strong expressions of anti-intellectualism' (Thompson 2012: 524), which consists of an amalgam of various traits born of the dogmatism caused by closed sociospatial structures, including conflict avoidance, an inability to partake in critical debate, lack of reflexive consciousness, and the need to ensure social conformity, which can lead to fear of those perceived as a threat because they are 'different'.

Many of these anxieties are personified in figure of US President Barack Obama, who is feared not only for his 'Otherness' – including 'his race, his foreign father, and his background as a college professor and community organizer' (Skocpol and Williamson 2012: 79) – but also because he is 'a symbol of many other things that Tea Partiers hate, including, in their view, over-educated, arrogant liberals who try to impose their views on the rest of the country through their control of the "liberal" media, government, and universities' (Dreier 2012: 760). Accordingly, 'the conservative mind will tend toward control, order, and simplicity in order to compensate for the disorienting world of change it experiences' (Thompson 2012: 524). And with its emphasis on 'the need for smaller government, support for radical tax cuts, for "free" markets, and so on' the Tea Party, as with other grassroots conservative groups, is an expression of 'rage against the changing social order where white, working, middle, and upper-middle class segments of the population are feeling a decay in their standards of living and a renewed air of economic insecurity' (Thompson 2012: 524). For Thompson (2012: 523), then, '[c]onservatism and non-urbanism become not so much causally necessary or inevitable as much as a likely outcome'.

References to anger, fear, anxiety, hate, and rage, among others, indicate clearly the significance of emotionality in Tea Party activism, which evokes some of the material we considered in Chapter 5, when we looked at how passion and emotion are important features of many social movements. Indeed, in that chapter we also saw how collective action can combine emotion and expression with strategy and cognition (Goodwin et al. 2001: 15; Kemper 2001: 69). Similarly, Cho et al. (2012: 105, 111) argue that the Tea Party movement has been simultaneously expressive and strategic, where strategy is defined in terms of success in the 2010 US election. Adopting a geographic perspective, they say that in their study they expected 'emotion to rival obvious electorally strategic considerations', hypothesizing that Tea Party activism might be strongest in areas suffering most economic hardship, and especially in those places with highest unemployment and mortgage foreclosure rates (Cho et al. 2012: 111). That hypothesis was partially born out by the 'remarkably higher Tea Party activity in "housing bubble" states such as Nevada, Florida, Arizona, and California' (Cho et al. 2012: 126). Accordingly, analysis of Tea Party events:

> . . . demonstrates that activity is highly correlated with expressive factors. First and foremost, it is expressive of economic restlessness, especially in areas where home foreclosures were running high from 2008 onwards. This helps explain the especially high rates of Tea Party activism in locations such as Florida, California, Nevada and Arizona.
>
> (Cho et al. 2012: 130)

Conversely, Cho et al. (2012: 131) conclude 'the geographic patterns of Tea Party activities do not reveal much evidence of strategic direction in 2010'. Locations where the Republican percentage of the vote in presidential elections is traditionally high did not show particularly high levels of Tea Party activity. In fact, 'Republican districts saw *less* activism' (Cho et al. 2012: 126, original emphasis). Moreover, grassroots energy and enthusiasm for Tea Party grievances 'was commonly found in areas where it was of little electoral benefit, e.g. in the districts of safe incumbents' (Cho et al. 2012: 131), which suggests, in this case, political activity is an expression of identity, that is, 'they are Republicans who identify with the small government, anti-debt, anti-regulatory message of the Tea Party' (Cho et al. 2012: 110).

While Cho et al. (2012: 130) 'are convinced that elites of some stripe were critical in helping to organize events', they say, 'it is very difficult to see the hand of traditional, political elites in the Tea Party patterns', which, interestingly, is a finding at odds with DiMaggio's (2011) view that the Tea Party is not a genuine grassroots social movement, but is a proxy for a Republican elite, backed by the right-wing US media. On the role of business elites (including billionaire reactionaries) and the conservative media (such as Fox News) Skocpol and Williamson (2012) agree with DiMaggio. However, they diverge from him in their disputation of the notion that the Tea Party came 'out of nowhere', since, they argue, many Tea Partiers already had deep ties to extant local conservative groups and Republican organizations. We shall return to look at the dispute over whether the Tea Party was media manufactured or is a genuine grassroots movement in the next chapter. For the time being, we will look at the importance of geography and space for the Occupy movement.

BOX 7.4 NIMBYS OR NIABYS?

A familiar example of geographically specific social movements is local Nimby (not-in-my-backyard) groups (see Figure 7.4). Not unlike the Tea Party movement, one might expect the grievances and goals of such groups to be 'exclusively narrow, single-issue, or reactive' (Shemtov 1999: 91). However, in some ways, these groups are more like indigenous peoples' movements, which, as we have seen, are often inclusive of a wide range of issues, and not limited to those typically associated with the struggles of native peoples, such as fighting for land rights, cultural recognition, and self-determination.

Indeed, in his study of local environmental (anti-incinerator) Nimby groups, Shemtov (1999) shows how many of these social movement organizations expand their goals to become proactive and future oriented, broadening their geographical scope, as well as offering solutions to pollution problems and prognoses about environmental threats. Hence, many activists reject the Nimby label, which they regard as parochial and stigmatizing (Shemtov 1999: 99). Key here is what Shemtov (1999: 92) observes as activists taking ownership of the problem, which affects a kind of 'cognitive liberation' (McAdam 1982: 34), such that we encountered in Chapter 5. Thus, '[b]y motivating NIMBY actors to cognitively break free from reliance on the "expertise" of elected officials, ownership frames empower local activists to develop an independent diagnosis and prognosis that helps them broaden their initial, collective agenda' (Shemtov 1999: 101).

Framing issues broadly has also been identified as an important factor in determining the relative success of small, local social movements. In his study of groups opposed to the siting of Wal-Mart superstores in their communities, Halebsky (2006: 453) found that 'broad framings were more successful than narrow framings'. Two particular types of broad framings were key to social movement success in anti-Wal-Mart disputes: (i) geographically broad framing; and (ii) those emphasizing the harmful effects of the superstore on the *entire* community (as opposed to insular campaigns that failed to elicit widespread support, since they spoke only to a small section of the community).

© Greg Martin

Figure 7.4 Protest of local residents in a suburb of Sydney, Australia, against the building of an aquatic centre in their neighbourhood

A major factor in the success of these groups was their influence over local government agencies – and especially the local city council – which shape political opportunity structures (Halebsky 2006: 444). Providing tangible evidence of widespread support for the movement's goals acts particularly upon politicians, 'who have a keen interest in being re-elected, by motivating them to bring their actions in line with their constituents' (Halebsky 2006: 455). In sum, Halebsky (2006: 456, original emphasis) says that 'broad framing influences politicians by indicating that the issue is of concern to *many* of their constituents, while it influences the public-at-large by compelling them to see the issue as a problem for *them* and not just for somebody else, and thus shifts the debate from NIMBY (Not In My BackYard) to NIABY (Not In Anyone's BackYard)'.

WHY SPACE MATTERS TO OCCUPY

Frustration over the bailout of Wall Street helped feed the frustrations of Tea Partiers who felt 'the reckless economic risks of bankers and mortgage defaulters were being unfairly subsidized by taxpayers' (Courser 2012: 52). Hence, the feeling that the established political order has stopped responding to the concerns of average voters has led to a call for populist democracy by the Tea Party. Indeed, insofar as the real issue driving the Tea Party is 'not partisan rage on the right but a profound sense of crisis of governmental legitimacy that should deeply concern us all' (Rasmussen and Schoen 2010: 15), there are stark similarities with Occupy, which is also a response to the significant 'legitimacy deficit' in modern societies, that, as we saw in Chapter 6, is regarded by Bryan Turner (2013: 80, 149) as the root cause of the Tea Party and Occupy Wall Street movements. It is no surprise therefore that the bipartisan nature of frustrations voiced by millions of Americans, initially, at least, caused pundits and journalists to consider the Occupy movement as the left-wing counterpart to the Tea Party (Dreier 2012: 761). And while the two movements do differ significantly with respect to their protest repertoires, grievances, goals, and so forth, both nevertheless contribute, albeit in different ways, to our understanding of the relationship between space and social movements.

For Sbicca and Perdue (2014: 310), Occupy is an example of the practice of *spatial citizenship*, which 'arises in opposition to the uneven processes of neoliberalization, specifically the state facilitation of capital accumulation through privatization, deregulation, financialization and trade liberalization'. On this view, '[s]patial citizens engage and reclaim public spaces in their quest for democracy' (Sbicca and Perdue 2014: 311). Similarly, according to Pickerill and Krinsky, 'making space' is one of the reasons Occupy matters. In London, for instance, 'the failed attempt to occupy space within the square mile of the City facilitated a public realisation that the financial corporate world was not only off-limits to most, economically and socially, but also quite literally' (Pickerill and Krinsky 2012: 280). Moreover, the tactic of setting up physical encampments was both strategic and symbolic: 'Occupy camps reasserted the spatial dimensions of exclusion and inequality by forcing society to recognise that capitalist accumulation happens in certain places, and that these places can be named, located and objected to' (Pickerill and Krinsky 2012: 280). The encampments thus 'reasserted the power of the tactic to camp, and the power of such encampments to identify the geography of capitalism' (Pickerill and Krinsky 2012: 280–281). Importantly, though, to Pickerill and Krinsky, this focus on space poses a challenge to social movement studies, which must:

> . . . move beyond merely conceptualizing the extent of space or the compression of space by time (as with discussions of globalization and 'scaling up' protest), and instead to more thoroughly explore the strategic use and occupation of space as symbolic.
>
> (Pickerill and Krinsky 2012: 281)

Another way Occupy expressed the symbolic significance of space and articulated opposition to the privatization of public space was, according to Pickerill and Krinsky, through the use of what we might call, 'carnivalesque protest repertoire', which, as we have seen at various junctures in this book, entail the reversal or overturning of dominant norms, codes, meanings, and structures. In Chapter 5, for example, we considered Pussy Riot's performance of a 'punk prayer' in the Cathedral of Christ the Saviour in Moscow as carnivalesque in nature, since it was about young women occupying a sacred space that is symbolic of patriarchal religious power and authority (Seal 2013: 295). Occupy's tactic of setting up camp at key points of capital accumulation, such as Wall Street and the City of London, is equally carnivalesque, for it inverts the primary use of those spaces and thereby poses a 'symbolic challenge' to dominant codes (Melucci 1996), including the prevailing organizational logic of capitalism. In short, locating itself at the heart of the City of London provided a 'counter-temporality' (Adams 2011), and 'reasserted the agency of territoriality based on social movements' (Halvorsen 2012: 431). Like Pussy Riot, Occupy London also protested in a sacred space at St Paul's Cathedral (Shackle 2011). However, the similarities do not stop here.

Although not directly relevant to our concern in this chapter with the spatial dimensions of social movements, the protests of Occupy and Pussy Riot both lend support to Eyerman and Jamison's (1991: 3–4) 'cognitive praxis' approach to social movements, which, it will be recalled, refers to a movement's success in diffusing its consciousness or spreading its knowledge interests. In Chapter 5, we saw how while she acknowledges the continued stereotyping of women and negative representation of femininity across Western societies, Seal (2013: 298) says the Western media's endorsement of Pussy Riot's feminism can be explained in terms of the incorporation of elements of feminism and post-feminism into news media discourse in the West over the past two decades. Similarly, by crafting and repeating slogans, such as 'we are the 99 percent' (whether correct or not), Occupy has been successful in spreading an 'incredibly powerful' message about the nature of inequality in capitalist societies and, according to Pickerill and Krinsky (2012: 281), that has been 'key to the success of the movement', since '[i]t is exactly through this repetition that slogans come to populate the discourse and establish their own truths'.

BOX 7.5 ALREADY OCCUPIED: INDIGENOUS PEOPLES AND OCCUPY MOVEMENTS

Earlier in the chapter, we were reminded of material presented in Chapter 6, showing how Native American women have forged 'unlikely alliances' with Christian Right groups on abortion issues (Smith 2008). Conversely, one might think indigenous peoples and Occupy's 99 percent would constitute a 'likely alliance', given their apparently congruent concerns, namely 'broad-based opposition to economic and political marginalization, strong sub-currents of environmentalism and direct democracy and antipathy towards state violence' (Barker 2012: 327). However, as Barker (2012: 327) shows, although groups of indigenous peoples have engaged with Occupy in North America, they 'have also raised powerful critiques of the goals, philosophies and tactics of various Occupy movements'. Indeed, many of the concerns of indigenous peoples remain unaddressed by Occupy, including, most significantly, legacies of historical colonization that are the cause of persistent colonial dynamics in contemporary settler societies (Barker 2012: 328). Hence:

> For settler states such as Canada and the USA, the reality of capitalist oppression is inseparable from the history of colonization; the concerns of Indigenous communities are not necessarily those of the 99% and 'occupation' as term and tactic needs to be fundamentally reconsidered.
>
> (Barker 2012: 329)

To Barker (2012: 329), the last point is most important, for Canada and the United States together constitute the northern bloc of settler colonialism, which is a space that 'was created and has been perpetuated through the production of a "structure" of invasion'. And, since '[t]hat invasion has never ended; this space is already occupied' (Barker 2012: 329). Noteworthy here is a poster entitled, 'Decolonize Wall Street', that was distributed widely by Occupy groups online. The poster, depicting a Native American, with accompanying text, 'Wall St. is on occupied Algonquin land', and 'defend Mother Earth', has been subject to much debate and criticism. Among other things, it is argued the poster presents a confused message by portraying an 'aesthetic commonly appropriated by Settler people in constructing myths of pure, noble savages', and using another overplayed trope to exhort supporters to defend Mother Earth, 'as if Indigenous concerns are strictly environmental, leaving economic and political critiques to others' (Barker 2012: 329).

Barker suggests it is important to remember occupying particular sites has a long history in indigenous peoples' struggles against colonial aggression. However, he says, these occupations are fundamentally different from those of the various Occupy movements, which 'seek to claim the spaces created by state power and corporate wealth – specific sites such as Zuccotti Park or Wall Street, and more general spaces of urban poverty and suburban collapse' (Barker 2012: 329). By contrast, indigenous occupations seek:

. . . to reclaim and reassert relationships to land and place submerged beneath the settler colonial world. Their occupations do not question simply the divisions of wealth and power in the northern bloc; they question the very existence of settler colonial nation-states.

(Barker 2012: 329)

Given the pervasiveness of settler colonialism, says Barker (2012: 330), its persistence within Occupy is unsurprising. And that is why although indigenous dispossession has its roots in capital accumulation, Occupy has focused on the abuse of power and position of individuals and corporations, which is a problem to be resolved by the 99 percent. However, indigenous peoples are not part of the 99 percent in the way most settler people are:

In order to enter the social space of the 99%, Indigenous peoples must ignore generations of difference making and marginalization by governments and Settler communities, and assume the role of a politicized 'minority' in solidarity with other minority groups making equivalent claims. Participation is contingent on abandoning fundamental aspects of indigeneity.

(Barker 2012: 331)

Indigenous activism constitutes 'the act of reconnecting with land, and through this, to identity, social cohesion and self-sufficiency [and] is practised through the direct, collective assertion of place-based relationships that inform a worldview encompassing individual and group identities, resource acquisition and use, and governance structures and social institutions' (Barker 2012: 332). While indigenous peoples are willing to include nonindigenous peoples in their struggle, Barker argues the goals of indigenous liberation and decolonization appear to be lost on the Occupy movements, which have engaged only partially with indigenous concerns:

> The Occupy protestors may be more than this, but thus far their unwillingness to engage with Indigenous concerns and settler colonial privilege in the main seems to reinforce the point. The nationalistic, racialized nature of Occupy movements in North America does not just leave Indigenous peoples out; it situates Occupy as another settler colonial dynamic participating in the transfer of land and space to the hands of the settler colonial majority.
>
> (Barker 2012: 333)

Interestingly, in their study of a local iteration of Occupy Wall Street, Occupy Gainesville, Sbicca and Perdue (2014) show how the 99 percent are divided in terms of privileged activists who choose to occupy public protest space and those who have no option other than to occupy that space, including homeless people. They show how this division was clearly evident in the policing of Occupy Gainesville (OG), when 'police originally chose to work with the mainly white OG protestors and not arrest them for sleeping on sidewalks, while arresting the largely black homeless people for the same, politically unmotivated behaviour' (Sbicca and Perdue 2014: 317). The control and policing of public protest space is discussed in the next section.

POLICING SPACE

According to Pickerill and Krinsky (2012: 285), another reason why Occupy matters relates to the politics of policing. Law enforcement responses to Occupy have tended to be harsh. In Oakland, for example, an activist nearly died after being assaulted by police. And although most Occupy camps were cleared on the pretext of health and safety grounds or the need to ensure public order, Pickerill and Krinsky (2012: 285) say the harsh treatment of Occupy activists is symptomatic of the increased securitization of society over the past decade, as well as 'an ongoing erosion of the right to dissent for much longer'. To

Pickerill and Krinsky (2012: 285), Occupy is pertinent to the politics of protest policing on three grounds:

> Occupy has illustrated the extent to which protest policing has evolved, the ways in which policing tactics have diffused across countries, and the very act of confronting the police has a central place in what could be called the 'Occupy' repertoire.

We will consider some of these issues in this section, which deals specifically with the policing of protest space. To be sure, in the book so far we have focused on the collective action of protestors, which has meant that, apart from a few exceptions when we have considered countermovement responses to social movements, we have not looked at state responses to social movements. And, in particular, we have not considered in any depth, at least, the ways protest is subject to state repression and social control by police. We did look briefly at this when in Chapter 5 we saw how the happiness and positivity generated during the theatrical protest performances of Peruvian women's grassroots groups differed from mainstream protests, which sometimes provoked an aggressive police response (Moser 2003: 185). Also in that chapter, we considered how accounts of violent clashes between New Age Travellers and police were retold by Travellers as a 'war story', similar to the way soldiers do after a battle (Fine 1995: 136; Martin 1998: 740–741). And, earlier in this chapter, we saw how police responded to protesters during Bolivia's water war in a similarly repressive fashion, as well as how authorities in France came down hard on the Sans-papiers movement.

Protest policing has evolved over time, and has done so partly in response to the changing repertoire or tactics of social movements (Martin 2011b: 28–29). It is argued there has been a move away from a 'hard' or 'escalated force' approach to public order and protest policing, which was prevalent during the 1960s, and a move towards a 'soft' policing style (della Porta and Reiter 1998: 17). Hence, commentators talk of police *handling* protest events, which is 'a more neutral description for what protestors usually refer to as "repression" and the state as "law and order"' (della Porta and Reiter 1998: 1; della Porta and Fillieule 2004: 217). Thus, it is suggested there has been 'a general softening of social control, as the velvet glove increasingly comes to replace, or at least cover, the iron fist' (Marx 1998: 255).

In this context, we witness the emergence of the 'managed incorporation of dissent' (Waddington and King 2007: 419), or the 'negotiated management' approach (Fernandez 2008: 14–15) to protest policing,

features of which include 'the protection of free speech rights, tolera-
tion of community disruption, ongoing communication between
police and demonstrators, avoidance of arrests, and limiting the use of
force to situations where violence is occurring' (Vitale 2005: 286).
Softer methods of police control also involve what Noakes and Gillham (2006: 111–114) call 'strategic incapacitation', which entails the
use of preemptive arrests, the demarcation of 'no-protest zones', and
the corralling (or 'kettling') of protesters.

A major shift in the policing of protest occurred after the now infa-
mous Battle of Seattle, when protestors successfully disrupted the
World Trade Organization (WTO) ministerial meetings in 1999.
While protest policing had been evolving throughout the 1990s in
response to the confrontational tactics of anti-globalization activists
(see Chapter 9) and their adoption of decentralized, nonhierarchical,
network-based forms of organizing (Fernandez 2008: 130, 137), after
the Battle of Seattle, law enforcement agencies radically revised their
strategies, devising techniques such as securing space, building barri-
cades, creating security (or frozen) zones, and conducting mass
preemptive arrests (Fernandez 2008: 92–93). Importantly, given our
focus in this chapter, instead of relying on negotiations and 'protest
permits' to engage protestors, states 'moved to control the physical
landscape around protest, aiming to prevent another Battle of Seattle'
(Fernandez 2008: 93).

While policing space and territorial control have always been
central to police work (Herbert 1997), and everyday policing now
entails the expansive use of 'soft' surveillance tactics across the urban
landscape (Beckett and Herbert 2008: 16), these developments are
amplified at high-profile international events, such as WTO, Group
of Eight (G8), and Group of Twenty (G20) meetings. Hence, the
policing of space at international events involves the use of increasingly
sophisticated modes of social control that are neither purely repressive nor entirely negotiated, which is captured by Luis Fernandez
(2008: 15), when he says that 'the current mode is an effective mixture of hard- and soft-line tactics, including the use of new
"non-lethal weapons" as well as laws, codes, regulations, and public
relations strategies that attempt to control protest spaces directly and
indirectly'. Many of these developments are evident at international
'mega-events' (Boyle and Haggerty 2009), where a particular policing style, or 'global protest policing repertoire', has emerged (Martin
2011a: 31, 43). The policing of space at the 2007 Sydney Asia Pacific
Economic Cooperation (APEC) meeting provides a case in point
(see Box 7.6).

BOX 7.6 POLICING PROTEST SPACE, SYDNEY STYLE

The APEC meeting held in Sydney in September 2007 provides an example of a high-profile international event where both hard and soft tactics were employed. In the lead up to the summit, the Australian government and the police undertook months of planning and preparation, which included running an intimidation campaign, harassing would-be protestors, and executing preemptive arrests (Martin 2011b: 34). At the meeting itself, security measures involved a huge police presence, rooftop snipers, 'ring of steel' fencing, water cannon, rolling prisons, and police frogmen on Jet Skis. The 'fortification' and 'militarization' of Sydney during the APEC summit is now common to many international protest events, where there tends to be an overwhelming police presence (Fernandez 2008: 123), and where the space around meetings 'resembles a war zone, with armored vehicles and police in full riot gear, including dark padded uniforms, sturdy helmets, and large see-through shields, and wielding batons and other weaponry' (Fernandez 2008: 122).

Another means of fortifying space is to create security, or frozen, zones, which enable police to secure entire areas of cities without fences, 'keeping close watch on everyone who enters the area' (Fernandez 2008: 127). Part of the 'soft', nonlethal weaponry of protest policing, the fortification and securitization of space can be provided for by laws, codes, and regulations. In the case of APEC, police powers were enshrined in legislation enacted especially for the Sydney summit, which gave police extraordinary authority in parts of Sydney's central business district from 30 August–12 September 2007 inclusive (Martin 2011b: 33). Within specially designated 'security areas', police had the power, for instance, 'to establish roadblocks, checkpoints and cordons; search people, vehicles and vessels; seize and detail prohibited items; give reasonable directions; exclude or remove people from APEC security areas' (Snell 2008: 5). The legislation also gave the New South Wales Police Commissioner authority to compile (and publish) an *excluded persons list*, 'comprising persons the Commissioner is satisfied would pose serious threats to the safety of persons or property (or both) in an APEC security area during the APEC period' (Snell 2008: 13).

Costing AUD170 million, the APEC summit also provided an example of what Fernandez (2008: 100–101) identifies as the 'economy of protest' that has grown up 'around training officers and cities hosting anti-globalization protests', which 'costs the local government millions of dollars'. As with other international events, it has been argued that the principal reason for spending so much on policing and security at the APEC summit was to provide reassurance that Sydney is a safe and unproblematic (i.e., protest-free) place for capital investment and tourism, which is increasingly imperative as external pressures from global neoliberalism are brought to bear on 'global cities' (Sassen 2001), such as Sydney, that 'now compete with one another to create hospitable environments for corporate investment, retail, tourism and other high-end services' (Martin 2011b: 31).

Hence, *showcasing security* becomes a vital means of publicity for cities competing in a global marketplace. Margit Mayer (2007: 94) sees this 'place promotion' as an aspect of public-sector austerity under neoliberalism, which has gone 'hand in hand with a limited urban policy repertoire'. Success in this competition depends on 'the packaging and sale of urban place *images*, which [. . .] keep downtowns and event spaces free of "undesirables" and "dangerous elements"' (Mayer 2007: 94, original emphasis). That not only involves excluding protestors occupying 'spaces of resistance' (Coleman 2005: 143), but also excluding any other elements that are deemed a threat to city spaces that are directed increasingly by private, commercial, and corporate interests (Martin 2011b: 38).

Thus, at the Sydney APEC meeting, protestors were excluded from the city, but so, too, were homeless people, most of whom moved away 'voluntarily' during APEC week (Martin 2011b: 39). Also affected were tourists and restaurateurs, the latter being told by police to remove butter knives and forks from outdoor tables in case they might be used as weapons (Martin 2011b: 42), thereby providing an example of what Vitale (2005: 284) refers to as the 'micro-management of demonstrations'. Ironically, international business leaders, who were delegates at the APEC meeting, also complained that the intense security hampered their ability to move around the city and mix freely (Martin 2011b: 39). Therefore, a serious question mark hung over possible police mishandling of the APEC event and whether the spectacle of security triumphed over the substance of security, a point made all the more poignant given what occurred at one point during APEC week:

> On 6 September 2007, a team of satirical comedians from the Australian TV show, *The Chaser's War on Everything*, breached the security cordon by driving a fake motorcade displaying Canadian flags within 10 meters of the Intercontinental Hotel where the US president, George W. Bush, was staying. The police arrested 11 members of the cast and crew only after the motorcade was turned around by the show's executive producer and one of the comedians alighted a vehicle dressed as Osama bin Laden.
>
> (Martin 2011b: 35)

CONCLUSION

Many of the developments in protest policing discussed earlier presuppose a blurring of police and intelligence security service functions, which is a process that predated the 'war on terror', although it has intensified since the terror attacks of 11 September 2001. Essentially, this has meant police forces now have at their disposal powers, techniques, and technologies that in the past were used primarily by security/spy agencies (Martin 2011b: 29, 40). Hence, reversing the traditional strategy of investigating past events to determine criminal responsibility, policing increasingly involves intelligence gathering and surveillance work to *preempt* crime, and thus prevent it from occurring in the first place (Martin 2011b: 29–30). In these circumstances, the use of surveillance technologies by law enforcement agencies has become a normalized part of everyday police work, as well as another tool used by police in public order settings and at protest events. However, as we shall see in the next chapter, the ubiquity of mobile phone video cameras in particular has leveled the playing field somewhat, enabling protestors and bystanders alike to turn the gaze back on the police, who are increasingly likely to be subject to public scrutiny if seen (and filmed) using excessive force or participating in misconduct.

Martin's analysis of the policing of space at high-profile international events, like the Sydney APEC summit, broadly reflects a critical approach, which we encountered when we looked earlier at indigenous peoples' struggles over space. It will be recalled that critical geographers are concerned with the 'relationships between space, power and social transformation' (Feldman 2002: 32), recognizing that power relations are infused in the social geographies of marginalization. His analysis also demonstrates a concern with political economy, which gives explanatory priority to social relations, 'seeing spatial patterns as the outcome of social struggle' (Miller 2000: 9) and, importantly, regarding space as *commodified* via capitalist social relations, as well as *territorialized* via the exercise of state military and police power (Miller 2000: 12).

According to this view, the police are not benign upholders of law and order, but are treated as coercive agents of the state, providing support, by force if need be, to establish conditions for the proper functioning of free markets in a neoliberal capitalist mode of production (Martin 2011b: 32, 40–41). Although that is something of a contentious point in some parts of the protest policing literature, the view that the social and the spatial are mutually constitutive and inseparable is widely accepted in the discipline of geography (Martin and Miller 2003: 144, 146), even if scholars express different views as to the precise nature of the configurations, permutations, and power relations involved here. The example of protest policing at major international events, then, provides a lens through which to view some of the key issues underpinning struggles over space that we have examined in this chapter. And, as we shall see, it also provides a springboard from which to examine some of the issues relating to media and movements that we look at in the next chapter.

SUGGESTED READINGS

The following texts and resources can be used to explore issues raised in this chapter.

Books

Miller, B. A. (2000) *Geography and Social Movements: Comparing Antinuclear Activism in the Boston Area.* Minneapolis, MN: University of Minnesota Press.

The first chapter of this book (co-written by Deborah G. Martin) provides a comprehensive overview of the field relating to geography, space, and social movements. It explores the key concepts of space, place, and scale. And it looks at some of the ways geographic research can contribute to our understanding of movement mobilization via an assessment of resource mobilization theory, political process models, and new social movement theory.

Nicholls, W., Miller, B., and Beaumont, J. (eds.) (2013) *Spaces of Contention: Spatialities and Social Movements.* Farnham: Ashgate.

This recent edited volume aims to provide a state-of-the-art analysis of how space plays a constitutive role in social movement mobilization.

Hamel, P., Lustiger-Thaler, H., and Mayer, M. (eds.) (2000) *Urban Movements in a Globalising World.* London: Routledge.

Leitner, H. Peck, J., and Sheppard, E. S. (eds.) (2007) *Contesting Neoliberalism: Urban Frontiers.* New York: The Guildford Press.

These two edited collections look at the important impact of globalization and neoliberalism on a variety of urban social movements in different geographical locations.

Davenport, C., Johnston, H., and Mueller, C. (eds.) (2004) *Repression and Mobilization.* Minneapolis, MN: University of Minnesota Press.

della Porta, D. and Reiter, H. (eds.) (1998) *Policing Protest: The Control of Mass Demonstrations in Western Democracies.* Minneapolis, MN: University of Minnesota Press.

These two edited volumes provide useful introductions to some of the key themes and issues in the policing of protest (della Porta and Reiter) and, more generally, the repression of social movements (Davenport et al.). The following book chapter offers another introduction to the field of policing protest:

della Porta, D. and Fillieule, O. (2004) 'Policing Social Protest' in D. A. Snow, S. A. Soule, and H. Kriesi (eds.) *The Blackwell Companion to Social Movements*. Oxford: Blackwell, pp. 217–241.

Journals

There are several journal special issues relevant to some of the topics discussed in this chapter, including:

Critical Sociology 38(4) (2012): 'Tea Party Politics in America'.
Mobilization 8(2) (2003): 'Space and Contentious Politics'.
Mobilization 11(2) (2006): 'Repression and the Social Control of Protest'.
Policing and Society 15(3) (2005): 'Policing Protest After Seattle'.
Social Movement Studies 11(3–4) (2012): 'Occupy!'

CHAPTER 8

Media and movements

INTRODUCTION

While the study of media has often been omitted from textbooks on social movements, some texts do now include material relating to the role of media in social protest, which has become necessary, especially given the advent of the Internet, new media, and social networking sites. In her brief commentary on the subject, Susan Staggenborg (2011: 45–47) shows how the issue of *newsworthiness* tends to preclude the grievances of social movements being aired in the mass media. The idea here is that because they are driven by a commercial imperative to produce stories that sell – which is heightened in the increasingly competitive 24/7 mediasphere marketplace – mainstream news media tend not to be interested in covering social movement issues of long-term policy relevance, such as tackling poverty or addressing environmental damage.

When the media does dedicate space to the activities of social movements, argues Koopmans (2004), it does so according to three main selective mechanisms, or 'discursive opportunities', which affect the diffusion chances of contentious messages: (i) *visibility* (the extent of coverage of a message by the mass media), (ii) *resonance* (the extent of reaction to a message by allies, opponents, authorities, and so on), and (iii) *legitimacy* (the degree of support for such reactions). Nevertheless, there remains a media bias against social movements, which are seen as 'endowed with little social capital (in terms of relati reputation as reliable sources) to benefit journalists' (dell 2012: 45). On the other hand, protests 'that succeed in drawing many people to the street signal a relevant social issue journalists cannot ignore', thus underscoring the finding of Wouters (2013: 99) that '[d]emonstration size appears to be the single strongest predictor of newsworthiness'.

When they do receive information on issues of social import, journalists tend to rely on official sources (e.g., government agencies), which provide a one-dimensional perspective, thereby missing alternative viewpoints, such as those provided by social movements. Indeed, in his study of Spanish anti-military mobilization, Sampedro (1997) found that government elites tend to trivialize movement challenges – hence reducing their newsworthiness – and that the tendency among established media actors to abide by journalistic rules serves to validate the political class, which, in the long run, dilutes social protest.

Gathering information from official sources may not only result in news organizations producing distorted or inaccurate stories, but can also result in them missing the existence of social movements altogether. For instance, Todd Gitlin (1980) has shown how the Students for a Democratic Society (SDS) existed five years prior to its 'discovery' by the mass media in 1965. This then could explain why some movements apparently lie in abeyance for long periods of time (as we saw in Chapter 4). It also goes some way to explain why certain movements, such as Tea Party (examined in Box 8.2 later), seem to appear 'out of nowhere'.

Because they tend to be ignored by the mainstream media, many social movements resort to dramatic tactics to get noticed. However, a problem associated with this, as Staggenborg (2011: 46) notes, is that standards for coverage may escalate too. Returning to Gitlin's (1980: 182) study, he argued that the increasingly flamboyant gestures used by the anti-Vietnam War movement in the 1960s raised the threshold of rhetoric and violence needed for coverage, such that, while 'a picket line might have been news in 1965, it took tear gas and bloodied heads to make headlines in 1968'.

The focus on sensationalist news stories is well documented in the media studies literature, which shows how some of the most salient 'news values' are those of sex and violent crime (Jewkes 2011: 51–53, 58–59). In the context of social protest, the requirement for sensationalist newsworthy stories that provide good copy is evident in the overemphasis on repressive state responses to social movements. We get a sense of this from some of the information provided by Wilson and Serisier (2010: 168) in their study of video activists, which 'refers to

people who use video as a tactical tool to deter police violence, document abuse and misconduct by police authorities, and in an effort to
influence and set the political agenda'. Wilson and Serisier's (2010:
174) findings highlight the oft-made complaint that the demands of
newsworthiness (and especially the media's preoccupation with violence) may decontextualize footage or lead to it being freighted with
meanings that distort the original intentions of those filming, with one
interviewee stating:

> . . . there're two issues. There's the issue around which the protest
> and the activism is happening and then there's the issue of police
> accountability and often we capture stuff which shows police
> behaving badly and the issue we're trying to get attention for gets
> ignored for the police stuff.

Towards the end of Chapter 7, we touched upon what Wilson and
Serisier (2010: 167) describe as the 'democratization and diffusion of
imaging technologies', which indicates there is now greater equality of
access to and use of surveillance equipment. And later we will consider
this development in more depth when we see how protestors and
ordinary citizens alike are now able to use new media technologies,
such as mobile phone video cameras, to surveil the police in protest/
public order settings. For now, we should note, as Wilson and Serisier
(2010: 170) do, the interactive nature of protestor-police relations,
described by them as a 'constant interplay of move and counter-move
between police and video activists [which] activates ascending spirals
of surveillance and counter-surveillance' in what Gary Marx (2007:
299) calls a 'surveillance arms race'. The example from Gitlin's study
also demonstrates the point not only that 'repertoires of contention'
(i.e., movement tactics) change or evolve over time – a point made
originally by Charles Tilly (see Chapter 3) and applied more recently
to the 'electronic repertoire of contention' of online social movements
(Rolfe 2005) – but that they do so via interactions with other collective actors in a wider, external environment, including the police, the
state, and media. We also looked at this in Chapter 7, when we saw
how police forces across the globe changed tactics and approach after
protestors successfully disrupted the World Trade Organization (WTO)
meetings in 1999 at the Battle of Seattle.

Along with showing how potentially pivotal the media are in discovering social movements in the first place, Gitlin's account of the
case of the SDS also shows how when the media do discover social
movements, they may not necessarily depict them in ways protestors
like. Hence, when the SDS was eventually discovered by the media, it

BOX 8.1 PUSSY RIOT REDUX

In Chapter 5, we saw how the medium of music has been used by social movements as a means of 'mobilizing traditions' (Eyerman and Jamison 1998: 2) and as a source of 'cognitive praxis', whereby it contributes 'to the ideas that movements offer and create in opposition to the existing social and cultural order' (Eyerman and Jamison 1998: 24). We also saw how the positive acceptance on Western news media websites of Russian feminist punk band, Pussy Riot, could be considered an example of the 'cognitive praxis' of the women's movement insofar as it demonstrates a successful diffusion of feminist ideas and knowledge interests (see Box 5.5). However, Pussy Riot's performance-based, media-savvy style of protest also highlights the increasing use of new social media in contemporary activism.

In this respect, and according to Seal (2013: 299), Pussy Riot's success lies 'in promoting their cause and mobilizing media and activist support'. While the band does communicate their ideas via interviews with journalists, their 'supporters have an online presence that does not rely on the mainstream news media, such as the website Free Pussy Riot!, YouTube video clips of the band's songs and performances, Facebook pages, and a Twitter account' (Seal 2013: 299–300). And, it is believed, because of its effective use of the Internet, Pussy Riot poses a genuine challenge to the Putin regime (Seal 2013: 300).

was portrayed only as an anti-war organization, even though it 'put itself forward in no uncertain terms as a multi-issue organization which worked in university reform, civil rights, and community organizing, as well as against war and corporate domination of foreign policy' (Gitlin 1980: 34).

GREENPEACE: A MEDIA-SAVVY SOCIAL MOVEMENT ORGANIZATION

Staggenborg (2011: 46) notes that '[m]ovement organizations that are more centralized and professionalized, and that learn how to conform to media norms and provide information or "stories" in a format acceptable to media organizations, are most likely to get coverage' (see also Gamson and Wolfsfeld 1993). However, even for professionalized movement organizations, she says, 'it is difficult to get movement frames represented accurately in the mass media, as journalists and news organizations apply their own frames to events' (Staggenborg

2011: 46). The paradigmatic example of a media-savvy social movement organization is Greenpeace.

Given the media's predilection for newsworthy stories, Greenpeace, like other campaigning organizations, has faced difficulties presenting issues of environmental concern in the media. Specifically focusing on the medium of television, Aaron Doyle (2003: 118–119) says these problems include that environmental issues often occur in geographically isolated locations, they have a slow onset, they are often invisible and technically complex, and they tend to implicate 'faceless villains', such as corporations and governments. Hence, and in accordance with what was said earlier about social movements responding to lack of media interest with flamboyant gestures and tactics to get noticed, Greenpeace has devised a repertoire of 'media stunts'.

Greenpeace's early direct actions were rooted in the Quaker idea of 'bearing witness' (Doyle 2003: 117), which, as mentioned in Chapter 6, is intended to present an audience with ideas and information that cannot be ignored. Greenpeace's media stunts subsequently evolved to become highly planned and organized; they are also announced well in advance of the stunts taking place and are timed to suit media deadlines. The media stunts consist of brief vignettes or 'micro-dramas' involving direct action, which is tailor-made for the TV medium, and they 'always involve visually striking, made-for-TV elements such as acts of physical daring, wearing of costumes, or unveiling of a banner with a very brief message' (Doyle 2003: 119).

To add to the drama, Greenpeace often also instigates strategic, non-violent law breaking, such as a sit-in or blockade, to prompt on-the-spot arrests. The organization has even produced a media handbook, which provides information about 'arrest scenarios' that include 'placing trained activists in highly visible situations from which they cannot be whisked away by the police' (Doyle 2003: 119). Sometimes arrest scenarios might be negotiated with police in advance and timed to meet TV deadlines. Greenpeace also has its own videographers who are able to provide footage to television outlets that are unable to send cameras to the scene of stunts. The net effect is what Altheide and Snow (1991) call, 'post-journalism', meaning Greenpeace's stunts are prepackaged to such an extent that journalists, whether sympathetic or not, are increasingly redundant, as the organization prepares its own provocative stories (see Figure 8.1).

Doyle shows how TV has helped shape Greenpeace and its tactics in a number of ways. First, as '[t]elevision tends to reduce politics to a spectacle', Doyle (2003: 125) says, Greenpeace produces simple bite-sized messages, which, during direct action stunts, frequently take the form of banners promoting the organizational brand, such as 'Let the whales

© Pete Maclaine/Alamy

Figure 8.1 Greenpeace activists unfurl banner during media stunt. As Shell executives and guests held a public relations event dinner in the National Gallery in London, UK, on 21 February 2012, Greenpeace activists abseiled from the building's roof and hung a massive 40-foot banner across its pillars. The protest was to highlight the dangers that drilling for oil pose to the Arctic region.

live – Greenpeace'. As discussed in Chapter 7, this strategic use of slogans has proved powerful more recently in Occupy's attempt to highlight issues of inequality and corporate greed by crafting and repeating the slogan, 'We are the 99 percent'. Second, TV has helped shape Greenpeace's organizational goals. For instance, it has focused on certain environmental issues and mediagenic images, such as baby harp seals being clubbed to death, rather than drawing attention to concern over the possible extinction of the giant earwig of St Helena (Doyle 2003: 127). In this way, Greenpeace has also used emotion to get its message across, which stands in stark contrast to the 'dispassionate politics' of animal rights activists studied by McAllister Groves (2001), which we looked at in Chapter 5.

Finally, the organization's reliance on media stunts has increased support from a *passive public* who are uninclined to take part in mass demonstrations, but are willing to support organizations like Greenpeace by donating money, for example. While this so-called 'couch potato activism' certainly has monetary advantages, Doyle (2003: 131) shows how the requirements of television have been such that they have also led to the taming and institutionalization of Greenpeace, which, as we have seen at various points in the book, is a dilemma for many social movements, as it can result in movements becoming less radical and more conservative, as their original demands and objectives are compromised to accommodate organizational imperatives and political goals. This is summed up by Doyle (2003: 130) when he says, 'Former president Robert Hunter's early philosophizing suggested that a change in "public consciousness" would be wrought by Greenpeace's media campaigns. This now seems very secondary to achieving the organization's financial and political goals'.

Similarly, Carroll and Ratner (1999: 14) have observed how Greenpeace's reliance on visual stunts has detracted from grassroots organizing, although it 'has increasingly used the Internet to bypass mass media'. Finally, Greenpeace activists' portrayal of themselves as heroic outlaws (e.g., eco-cowboys, 'rainbow warriors') pitted against giant corporate villains (i.e., in David and Goliath scenarios) belies the organization's 'latter-day status as a large multinational organization' (Doyle 2003: 122). Notwithstanding this, the notion that Greenpeace's media stunts are conceived of as *dramas* and *vignettes* highlights the importance of storytelling and narrative (examined in Chapter 5) in the tactical repertoire of the organization.

BOX 8.2 TEA PARTY: MEDIA MANUFACTURED OR GENUINE GRASSROOTS MOVEMENT?

In Chapter 6, we looked at the Tea Party movement as an example of the relative convergence of social and religious issues, and, in Chapter 7, we looked at spatial and geographic explications of the emergence of Tea Party. Much has also been written about the relationship between the Tea Party movement and the US media. A central point of contention here has been whether Tea Party constitutes a genuine grassroots movement, or whether it is a media-manufactured phenomenon.

To recap, in Chapter 7, we saw how commentators are at odds with one another as to the origins of the Tea Party movement. On the one hand, Cho et al. (2012) argue that nontraditional elites were crucial to Tea Party's emergence. On the other hand, DiMaggio's (2011) view is that rather than being a genuine grassroots movement, the Tea Party is a proxy for an entrenched Republican elite, bolstered by the right-wing US media. Banerjee (2013) provides a variant of this view, arguing that rather than being a post facto consequence of news, coverage tended to precede Tea Party mobilization, and thus was its most important predictor. A middle-range perspective is presented by Skocpol and Williamson (2012) who agree with DiMaggio on the pivotal role played by business elites (including billionaire reactionaries) and the conservative media (e.g., Fox News), but differ from him in disputing the idea that the Tea Party came 'out of nowhere', since, they argue, many Tea Partiers had deep ties to preexisting grassroots conservative groups and Republican organizations.

This argument confirms the view of resource mobilization theorists, such as Doug McAdam (1982) and Anthony Oberschall (1973), who stress the importance of extant networks for movement mobilization (see Chapter 3), as well as Verta Taylor's (1989) idea that movements are sustained by 'abeyance structures', which, as we saw in Chapter 4, is her antidote to the 'immaculate conception' of social movements, or the notion that collective action emerges suddenly, as if from nowhere. Moreover, Skocpol and Williamson's take on the relative speed by which the Tea Party came to prominence and gathered momentum could be seen to complement the view of Thompson (2012: 512), discussed in Chapter 7, who accounts for the quickness with which the Tea Party generated and organized, as well as the homogeneity of their beliefs, in terms of the nonurban spatial environment inhabited by a 'certain strata of American society that predisposes individuals to feel outraged at specific political institutions, social policies, and social groups'.

Skocpol and Williamson's vision of a tripartite Tea Party (i.e., elites, media, grassroots) also helps explicate the prima facie hypocrisy of Tea Partiers, who are, at once, angry at government spending on those they perceive as 'undeserving' (e.g., younger generations and poor people) and angry at cuts to government spending on schemes they feel entitled to as 'rightfully earned compensation for years of hard work and contributions' (Fetner 2012: 764). The contradiction is exemplified in the clash between the Tea Party grassroots and the extreme-right billionaires who support the movement:

> . . . most grassroots supporters are in favour of government-run Medicare and Social Security programs, while the business elite faction, aided by ultra-conservative Republican legislators, would like to destroy these programs, privatizing health care and retirement savings for the elderly.
>
> (McVeigh 2012: 767)

Contrary to DiMaggio's (2011) view of the Tea Party as a media-manufactured fiction created by powerful elite interests, Courser (2012: 48) sees Tea Partiers as being driven by a profound distrust of politicians and partisan elites. While Tea Partiers are overwhelmingly conservative, Courser disputes the popular characterization of them as being engaged in a 'culture war' focused on moral and religious issues. Instead, he argues, the war 'is one for populist democracy against elite domination of politics' (Courser 2012: 50). Moreover, he says, distrust of the political class and elite interest groups is found on the right *and* left sides of American politics, both of which express disillusionment at the disconnect between government and the people it purports to represent.

To be sure, the Tea Party movement operates in a political context perceived of as being dominated by entrenched interest groups that are unresponsive to public opinion, which is why '[t]he frustration Tea Partiers felt over the federal bailout of Wall Street, the rescue of General Motors, or the convoluted manner the healthcare reform bill was passed into law, all reflect the responsiveness of government to the demands of interest groups' (Courser 2012: 51). This is not to say, however, that elite domination is a problem only affecting the right, since the problem goes to the heart of American democracy, such that '[w]riters from the left have observed a growing distrust by voters of the established political order, especially among the white middle class' (Courser 2012: 51).

HACKERS AND HACKTIVISTS

In the chapter so far we have focused mostly on relationships between social movements and what might be regarded as 'traditional' forms of media and information technologies. However, interest in media-movement relations has risen exponentially in recent times, mainly since the emergence of new social media and digital technologies, and their increasing use *as a resource* for movement mobilization and goal attainment. Indeed, Staggenborg (2011: 47) states that 'the issue of how movements can use the mass media effectively is a critical one for social movement studies', where an 'important development is the availability of the Internet as a direct form of mass media for social movements'. She continues:

Movements have always used internal communications such as newsletters to convey their messages, but the Internet provides a quick, low-cost means of reaching a large number of potential supporters and of organizing events through email and websites. The global justice movement, for example, has made extensive use of the Internet to organize its international campaigns. In some instances, collective actions or 'e-movements' have been organized strictly online with little formal organization. The strengths and limitations of this type of organizing, which bypass the mainstream media, are an increasingly important topic for social movement research.

(Staggenborg 2011: 47)

In subsequent sections of this chapter we will consider various ways in which protestors and social movements have used not only the Internet but also other new information technologies and social media forms beyond the mainstream media. The focus in this section, however, is on early studies of 'hackers' and 'hacktivism', which have examined the relationship between activism and new media technologies and, in particular, activists' use of the Internet. Interestingly, these studies provide an alternative take on the view that microserfs and hackers tend to be conservative and apolitical. It will be recalled how in Chapter 4 we saw that although they are a core constituent of an increasingly precarious workforce in post-industrial societies, high-tech and information technology (IT) workers tend to regard trade unions as antiquated and irrelevant to their profession. Moreover, in his study of Microsoft workers, Brophy (2006: 631) shows how they are also critical of progressive social movements, such as the global justice movement. Studies of hackers and hacktivism provide a very different view.

Insofar as the hacker generation that emerged in the mid-1980s actually had a political agenda, it concerned the control and liberation of information (Jordan 2007: 74). Hacktivism grew out of hacking in the mid-1990s. It entails 'the combination of hacking techniques with political activism' (Taylor 2005: 626). Hacktivists speak out on political matters and as such are more outwardly focused than hackers, in that they connect 'hacking to a politics outside that of informational freedom' (Jordan 2007: 75). Tim Jordan (2007) argues there are two strands of hacktivism: *mass action* and *digital correctness*.

Mass-action hacktivism translates the classic tactic of civil disobedience into electronic civil disobedience (Garrett 2006: 208–209). In 1998, the Electronic Disturbance Theatre (EDT) staged a series of web sit-ins in support of Mexico's Zapatistas, who have themselves employed the Internet as a prefigurative method of organizing (Atton 2003; see also Kulick 2014). EDT created a piece of software called Floodnet, which, once downloaded to a computer, connected the surfer's web browser to a preselected website and automatically reloaded the web browser every seven seconds (Taylor 2005: 634–635). When large numbers of people participate in virtual sit-ins of this nature, it has the effect of slowing down or even closing down targeted websites. Mass action also gives legitimacy to the cause. Another EDT virtual sit-in was targeted against an organization that opposed migration across the US-Mexican border. This virtual sit-in involved 27,000 participants who managed to close access to key sites, including the US Border Patrol website and the North American Free Trade Agreement (NAFTA) website (Jordan 2007: 76).

A similar action was staged by the Electrohippies, whose virtual sit-in against the 1999 Seattle WTO meeting involved 450,000 participants over five days, having the effect of slowing down the WTO network, and even stopping it on occasion (Jordan and Taylor 2004: 74–75). This action is important, among other things, for highlighting the connection between hacktivism and the anti-globalization/global justice movement. Indeed, for Jordan (2007: 76–77), 'the vast majority of mass hacktivism actions have been launched within the context of the alter-globalization movement', making a 'historical association [. . .] based on the emergence of hacktivism in the mid-1990s at the same time that the alter-globalization movement was blossoming'. Nonetheless, according to Jordan (2007: 76), hacktivism should be viewed more as a tactic or repertoire than an ethical or social movement with its own collective identity and goals, for, 'any cause may find hacktivist repertoires of action useful', including, he says, campaigns against the death penalty in the United States.

Virtual sit-ins such as those of EDT are 'a form of electronic civil disobedience in which the social form of the protest takes precedence over its technological content' (Taylor 2005: 635). Digitally correct hacktivism, on the other hand, is not concerned with replicating offline modes of protest like civil disobedience, but is focused on the technology. Digitally correct hacktivism is more hackerlike than mass-action hacktivism. It tends to be online based and technology focused, and concerned with 'a politics of free, secure access to information on the Internet enacted through the production of software' (Jordan 2007: 79). Accordingly, their main targets are national governments that try to censor and restrict access to the Internet as well as surveil people's traffic. However, they also target corporations such as Microsoft, which as a result of the activities of some hacktivists has been forced to face up to security issues associated with its Windows operating system (Jordan and Taylor 2004: 111–114). Digitally correct hacktivists, then, 'implement a politics with software' (Jordan 2007: 81), inventing and utilizing specially encrypted software to ensure free and secure access to the Internet.

Jordan (2007: 84) points out that, like other social movements, the hacktivist movement is 'internally varied'. Indeed, both he and Paul Taylor show how tension exists between different types of hacktivists. Digitally correct hacktivists are critical of mass-action hacktivists' use of inefficient and resource-hungry programs such as Floodnet. Protest of this sort, they argue, becomes a form of censorship because it interferes with people's bandwidth (access) rights and the rights of digital information. For groups such as EDT, however, digitally correct hacktivists 'are nerdishly missing the point' (Taylor 2005: 635). To Taylor

(2005: 635), this represents the 'politically myopic' nature of the digitally correct position 'and its failure to separate technological means from social ends'. However, Jordan (2007: 83) argues mass-action hacktivists' caricature of the digitally correct as more concerned with the rights of machines than the rights of humans misrepresents digitally correct hacktivists who are, in fact, concerned with 'the human right to free speech in the age of the Internet'. For example, the digitally correct hacktivist group, Hacktivismo, named their Six/Four project after the Tiananmen Square massacre, which took place on 4 June 1989, and their CameraShy project – ostensibly a means by which users could hide information in graphic files and then swap them – had human rights as its chief purpose, 'illustrated by the dedication integrated into CameraShy to Chinese human rights activist Wang Ruowang' (Jordan 2007: 81).

BOX 8.3 CULTURE JAMMING

As a form of hacktivism (Taylor 2005: 634), 'culture jamming' entails 'the practice of parodying advertisements and hijacking billboards in order to drastically alter their messages' (Klein 2000a: 280). In so doing, it subverts a corporation's own image and advertising in what Naomi Klein (2000b) refers to as a kind of 'brand boomerang' whereby culture jammers adapt the messages corporations wish to convey about themselves. For instance, the 'Think Different' campaign of Apple, Inc., acquires a photograph of Stalin, accompanied by the slogan, 'Think Really Different':

> The process forces the company to foot the bill for its own subversion, either literally, because the company is the one that bought the billboard being altered, or figuratively, because whenever anyone messes with a logo, they are tapping into the vast resources spent to make that logo meaningful.
>
> (Klein 2000b)

Culture jamming is a form of anti-corporate activism, which we have looked at in various parts of the book, including via the work of Soule (2009) and in relation to the anti-sweatshop movement (Ross 2008: 43), which we examined in the context of precarity in Chapter 4. As such, it is a technique used on some anti-corporate websites, which align themselves with the culture jammers movement. For example, McSpotlight, which targets McDonald's, uses it, as does Adbusters, which is a Canadian anti-consumerism organization that runs its own website and is involved in the CokeSpotlight campaign targeting the Coca-Cola Company (Rosenkrands 2004: 72; see also Leizerov 2000).

█ WIKILEAKS: HACKTIVISM AND COUNTERVEILLANCE

Although founded by controversial figure Julian Assange in 2006, Wikileaks came to prominence in April 2010 when it published on its website the controversial video, *Collateral Murder* (www.collateralmurder. com/). Taken during an airstrike carried out in the Iraqi suburb of New Baghdad on 12 July 2007, the video consists of US military–classified gunsight footage from an Apache helicopter, which depicts the killing of a dozen people (including two Reuters journalists) in clear breach of the military's rules of engagement.

According to its website (https://wikileaks.org/About.html), Wikileaks describes its purpose as being 'to bring important news and information to the public' by providing 'an innovative, secure and anonymous way for sources to leak information to our journalists'. It adds that the broader principles upon which its work is based 'are the defence of freedom of speech and media publishing, the improvement of our common historical record and the support of the rights of all people to create new history'. These principles derive, it says, from Article 19 of the Universal Declaration of Human Rights, which 'inspires the work of our journalists and other volunteers', for it states 'that everyone has the right to freedom of opinion and expression', which is a right that 'includes freedom to hold opinions without inter-ference and to seek, receive and impart information and ideas through any media and regardless of frontiers'.

Wikileaks sees one of its most important activities as publishing 'original source material alongside our news stories so readers and historians alike can see evidence of the truth' (https://wikileaks.org/ About.html). The media, and particularly Wikileaks, is significant in this respect because:

> Publishing improves transparency, and this transparency creates a better society for all people. Better scrutiny leads to reduced cor-ruption and stronger democracies in all society's institutions, including government, corporations and other organizations. A healthy, vibrant and inquisitive journalistic media plays a vital role in achieving these goals. We are part of that media.
>
> (https://wikileaks.org/About.html)

Clearly, Wikileaks sees itself as a journalistic organization, a concep-tion about which there has been much debate, with opponents of Wikileaks claiming it does little to improve transparency, but instead releases information that has the potential to endanger national secu-rity, damage diplomatic relations between nations, and risk peoples' lives

(Fenster 2012). Moreover, despite providing 'a high security anonymous drop box fortified by cutting-edge cryptographic information technologies' to protect journalists, whistleblowers, and other anonymous sources of information (https://wikileaks.org/About.html), Wikileaks was unable to prevent the arrest in May 2010 of Private First Class Bradley Manning (now Chelsea Manning). A 22-year-old

© Greg Martin

Figure 8.2 Superleakers: Julian Assange (top), Edward Snowden (left), Bradley Manning (right)

intelligence analyst with the US Army in Baghdad, Manning was subsequently charged with disclosing the *Collateral Murder* video to Wikileaks, and was suspected of supplying the organization with various classified documents. Notwithstanding Wikileaks' use of novel media technologies to further its cause, it has been noted that the Manning case is only the most recent example of state victimization of a whistleblower, the landmark case being Daniel Ellsberg's leaking to *The New York Times* in 1971 of the 'Pentagon Papers', which contained sensitive information about US military involvement in the Vietnam War (Rothe and Steinmetz 2013).

In some respects, the activities of Wikileaks can also be seen as a form of hacktivism (Ludlow 2010) and, in particular, 'digitally correct' hacktivism, which, as described earlier, includes the targeting of national governments that try to censor and restrict access to information. Another way of conceiving of Wikileaks is as an example of 'counterveillance', which 'refers to a form of protest that reverses the visual field not only as a challenge to penal power but also toward institutional reform' (Welch 2011: 304). For Welch, counterveillance consists of two main inversions: (i) turning the prison inside out, and (ii) watching the watchers:

> In the first inversion, counterveillance turns unwanted attention to inhumane conditions of imprisonment – which the state deliberately hides from public view. In so doing, prisoner neglect and abuses of state power are exposed to a wider audience; therefore, contributing to greater transparency of the State's penal operations.
>
> (Welch 2011: 304)

The second inversion (i.e., watch the watchers) shares an important dynamic with what Thomas Mathiesen (1997) terms the 'synopticon', whereby the *many watch the few*. The synopticon concept itself constitutes a reformulation of Michel Foucault's (1977) calculus of the 'panopticon' in which the *few watch the many*: 'Together the two-way – or double – process speaks to the magnetic quality of power when exercised visually, and equally important its potential to reduce, balance, or invert asymmetries of observation' (Welch 2011: 303).

Mathiesen (1997: 219), then, provides an important corrective to Foucault's idea that modern society is predominated by various forms of panoptic surveillance, or 'his whole image of society as surveillance'. Given the ubiquity of mass media, Mathiesen urges us to think in terms of a 'viewer society', which 'does not dismiss the vector of surveillance but provides a fuller picture of the public sphere by recognizing that visibility is also synoptic' (Welch 2011: 303). In particular, Mathiesen stresses the electronic media and their role in the viewer society, espe-cially with respect to celebrities and entertainment (and voyeurism). He also emphasizes the coupling of panopticism with synopticism, thereby producing a two-way – reciprocal – framework. However, Michael Welch (2011: 304) argues that while:

> . . . it is true that there are instances of the many watching the few and the few watching the many, both Mathiesen and Foucault neglect an important dimension of modern society. That is, there are also instances in which those being watched also watch back.

The result is what Monahan (2006: 515) describes as 'counter-surveillance', which denotes 'intentional, tactical uses, or disruptions of surveillance technologies to challenge institutional power asymme-tries'. Welch applies these ideas to the context of prisons:

> By *watching the watchers*, key officials governing the penal apparatus themselves are monitored by a collective of prisoners, ex-cons, and activists. With that switch in attention, state officials are put on the defensive. That reduction of the symmetry of power has the capac-ity to enhance levels of official accountability.
>
> (Welch 2011: 304, original emphasis)

Although he is writing about counterveillance in the penal context, the general principles relating to counterveillance can be applied to other forms of protest – or 'optical activism', to use Welch's (2011: 304–305) term – against surveillance, examples of which include 'dis-abling or destroying surveillance cameras, using video recorders to monitor surveillance personnel, and staging public plays to draw atten-tion to the prevalence of surveillance in society' (Welch 2011: 303). Importantly, however, as Fiona Jeffries (2011) argues, a number of contemporary social movements articulate resistance to surveillance even though they are not anti-surveillance per se.

One example she cites is called Fulana, a group of female activists based in New York City that 'has sought to provoke reflection and pose alternative perspectives on war and imperialism, immigration and migrant justice, gentrification and displacement, social inequality, rac-ism, sexism, and the commercial colonization of the popular cultural environment' (Jeffries 2011: 185). While Fulana is not an anti-surveil-lance organization, Jeffries (2011: 185) says, 'its use of media activism, the broad multi-dimensional content of its political critique and the historical context in which the group was formed, situates its form and strategy of critique within the renaissance of radical thought and practice that erupted into public view during the high point of the alter-globalization protests'.

Interestingly, Fulana has used the technique of culture jamming (see Box 8.3), to alter and 'hijack' the slogan, 'If You See Something, Say Something', which formed part of a post-9/11 poster campaign run by New York City's Metropolitan Transportation Authority. Hence, Fulana's 'Fear Something, See Something' poster intends 'to seize the language of the fear-promoting spectacle and play with it so that it can be turned against itself' (Jeffries 2011: 185). The poster asks viewers to reflect upon 'the dangerous normalization of the citizen-informer model of social participation and public responsibility', and warns that 'prejudices fuelled by sensational commercial media portrayals of who is designated as dangerous and what constitutes suspicious behavior can combine toxically with desires to stay safe' (Jeffries 2011: 186). Put simply, by 'raising concerns about surveillance as a social technology that purports to enhance public safety, the poster sought to contest the repressive definition of security that shaped the government and media response to the 9/11 attacks' (Jeffries 2011: 186). And, in particular, 'it served as an intervention in the debate about the effects of surveillance as a discourse of security in a fear-drenched climate thought by many commentators to be perilous to democracy' (Jeffries 2011: 186).

Wikileaks can be seen as another example of counterveillance, since it aims to turn the surveillant gaze back on the watchers – to watch the watchers. In so doing, it seeks to challenge institutional power asymmetries involved in the keeping secret of information, disclosure of which, it is argued, enhances transparency and official accountability, and ultimately contributes to the building of stronger democratic structures. In highlighting the dangers posed to democracy by secrecy and surveillance, Wikileaks is similar to activist groups like Fulana. However, as a form of digitally correct hacktivism, Wikileaks differs from Fulana, since it resembles more an anti-surveillance organization, which not only contests the ubiquity and nefariousness of surveillance technologies, which, among other things, create a compliant and complacent (or docile) public, but it does so by using those very technologies.

CITIZEN JOURNALISM AS SOUSVEILLANCE

Towards the end of Chapter 7, we saw how the police increasingly use surveillance technologies, not only in public order/protest settings, but also as a part of everyday policing. In this way, the police have become implicated in what Haggerty and Ericson (2000: 606) call the 'surveillant assemblage', which refers to 'the convergence of what were once discrete surveillance systems' and involves, among other things, police organizations (and intelligence services) having increased access to information stored on a host of nonpolice databases, including those from insurance companies, financial institutions, and schools. Combining information sources via computerized data matching allows for an exponential increase in the amount of information police now have at their disposal:

> Files from telephone and utilities companies can be used to document an individual's lifestyle and physical location, and marketing firms have developed consumer profiling techniques that contain precise information on a person's age, gender, political inclinations, religious preferences, reading habits, ethnicity, family size, income, and so on.
>
> (Haggerty and Ericson 2000: 617)

Given these developments, Haggerty and Ericson (2000: 613) argue that today 'we are witnessing the formation and coalescence of a new type of body', known as a 'data double', which is 'a form of becoming which transcends human corporeality and reduces flesh to pure information'. Indeed, Haggerty and Ericson (2000: 619) point out that '[t]he coalescence of such practices in the surveillant assemblage marks the procession to the "disappearance of disappearance" – a process whereby it is difficult for individuals to maintain their anonymity or to escape the monitoring of social institutions'. One would think therefore that the sheer scale and ubiquity of surveillance in modern societies would render resistance futile.

However, as mentioned previously, the increased availability of mobile surveillance devices, such as camera phones, has brought about a degree of democratization, or 'digital democracy' (Loader and Mercea 2012: 2), which has leveled the playing field, enabling ordinary citizens (including protesters) to turn the surveillant gaze back on the watchers, that is, to watch the watchers. And of all of the watchers, it is the police who are most likely to be subject to counterveillance of this sort, since it is the police who most frequently come into contact with activists at protest events in public spaces. The transformations in public order and protest policing discussed in Chapter 7 are captured by what de Lint and Hall (2009: 267–270) call 'intelligent control', which includes increased use of preemptive surveillance. Moreover, as stated earlier, the repertoires of police and protestors tend to evolve and interact with one another. Hence, it is unsurprising that protestors have responded to the police practice of intelligent control.

209

We have already discussed briefly Wilson and Serisier's (2010: 168) study of video activists, who use video as a tactical tool to document instances of police misconduct and abuse, and to deter police violence. Another response has been the relatively recent phenomenon of 'citizen journalism', which is a 'form of reportage that blends on-the-ground citizen news collecting, analyzing, and disseminating, with a form of participatory surveillance' (Dennis 2008: 349). Also known as 'partici-patory journalism', this type of coverage constitutes a form of counterveillance – itself a variant of 'sousveillance' – which is a term coined by Steve Mann (1998) to describe unmediated forms of bottom-up surveillance.

A key moment in the modern history of this kind of surveillance was the case of Rodney King, who, in March 1991, upon being stopped after a high-speed car chase with California Highway Patrol, disobeyed police commands to lie down, which resulted in him receiving a pro-longed beating by Los Angeles Police Department officers that was videotaped by a bystander. Almost a year later, in April 1992, the police officers were acquitted by a jury, sparking the Los Angeles riots, which lasted just under five days and ended with 50 people killed, more than 2,000 injured, and over 8,000 arrested. To Dennis (2008: 348), this most memorable event in spectator recordings 'heralded the power of the handheld video recorder to capture, store, and transmit images that could now be reproduced globally in almost an instant [and] gave out a message: that living in the eye of the camera meant a person, people, institutions, and organizations were no longer insular and immune'.

The advent of digital media technologies clearly provides greater scope than ever before for police accountability, not only in everyday scenarios, such as the King case, but also in protest and public order settings. New digital technologies thus transform capabilities for 'dis-ruptive disclosure', for the surveillance of policing, and mean 'the tactics of maintaining secrecy, keeping silent and practicing conceal-ment are less available to police now' (Goldsmith 2010: 920). In short, these technologies enable the exposure of alleged police misconduct to mass audiences. Importantly, this 'new visibility', as Goldsmith (2010: 925–926) calls it, relates largely to police use of force and police bru-tality, which, we might add, is accentuated in public order and protest policing, simply because that type of policing is, by definition, more visible.

While maintaining silence and preserving secrecy are legitimate police practices in lawful covert operations, for example, they can also be defensive manoeuvres to avoid public embarrassment and formal accountability (Goldsmith 2010: 915). However, the police's 'accountability' (i.e., keeping up normal appearances via forms of impression management within the control of the police) has been greatly diminished and, in turn, their accountability to the court of public opinion greatly increased with the advent of mobile phone cameras, video-sharing platforms like YouTube, and social networking sites such as Facebook. Indeed, while Haggerty and Ericson (2000: 618) recognize these developments have not led to 'a complete democratic levelling of the hierarchy of surveillance', they nevertheless constitute a positive and productive effect of the surveillant assemblage:

> . . . the monitoring of the powerful has been eased by the proliferation of relatively inexpensive video cameras. These allow the general public to tape instances of police brutality, and have given rise to inner-city citizen response teams which monitor police radios and arrive at the scene camera-in-hand to record police behaviour.
>
> (Haggerty and Ericson 2000: 618)

BOX 8.4 POLICING'S NEW VISIBILITY: THE CASE OF IAN TOMLINSON

Since the Battle of Seattle in 1999, Indymedia, the Internet-based network of Independent Media Centres, has played a prominent role in anti-globalization demonstrations that have taken place at high-profile protest events, such as at the Group of Eight (G8) meeting in Genoa in 2001 where 'amateur journalism' and 'native reporting' – both species of citizen journalism – 'provided a powerful counter to the dominant mainstream media coverage of the protests' (Atton 2003: 10). The relationship between citizen journalism and the new visibility of policing at international protest events was also evident at the 2007 Asia-Pacific Economic Cooperation (APEC) Sydney summit, which we looked at toward the end of Chapter 7 (see also Figure 8.3). However, the recent case of the death of Ian Tomlinson provides a powerful example of how citizen journalism can effect real change, such as intervening in the administration of justice.

During the protests surrounding the London Group of Twenty (G20) summit in 2009, Tomlinson was filmed being struck with a baton and pushed to the ground by a police officer. Soon after, he died. Tomlinson was not a protestor (he was, in fact, walking home from work at the time), and although most citizen journalism tends to be practiced by activists and other people committed to political causes (Loader and Mercea 2012: 4), the video footage was shot by an American tourist, Christopher La Jaunie, who initially failed

© Russotwins/Alamy

Figure 8.3 Police officer and camera crew during the APEC protests in Sydney, Australia, September 2007

to realize the significance of the video, but, when he did, he forwarded it to *The Guardian* newspaper (Scott Bray 2013: 457, 468). This altered the formal course of events, revealing the power in citizen journalism.

Prior to the release of the footage, the UK Home Office pathologist determined Tomlinson died of natural causes, and his death was subject to a review by the Independent Police Complaints Commission (IPCC). After the video's release, however, the IPCC assumed investigative control of the case and subsequently conducted three other independent investigations in response to complaints from Tomlinson's family. The video release also precipitated further autopsies and informed a coronial verdict of 'unlawful killing' (Scott Bray 2013: 455). That verdict led the Crown Prosecution Service (CPS) to review its original decision not to prosecute the police officer, PC Simon Harwood, shown striking and pushing Tomlinson, and charge him with manslaughter; although ultimately Harwood was acquitted, resulting in what has been described as an instance of 'paradoxical justice' (Scott Bray 2013: 471).

Like the earlier case of Jean Charles de Menezes, the Brazilian illegal migrant who was shot dead by Metropolitan police officers on London's Underground in 2005, controversy surrounded the original decision of the CPS not to prosecute in the Tomlinson case (Greer and McLaughlin 2012: 284–285). Indeed, the viral spread of the Tomlinson G20 footage via the Internet caused Brazilian viewers to reflect upon the de Menezes shooting and led to the formation of a Facebook group (Goldsmith 2010: 923–924). Although that fell short of an Internet campaign for justice, in other contexts the Internet has been used as an extra-legal means of campaigning for justice (Tyson 2009).

In certain respects, citizen journalism resembles Altheide and Snow's (1991) notion of 'post-journalism', as described earlier in relation to Greenpeace's media stunts, which are prepackaged to such a degree as to obviate the need for professional journalists. Indeed, although in its pure form citizen journalism entails unmediated bottom-up surveillance (sousveillance), it is also a mode of civic participation that is increasingly incorporated into mainstream news media (see Dennis 2008: 349–350), as attested to by Alan Rusbridger, editor-in-chief at *The Guardian*, who, recognizing its significance in the case of Ian Tomlinson, has said: '"I am sometimes giddy with the possibilities new technologies offer us . . . for being embedded in the most astonishing network of information the world has ever seen or could ever have imagined"' (Wilby 2012: 37). To illustrate his point, Rusbridger noted how *The Guardian*'s exposé of the police's role in the death of Ian Tomlinson at the G20 protests in London 2009 was based on eyewitnesses' use of mobile phone camera footage, which amounted to a situation where '"old-fashioned reporting was allied with the mass observation of people we wouldn't call reporters but who were, on the day, able to do acts of journalism"' (Wilby 2012: 37).

THE 2011 ENGLISH RIOTS: DIGITAL MOB OR MEDIATED CROWD?

While citizen journalism and other forms of sousveillance can be used productively and positively for good purposes, Kingsley Dennis (2008: 348) shows these forms of surveillance may also have 'dark undertones', some of which reawaken old fears of early collective behaviour theories relating to the perceived dangers of the mass psychology of mobs and crowds that we examined in Chapter 2. Hence, the increased ubiquity of and access to 'miniaturised and mobilized surveillance devices is thus empowering both individualistic acts of "good intentions" as well as encouraging mob activism' (Dennis 2008: 350). Accordingly, we witness the emergence of 'digital mobs' (Dennis 2008: 35), evident in instances of 'virtual-vigilantism' (Dennis 2008: 348, 351, 355), which involve forms of public Internet humiliation, such as naming and shaming, reminiscent of community punishments meted out in medieval times.

Stephanie Baker (2012) has shown how this use of new media played a role in the wake of the riots that occurred in England in August 2011. She argues that despite the apparent intelligence failure of the police, who did not integrate social media services into their tactics for policing the riots, new social media nevertheless played a part in the policing of the riots, whereby 'social networking sites operated as public surveillance platforms to locate those responsible for the unrest. The blogging platform Tumblr, for example, hosted an account called "Catch a Looter", which encouraged users to disseminate photos of looters and thereby expose their identities to the police' (Baker 2012: 185).

Just as the perceived injustice of the acquittal of the officers filmed beating Rodney King sparked the Los Angeles riots in 1992, the 2011 riots in England were triggered by the fatal shooting of Mark Duggan by police in Tottenham, North London (Martin and Scott Bray 2013: 642). The widespread sense of social injustice surrounding this 'social tragedy' was a key factor precipitating the riots, with social media contributing to the ensuing disorder 'by facilitating feelings of solidarity and empowering collective action' (Baker 2012: 176). Clearly, says Baker (2012: 175), new social media had a notable effect in contributing to the riots evidenced, for instance, by:

. . . symbolic images posted on Facebook of burning police cars in Tottenham, and protestors calling on members of the community to avenge Mark Duggan's death [which] engendered a sense of social cohesion by connecting actors from disparate geographies into a common symbolic space.

In an argument reminiscent of Mario Diani's (2000) earlier ideas about the impact of 'computer mediated communication' on social movement networks, Baker (2012: 176) argues that the protests associated with the 2011 riots gave rise to the formation of a *mediated crowd*, 'wherein the interactive online relationships enabled by social media connected aggrieved users into intense relationships that transpired offline'.

For Baker (2012: 172–173), it is important to recognize both the online and offline aspects of this new form of mediated crowd membership so as to counteract 'technological determinism', which, in the case of the English riots, gave rise to a common perception in the mainstream media and among commentators that social media was solely to blame for recruiting rioters and looters – thus gainsaying the human agency and emotionality of the *people* who were motivated to riot. A more nuanced approach, she argues, enables us to appreciate the role of new social media, not only in contributing to the speed and scale with which the riots emerged, but it also allows us to understand how some used social media as a form of resistance, choosing not to participate, as well as helping to orchestrate the cleanup in the immediate aftermath of the riots. In this sense, Baker (2012: 182) argues, 'Twitter operated as an extension of the public sphere'. The establishment via Twitter of Riot Cleanup, for example, 'operated as a collective act of resistance against rioters with online social networks transpiring into an offline social movement' (Baker 2012: 183).

ARAB SPRING

Technological determinism during and after the English riots of 2011 led to calls for authorities to censor social networking services, such as BlackBerry's instant messenger service, 'by removing hashtags, temporarily shutting down services, and banning individual users thought to be responsible for inciting the riots' (Baker 2012: 171). Baker (2012: 171–172) shows how this not only appeared to contradict the liberal democratic principles of British society, but also how '[t]alk of such a move drew parallels to contemporary methods of censorship used by authoritarian regimes during the Arab Spring, and was consequently publicly criticized'. However, the parallels do not end there.

Referring to the uprisings against despotic regimes across the Middle East and North Africa during 2011, it has been said of the Arab Spring that the 'constant narrative arc of the uprisings involves digital media' (Howard and Hussain 2011: 46). Accordingly, repressive governments across the region adopted what Howard and Hussain (2011: 44) call the 'desperate tactic' of attempting to block Internet access and Facebook use, a strategy that was foiled by hacktivist groups Anonymous and Telecomix 'by building new software to help activists get around state firewalls' (Howard and Hussain 2011: 37; see also McBain 2014).

Given the centrality of new social media in the Arab Spring, it is hardly surprising those 'countries that experienced the most dramatic protests were among the region's most thoroughly wired, and their societies boasted large numbers of people with the technical knowledge to use these new media to strong effect' (Howard and Hussain 2011: 46). In Egypt and Tunisia, for instance, almost everyone has access to a mobile phone (Howard and Hussain 2011: 37–38). On the other hand, say Howard and Hussain (2011: 47), 'the countries with the lowest levels of technology proliferation have also tended to have the weakest democratization movements'.

Although Howard and Hussain (2011: 47) believe it is too early to claim the Arab Spring represented a wave of democratization – indeed, a year on from the Arab Spring, it was argued the protests for democracy had been hijacked by Islamist parties, such as Egypt's Muslim Brotherhood (Roy 2012; see also Gerges 2011) – they argue, '[d]igital media are important precisely because they had a role in popular mobilizations against authoritarian rule that were unlike anything seen before in the region'. That is why, as stated in Chapter 6, the use of social media during the Arab Spring could be considered as adding to the protest repertoire of Islamic activism. Indeed, while discontent had existed prior to the Arab Spring (Kurzman 2012), the role of digital media, and especially the Internet and mobile phones, was a pivotal contributing factor:

> . . . spreading protest messages, driving coverage by mainstream broadcasters, connecting frustrated citizens with one another, and helping them to realize that they could take shared action regarding shared grievances. For years, discontent had been stirring, but somehow the drivers of protest never proved sufficient until mobile phones and the Web began pervading the region.
>
> (Howard and Hussain 2011: 41)

Howard and Hussain (2011: 41) go on to say that although it is never wise 'to look for simple, solitary causes of a revolution, to say nothing of a string of revolutions [. . .] the use of digital media to rouse and organize opposition has furnished a common thread'. Two things should be noted from this comment and the previous quotation. First, while digital media were crucial to the Arab Spring, as with movements in other contexts (Funke and Wolfson 2014), traditional media sources also played their part. However, unlike the 2011 En, riots, where 'old' media tended to focus negatively on working-cla and minority groups (Baker 2012: 179), thereby reinforcing extant power structures (Baker 2012: 187), the role of mainstream news media in the Arab Spring was altogether more positive (cp. Almeida and Lichbach 2003). For example, Al Jazeera had a highly innovative new media team, which transposed its traditional news product to social media sites and made use of the preexisting social networks of its online users:

> But a key aspect of its success was its use of digital media to collect information and images from countries in which its journalists had been harassed or banned. These digital networks gave Al Jazeera's journalists access to more sources, and gave a second life to their news products.
>
> (Howard and Hussain 2011: 45)

Second, it should be noted that, as Baker (2012) does with respect to the English riots (see earlier), the Arab Spring was not only an online, digital revolution. Certainly, as with the English riots, the speed and viral spread of the uprisings during the Arab Spring can be accounted for by the use of new social media such as Twitter, YouTube, and Facebook. However, it is equally important to recognize that alongside the virtual spaces created by bloggers and activists to produce alternative newscasts and a place for political discussion, protests also occurred in actual public spaces (Howard and Hussain 2011: 36). Indeed, this is also something the Arab Spring had in common with Occupy, which was inspired partly by the Arab Spring (Gaby and Caren 2012: 368; Kerton 2012: 302; Pickerill and Krinsky 2012: 284). Eltantawy and Wiest (2011: 1212) draw directly upon resource mobilization theory to argue 'a significant resource for the Egyptian revolution that was utilized effectively was social media'. Similarly, Gaby and Caren (2012) contend that by allowing Occupy activists to post shocking images online, social networking sites such as Facebook and Twitter proved important recruitment tools and powerful resources that enabled the rapid and widespread reach of information (see also Tremayne 2014). According to Thorson et al. (2013), Twitter and YouTube also provided media sharing across large-scale networks of videos, which acted as repositories of movement resources that allowed activists, armed with cell phones and digital cameras, to produce footage as eyewitness accounts of protest (and police) activity. Insofar as video footage was used to monitor the policing of Occupy, Thorson et al. (2013: 426) say, it fit squarely with the notion of sousveillance, which 'keeps watch on those in power in an effort to equalize the asymmetrical nature of the relationship'.

Notwithstanding the significant role played by digital social media in the Occupy movement, like the Arab Spring (and the English riots), offline activity also constituted an important part of the protest. To Pickerill and Krinsky (2012: 285), 'Occupy was mediated through a mix of "old" and "new" methods of diffusion [which] worked with electronic media, and also through interpersonal ties and existing alliances'. Thus, alongside so-called Facebook activism, as we saw in Chapter 7, offline activity was a central element of the Occupy protests, 'involving activists gathering in central city locations for hours, days or even months on end' (Gaby and Caren 2012: 369). Hence, Pickerill and Krinsky (2012: 285) say:

> . . . Occupy will doubtless be celebrated as a product of an online age of 24/7 interaction and rampant social networks, but there remains an interesting tension between the utility of online social networks for protest and the place-based utility of personal ties.

CONCLUSION

In his review of the literature on social movements and new information and communication technologies (ICTs), Garrett (2006: 209) suggests the ability provided by new ICTs to disseminate information rapidly may increase political accountability, since '[e]lites are more likely to behave in a manner consistent with citizen concerns if they work in an environment where they must assume their actions are being observed and that news of any inappropriate actions – even those traditionally outside the media spotlight – will quickly reach the public'. Clearly, this resonates with ideas discussed earlier to do with sousveillance, counterveillance, and citizen journalism. On the other hand, he argues, activists' reliance on ICTs also provides opportunities for 'demobilization'. For instance, when cyber activists become too threatening, they could be denied access to resources by elites and their allies who often own and/or control the ICT infrastructure (Garrett 2006: 210). Alternatively, network architecture, such as firewalls and controlled gateways, can be modified by states to preserve censorship (Garrett 2006: 214). We have seen how that occurred in several countries during the Arab Spring and how this kind of state control over access to information is something Wikileaks was set up to oppose.

As well as providing for more political accountability, Garrett argues the use of ICTs tends to increase levels of political participation by facilitating the creation of new low-cost forms of participation, such as accessing information on the Internet (see also Rosenkrands 2004: 72; Loader 2008). This provides some resolution to the 'free rider' problem, which, it will be recalled from Chapter 2, provides that people only participate in collective action if the benefits to them of participation outweigh the costs. Hence, Garrett (2006: 206) shows how ICTs 'allow very small contributions to be effectively aggregated'. Examples of such 'micro-contributions' include 'click and give' websites. Moreover, he suggests, the act of making even small contributions may foster a greater sense of obligation and commitment to a cause (Garrett 2006: 206–207).

This idea appears to resonate with Greenpeace's reliance on a passive public, which, fatigued by street protesting, is more inclined to 'couch potato activism' (as discussed earlier). While this model applied originally to Greenpeace's television campaigning, digital technologies such as the Internet and new social media will conceivably only intensify privatized forms of political participation. Indeed, as Loader and Mercea (2012: 3) state, the citizen equipped with social media 'no longer has to be a passive consumer of political party propaganda, government spin or mass media news, but is instead actually enabled to challenge discourses, share alternative perspectives and publish their own opinions'. However, we must not fall prey to the kind of 'technological determinism' described earlier, recognizing the human agency behind the use of new media, and understanding that the 'acquisition of an iPhone or access to a social networking site does not in itself determine the engagement of citizens' (Loader and Mercea 2012: 3).

In the case of Occupy, online media 'enabled a large audience to register support without physically joining a camp, and for ideas and strategies to be shared more easily' (Pickerill and Krinksy 2012: 285). However, as the examples of Occupy, the Arab Spring, and the English riots demonstrate, even in the digital age, offline activism nevertheless remains an important feature of public protest and social movement activity. Therefore, as discussed in Chapter 7, space, whether physical or virtual, is an important aspect of the study of social movements, which, in the era of new social media, say Pickerill and Krinsky (2012: 285), needs 'to move beyond the superficial celebration of digital mediation and unpack the (particularly scalar) implications of this use of mixed media'.

This brings us to a final point with which to segue into the next chapter. It is something of a cliché now that, as Garrett (2006: 207) puts it, ICTs facilitate community creation, reinforce existing social networks, and help maintain geographically dispersed networks. Hence, as well as increasing individual participation, new ICTs give rise to decentred, nonhierarchical forms of organization, increasing the likelihood of what Gerhards and Rucht (1992) call 'mesomobilization', that is, 'a high degree of co-ordination between movement networks across a broad geographical range without creating fixed hierarchical organizational forms (a network of networks)' (Scott and Street 2000: 231).

Certainly, a noted feature of contemporary protests relying on new social media, such as Occupy and the Arab Spring, has been their nonhierarchical and amorphous form (Howard and Hussain 2011: 37, 48; Kerton 2012: 307). Moreover, while Occupy, in particular, has been celebrated for its international reach, as Pickerill and Krinksy (2012: 284) rightly point out, 'that does not mean it was a global movement per se'. Indeed, while Internet-based diffusion was crucial to Occupy's globality, 'questions remain as to how international solidarity can be usefully practiced across such vast distances' (Pickerill and Krinsky 2012: 284). We will take up this and other matters relating to transnational activism and global social movements in the next chapter.

SUGGESTED READINGS

The following texts and resources can be used to explore issues raised in this chapter.

Books

Webster, F. (ed.) (2001) *Culture and Politics in the Information Age: A New Politics?* London: Routledge.

This is an early edited volume that considers how new media and information technologies, like the Internet, are reshaping political mobilization, protest, and communication in the twenty-first century.

Gerbaudo, P. (2012) *Tweets and the Streets: Social Media and Contemporary Activism.* London: Pluto Press.

Gillan, K., Pickerill, J., and Webster, F. (2008) *Anti-War Activism: New Media and Protest in the Information Age.* Houndmills: Palgrave Macmillan.

Han, S. (2011) *Web 2.0.* London: Routledge.

van de Donk, W., Loader, B. D., Nixon, P. G., and Rucht, D. (eds.) (2004) *Cyberprotest: New Media, Citizens and Social Movements.* London: Routledge.

Each of these books explores the impact of new media technologies on social movements, activism, and informational politics.

Briggs, D. (ed.) (2012) *The English Riots of 2011: A Summer of Discontent.* Sherfield: Waterside Press.

In this chapter, we have focused only on the role of new social media during the 2011 English riots. This edited book contains a number of essays about other aspects of the riots.

Journals

Dennis, K. (2008) 'Keeping a Close Watch – The Rise of Self-Surveillance and the Threat of Digital Exposure' *The Sociological Review* 56(3): 347–357.

This article provides a brief introduction to some key ideas in the surveillance literature, including panopticism, sousveillance, and citizen journalism.

Garrett, R. K. (2006) 'Protest in an Information Society: A Review of Literature on Social Movements and New ICTs' *Information, Communication and Society* 9(2): 202–224.

Although now a little outmoded by recent events discussed in this chapter, such as Occupy and the Arab Spring, Garrett's literature review still provides some useful ways of thinking about the relationship between new media technologies and social movements. The following article also contains a brief discussion of some key themes in the field:

Loader, B. D. (2008) 'Social Movements and New Media' *Sociology Compass* 2(6): 1920–1933.

The following journal special issues provide in-depth analyses of some of the issues considered in this chapter:

Information, Communication and Society 12(6) (2009): 'Changing Politics Through Digital Networks'.
Interface 4(1) (2012): 'The Season of Revolution: The Arab Spring and European Mobilizations', available at: <www.interfacejournal.net/2012/05/interface-volume-4-issue-1-the-season-of-revolution-the-arab-spring-and-european-mobilizations/>.
Mobilization 17(4) (2012): 'Understanding the Middle East Uprisings'.
Surveillance and Society 6(3) (2007): 'Surveillance and Resistance'.

CHAPTER 9

Global activism

INTRODUCTION

At the end of the last chapter, we considered briefly the important role played by new media and information technologies in transnational mobilization. And we looked at the Arab Spring and Occupy movements as prime examples. Because the use of new media, information, and communication technologies looks likely to continue to influence future global protest, this is one of our concerns in this chapter, too, where, among other things, we look at how the global justice movement has used the Internet extensively to organize international campaigns (Staggenborg 2011: 47).

Another issue we touched upon in the last chapter, which also concerns us here, has to do with whether social movements that have an international reach can be considered truly *global* movements. Put another way, we ought not assume transnational activism necessarily equates to concern with globalization. Indeed, transnational mobilization may originate in concerns that are of a local or national nature. Not surprisingly, then, issues relating to transnational activism and global mobilization that we examine in this chapter are relevant, in some way or other, to questions of *scale*, which we looked in Chapter 7, when we considered struggles over space.

Consideration of many of the issues explored in this chapter requires some knowledge and understanding of globalization, which is discussed later in terms of its technological, economic, political, and cultural dimensions, as well as in relation to its positive and negative effects. Generally speaking, anti-globalization/global justice activists regard the hegemony of neoliberal capitalism to be the principal cause of many of the ills of globalization. Although when confronted by the seemingly unstoppable juggernaut of globalization, resistance may appear futile, effective opposition to globalizing processes has been evident at the local grassroots level. Moreover, transnational advocacy networks and social movements have been able to take advantage of international structures of opportunity created by the formation of a 'global civil society', which houses international institutions, such as the United Nations (UN), that are receptive to the demands of transnational nongovernmental organizations (NGOs) and movements. One development here that has gathered momentum, which may continue into the future, is global activism around international human rights. We look at this towards the end of the chapter.

TRANSNATIONAL ACTIVISM AND GLOBALIZATION

In Chapter 8, we considered Pickerill and Krinsky's (2012: 284) contention that, although movements such as Occupy have an extensive international reach, this does not necessarily make them global social movements per se. On this issue, Olesen (2005: 49) argues that while:

There is widespread agreement that social movements are becoming increasingly transnational and that this development is somehow linked with globalization [. . .] instances of transnational activism are rarely transnational in the same way and for the same reasons and are not even necessarily related to globalization.

For example, he says, transnational activism may be spurred by a local or national event or situation, which is what happens when activists react to human rights violations in far-off places, or when they respond to issues relating to global warming:

What emerges from these points is that transnational mobilization does not have a necessary direction from the global to the local or vice versa; nor does it take place only in some abstract global sphere. Rather, transnational mobilization takes place simultaneously on local, national and global levels.

(Olesen 2005: 50)

To Olesen (2005: 50), '[h]ow (and whether) these levels are inte-grated is [. . .] a question of the issues at play and the way in which social actors construct them'. In other terms, globalization 'does not necessarily lead to transnational mobilization; the missing link between globalization and transnational mobilization is a process of social construction that links the local, the national and the global' (Olesen 2005: 50).

Olesen's (2005: 50) main objective, then, is to integrate the global-ization literature and the social constructivist framing approach to social movements (see also Chapter 3), as well as, more generally, 'to improve our understanding of the relationship between the concepts of globalization and transnational mobilization'. He identifies one of the most troubling ways the concept of globalization has been misused in analyses of transnational mobilization as the way in which global-ization is endowed with a strong degree of agency, which effectively 'reifies globalization and draws an image of it as a force at work outside the reach of social actors; something that forces them in certain direc-tions and increasingly divides the world into global and local spaces' (Olesen 2005: 52). This is something we have encountered previously in Chapter 7, when we saw how Feldman (2002: 42) argues that in contrast to top-down approaches portraying social movements as reac-tive to globalizing pressures, the international indigenous peoples' movement has played a very active (bottom-up) role in what 'ulti-mately amounts to centuries of indigenous peoples' efforts to shape and force open international institutions and fields of mobilization'.

To integrate globalization and framing perspectives, Olesen looks at transnational mobilization through the lens of 'injustice frames' (see Chapter 3), which, in the context of globalization, operate as 'trans-national injustice frames'. The example of neoliberalism is especially relevant here, since neoliberal restructuring processes during the 1970s and 1980s have been used extensively as 'the axis of transnational injus-tice frames' (Olesen 2005: 55). Hence, notwithstanding national and regional differences:

> . . . it is fair to say that never in the course of human history have a larger number of people been affected by the same complex of political and economic ideas. This situation has facilitated the potential for constructing transnational injustice frames with a broad appeal on a world scale.
>
> (Olesen 2005: 55)

While the extensive impact of neoliberalism on a world scale is an empirical fact, argues Olesen (2005: 55), its greater significance lies in the fact the people across the globe have become increasingly aware of the influence and negative consequences of neoliberalism, and it is this 'global consciousness' that presupposes the construction of the transnational injustice frame of neoliberalism. Moreover, he says, the injustice frame of neoliberalism falls under the broader 'radical democratic action master frame' (Olesen 2005: 57), which, although Olesen does not state as much, could presumably be conceived of as a 'transnational master frame'.

Similar arguments have been made about the 'movement of movements' against neoliberal global capitalism, also described as alter-globalization, anti-capitalist, or global justice movements (Cox and Nilsen 2007: 424). For instance, Gemma Edwards shows how what she calls the 'alternative globalization movement' originated in the global south in the struggle of the Zapatistas (Edwards 2014: 161), who were themselves involved in creating a global 'master frame' (Benford and Snow 2000), 'arguing their struggle was best cast as part of a global struggle against "neoliberalism"' (Edwards 2014: 176). This is why despite being labeled the *anti*-globalization movement by the media, activists preferred to call it the *alter*-globalization movement, since it was not against globalization per se, but 'was specifically rejecting dominant neoliberal forms of capitalism, whilst creating a diversity of alternative networks' (Halvorsen 2012: 429). Before considering opposition and resistance to neoliberal globalization/global neoliberalism, we should first outline some of the principal features of globalization.

WHAT IS GLOBALIZATION?

One could devote an entire book to the topic of globalization. For our purposes, though, it is sufficient to provide a brief overview of its main elements and set out some of the reasons globalizing processes have attracted criticism and been the target of social protest. The first thing to note is that although there was a steep change in interest in globalization from the 1980s, processes of globalization had been occurring for some time before that. This was something recognized by Immanuel Wallerstein (1976), among others, who noted that, historically, modernity has involved the interdependence of world economies, nation-states, and cultural systems. Certainly, however, the technological revolution of the 1980s caused an intensification of global interdependence, allowing, for instance, greater flows of capital in international markets and information flows via the Internet. In this sense, then, the *technological* and *economic* transformations that took place towards the end of the second millennium are two moments of historical significance in the process of globalization:

> A technological revolution, centred around information technologies, began to reshape, at accelerated pace, the material basis of society. Economies throughout the world have become globally interdependent, introducing a new form of relationship between economy, state, and society, in a system of variable geometry.
>
> (Castells 1996: 1)

Among other things, *economic globalization* involves increased mobility of capital and labour. Transnational corporations, in particular, have taken advantage of this, locating the production arm of their operations in the 'free trade zones' of developing countries, which have few, if any, labour standards (e.g., no minimum wage), as well as providing tax breaks as financial incentives for the 'inward investment' of these corporations. This, in turn, has given rise to an 'international division of labour', whereby the vast majority of goods consumed in the developed world are now produced in developing countries, while the economies of developed countries are geared increasingly to the provision of services. Consequently, globalization has led to polarization, which, for Bauman (1998: 2), is epitomized in the distinction between the *tourist*, whose experience is one of post-modern freedom, and *vagabonds*, who 'are on the move because they have been pushed from behind – spiritually uprooted from the place that holds no promise'.

Against Bauman's somewhat fatalistic view, Hardt and Negri (2000) regard the mass movement of nomadic proletarians as a potential source of threat to capitalism, which is unable to control the rebellious and autonomous flows of highly mobile 'immaterial labour'. In his review of their work, Kalyvas (2003: 269) explains that Hardt and Negri celebrate mass worker nomadism 'as a supreme emancipatory, anti-capitalist force', since '[t]he more labour moves, the more it enters into an unmediated confrontation with global capitalism [which] also explains why the power to move is portrayed by the authors as an affirmation of freedom, cooperation, spontaneous networks, and creative mixtures'. Social movements play a part here, too. The activities of transnational corporations are the target of anti-corporate protestors, including anti-sweatshop activists (discussed in Chapter 4), who, in turn, can be considered part of a broader anti-globalization/anti-capitalist movement that is critical of global neoliberalism, which provides the context within which transnational corporations operate.

Neoliberalism is both an *economic* and a *political* phenomenon. Accordingly, in his book on the subject, Harvey (2005: 2) defines neoliberalism as a 'theory of political economic practices', whose project, as we saw in Chapter 4, has been 'to re-establish the conditions for capital accumulation and to restore the power of economic elites' (Harvey 2005: 19) by setting up 'those military, defence, police, and legal structures and functions required to secure private property rights and to guarantee, by force if need be, the proper functioning of markets' (Harvey 2005: 2). The focus on free markets heralds what Michael Pusey (1991: 10) has called 'the triumph of economic rationalism', such that, 'primacy is given to "the economy", second place to the political order, and third place to the social order'.

The increasing global hegemony of neoliberalism since the 1970s has seen deregulation, privatization, and state withdrawal from many areas of social provision become commonplace across the Western world (Harvey 2005: 3), which is one reason why, as we saw in Chapter 4, some contemporary social movements remain focused on 'old' and newly relevant survival issues to do with material (rather than post-material) well-being. Indeed, while proponents of neoliberalism contend human well-being is best advanced and protected by 'liberating individual entrepreneurial freedoms and skills within an institutional framework characterized by strong private property rights, free market and free trade' (Harvey 2005: 2), its detractors argue the economically reductionist individualism of neoliberalism has had multiple deleterious social effects. For example, it has caused a hollowing out of civil society and concomitant decline in the influence of 'social capital', including less engagement in politics and government, less involvement in volunteer organizations, and a general trend to social and civic disengagement (Putnam 1995). Arguably, too, the widespread accommodation of neoliberalism in mainstream politics and broad acceptance that there is no alternative to the present system – what Mark Fisher (2009) calls 'capitalist realism' – has led to an impoverishment of the public sphere, as well as widespread disillusionment with politics (see Dean 2014), which we discussed in Chapter 1.

The ultimate consequence of the operation of neoliberalism, on a global scale, was the global financial crisis (GFC) of 2008, which led many liberal democratic governments to introduce austerity measures, the effects of which, as we have seen in previous parts of this book, were opposed by movements such as Occupy and the Indignados. However, despite the protests, the funding of the bank bailout by austerity measures continued unabated, highlighting just how hard it is, in practice, to resist neoliberal globalization and pose a genuine challenge to the current system, let alone offer a viable alternative (issues we consider shortly). It also underscores Harvey's (2005: 19) point, made earlier, about the purpose of neoliberalism being to reestablish conditions for capital accumulation and restore the power of economic elites.

BOX 9.1 GLOBAL CIVIL SOCIETY

One of the most important *political* effects of globalization has been the apparent decline of the sovereign nation-state. According to Martin Shaw (1994: 649), that 'has been accompanied by an increasing crisis of civil societies: traditional national symbolic systems have declined in potency, and traditional institutions like parties and churches have lost support'. Hence, argues Shaw (1994: 649), '[t]he debate about global society has brought into focus the issue of an emerging "global civil society"'. Shaw (1994: 650) thinks about global civil society in terms of a civil society that 'increasingly represents itself globally, across nation-state boundaries, through the formation of global institutions'. He proposes at least three major types of organizations that comprise the emergent global civil society:

> . . . formal organizations linking national institutions (organizations of parties, churches, unions, professions, educational bodies, media, etc.); linkages of informal networks and movements (e.g. of women's, gay and peace groups and movements); and globalist organizations (e.g. Amnesty, Greenpeace, Médecins sans Frontières), which are established with a specifically global orientation, global membership and activity of global scope.
>
> (Shaw 1994: 650)

Just as social movements are important collective actors in civil society, they also play a key role in global civil society, which 'can be seen as a response to the globalization of state power and a source of pressure for it' (Shaw 1994: 650). An example, here, is the international indigenous peoples' movement, which, as discussed in Chapter 7, has carved out a space for itself globally, actively shaping and forcing open international institutions and fields of mobilization. Hence, Feldman (2002: 39) says, we have 'seen the prospering of co-operative projects between indigenous NGOs and communities, state agencies and organs like the UN Development Program, UNICEF, the International Labour Organization and the World Bank, International Monetary Fund, Organization of American States'.

The preeminent scholar in this field is John Keane (2003: xi–xii), who has observed the promiscuousness of the concept of global civil society for attracting a wide variety of supporters the world over, so that '[w]hen used by its friends as an ethical standard [. . .] it champions the political vision of a world founded on non-violent, legally sanctioned power-sharing arrangements among many different and interconnected forms of socio-economic life that are distinct from governmental institutions'. In order to consolidate its various meanings, Keane has devised the following ideal-typical definition of global civil society:

> . . . a dynamic non-governmental system of interconnected socio-economic institutions that straddle the whole earth, and that have complex effects that are felt in its four corners. Global civil society is neither a static object nor a *fait accompli*. It is an unfinished project that consists of sometimes thick, sometimes thinly stretched networks, pyramids and hub-and-spoke clusters of socio-economic institutions and actors who organise themselves across borders, with the deliberate aim of drawing the world together in new ways. These non-governmental institutions and actors tend to pluralize power and to problematize violence; consequently, their peaceful or 'civil' effects are felt everywhere, here and there, far and wide, to and from local areas, through wider regions, to the planetary level itself.
>
> (Keane 2003: 8)

From this rather abstract definition, Keane (2003: 8–17) distils the following five key features of global civil society that highlight its historical distinctiveness:

1. It refers to *nongovernmental* structures and activities;
2. It is a form of *society*, which 'refers to a vast, sprawling non-governmental constellation of many institutionalized structures, associations and networks within which individual and group actors are interrelated and functionally interdependent';
3. It involves *civility* or 'respect for others expressed as politeness towards and acceptance of strangers';
4. It contains both strong traces of *pluralism* and *strong conflict potential*; and
5. It is *global*, which refers to 'politically framed and circumscribed social relations that stretch across and underneath state boundaries and other governmental forms'.

Global civil society is an important aspect of *political globalization*, and we will return to consider it again in various parts of this chapter when we look at transnational advocacy networks, international opportunity structures, and the institutionalization of international human rights.

Along with its economic and political aspects, globalization also has important *cultural* dimensions. Much of the criticism here has been directed at the flattening and homogenizing of local cultures by the juggernaut of global capitalism. An oft-cited example is George's Ritzer's (1993: 1) notion of McDonaldization, by which he means 'the process by which the principles of the fast-food restaurant are coming to dominate more and more sectors of American society as well as the rest of the world'. In this way, Ritzer uses McDonald's as a metaphor for the increasing standardization that is taking place across societies, which some see as a process synonymous with Americanization.

However, even McDonald's caters for local tastes. So, in France you can have a glass of red wine with your Big Mac, while you can order an Aussie Burger in Australia. Hence, 'globalisation is marked cultur-ally by processes of "glocalization", whereby local cultures adapt and redefine any global cultural product to suit their own particular needs, beliefs and customs' (Giulianotti and Robertson 2004: 546). In their study of football, Giulianotti and Robertson show how although the world's major clubs are transnational corporations that drive the game's contemporary globalization, the 'glocality' of these transnational cor-porations is also observable. Hence, all clubs are 'ethnocentric', in that they retain key symbolic ties to 'home' (Giulianotti and Robertson 2004: 552). They do so most notably through name, headquarters, home stadia, branding, strip colours, and by emphasizing their local support base:

> However, as clubs like Manchester United establish marketing out-lets in Asia and North America, more 'polycentric' marketing possibilities arise. Deterritorialization would intensify if clubs were to play 'home' fixtures outside of their 'home' city, or to obfuscate their geographical origins.
>
> (Giulianotti and Robertson 2004: 552)

The concept of glocalization highlights the very real sense in which globalization does not merely steamroll local cultures, which experi-ence globalization in a variety of ways, adapting accordingly. Moreover, it calls attention to the fact that globalization is not all bad: for instance, technological developments associated with globalization, such as the Internet, have increased access to information, positively enabling peo-ple to gain greater insights into and understanding of 'other' cultures.

Glocalization also brings into relief questions of *scale*, which were discussed in Chapter 7 when we looked at struggles over space. Hence, for example, anti-globalization movements of 'the local', observes Mayer (2007: 93), 'increasingly see localities as the scale where global neoliberalism "touches down" to make itself felt, where global issues become localized'. In this way, then, 'the experience of neoliberalism is nuanced, subject to local variations and played out differently in differ-ent countries and cities across the world' (Martin 2011b: 39). In the case of urban movements in a globalizing world, Hamel et al. (2000: 2) have contested the typical view of urban social movements as being preoccupied with local issues, arguing they have always been 'extra-local', although admittedly that is more pronounced in the present period of globalization.

More recently, Uitermark and Nicholls (2012) have shown how local activist networks in Los Angeles and Amsterdam shaped the global trajectory of the Occupy movement, arguing that the relatively rich social movement milieu in Los Angeles as compared to the less rich 'associational soil' in Amsterdam, has meant that, in Los Angeles, Occupy's message continues to circulate, whereas, in Amsterdam, it has all but disappeared. By contrast, in their study of the global justice movement, Hadden and Tarrow (2007: 371) have shown how after 9/11 and in the wake of the Iraq War, the movement flourished in Europe, yet stagnated in the United States for the following three reasons: (i) a more repressive response to transnational protest, (ii) the negative effect of US politicians linking global terrorism with all kinds of transnational activism, and (iii) 'social movement spillout' whereby US activists became involved in a resurgent peace movement, turning their attention from the fight against global neoliberalism and towards domestic electoral politics 'to try to defeat the administration that had brought the country into an immoral and unwinnable war'.

BOX 9.2 THINK GLOBALLY, ACT LOCALLY: RESISTING GLOBALIZATION 'FROM BELOW'

While Uitermark and Nicholls (2012) are interested in local networks shaping a global movement, a consideration of global-local relations can equally raise the prospect, mentioned earlier, as to whether, and to what extent, it is possible to resist or challenge globalization. In his early attempt at theorizing the relationship between globalization and social movements, Leslie Sklair (1995) argued that although capitalism is increasingly organized on a global scale, opposition to capitalist practices tends to be most effective if it is locally based, which has come to be known as 'globalization from below' (Martin 2004: 42; della Porta et al. 2006). According to Sklair (1995: 501), this explains, in part, why movements working against global capitalism, such as the labour movement, have had some notable successes, but have generally failed globally (cf. Ayres 2001: 55). His point is this:

The dilemma is that the only chance that people in social movements have to succeed is by disrupting the local agencies with which they come into direct contact in their daily lives, rather than the more global institutions whose interests these agencies are serving directly, or, more often, indirectly.

(Sklair 1995: 499)

Moreover, 'while workers are often confused about whom (which representation of capital) to oppose when their interests (conditions of labour, livelihoods) are threatened [. . .] as capitalism globalizes, subordinate groups find difficulty in identifying their adversaries' (Sklair 1995: 499). Thus, Sklair (1995: 501) concludes that 'movements working against global capitalism have been singularly unsuccessful globally, though their prospects of challenging global capitalism locally and making this count globally, globalizing disruptions, seems more realistic'.

Hence, while the global organization of transnational corporations (TNCs) is far too powerful for locally organized labour to resist, when transnational corporations have been challenged, 'it has usually been due to local campaigns of disruption and counter-information against TNC malpractices which have attracted world-wide publicity' (Sklair 1995: 501). The campaign against the promotion by Nestlé of its infant formula in developing countries is a case where the local disruption of a transnational corporation's activities led to a widespread global challenge, the general boycotting of Nestlé products, as a form of resistance to capitalist consumerism, or 'disrupting consumerism' (Sklair 1995: 504–507).

A similar ethos underpins the Fair Trade movement, which is about consumers in affluent nations exercising their power by purchasing goods made by local producers in preference to goods produced by multinational corporations. In this way, Fair Trade is part of a wider 'social responsibility movement' – a subset of 'lifestyle movements', which we looked at in Chapter 6 – that 'encourages participants to "vote" with their dollars, buying from socially responsible companies (and boycotting others), supporting locally owned businesses, purchasing "fair trade" products, and making socially responsible investments' (Haenfler et al. 2012: 6). However, as Huey's research into the website linking of global and local food movements shows, there can be a disparity between global rhetoric and local engagement.

Sometimes, she says, global environmental organizations' opposition to agribusiness does not adequately offer links to local alternatives and projects. While local farmer's markets do connect to organizations with broader agendas, like Greenpeace, they do not link with other farmer's market associations beyond their part of the world. Hence, 'instead of crafting a movement to provide local alternatives globally, their global work is projected onto organizations with very broad missions to protect the environment and the rights of citizens in non-industrialized regions from the depredations of big business' (Huey 2005: 135).

TRANSNATIONAL ADVOCACY NETWORKS AND INTERNATIONAL OPPORTUNITY STRUCTURES

In various parts of this book, we have seen how a key goal (and dilemma) for many social movements is maintaining autonomy in the face of political incorporation or co-optation. Especially in Chapter 4, we saw how autonomy is reckoned to be crucially important to new social movements, although it has also been observed that to be successful all movements must connect their demands to 'institutionally imminent possibilities' (Giddens 1991a: 155). We can frame this controversy in terms of *political globalization* and global civil society, which, as we saw in Box 9.1, comprises international institutions, such as the UN, World Bank and International Monetary Fund (IMF), as well as international NGOs and global social movements, with the latter being regarded 'as the principal hope for the democratization of a newly forming global civil society' (Nash 2002: 438). In these terms, global civil society may be seen as an institutionally immanent transnational opportunity structure for global movement demands. Equally, global civil society could be thought of as the transnational equivalent of the new political space Alberto Melucci (1985: 815) sees contemporary movements occupying; that is, the intermediate public space between state and civil society, wherein movements strive to maintain their autonomy (see Chapter 4).

On globalization and social movements, Melucci (1992: 53, emphasis in original) has stated that 'how to *exist with the other* in a planetary world is the moral challenge of our time'. In other words, he argues, we need an ethic of coexistence: 'a situational ethic, capable of lending dignity to the individual decision and repairing the links between genders, cultures, the individual and the species, living beings, the cosmos' (Melucci 1997: 66). Therefore, it would seem that, to Melucci, a globalized world is simply a bigger version of 'complex society', and that his ideas about coexistence are quite similar to his ideas about the recognition and acceptance of difference and autonomy, albeit on a larger scale. Accordingly, global civil society might be thought of as a space that is autonomous of individual nation-states within which international organizations and transnational movements (co)operate.

While, as we saw earlier, globalization is a deep-rooted historical process, the formation of global civil society began, more recently, in the decades after the Second World War. This was a period when international NGOs proliferated, playing a key role in what Keck and Sikkink (1998) call 'transnational advocacy networks', which have been formed around human rights, peace, environmental, women's rights, and economic justice issues. As well as working through international institutional structures, such as those at the UN, these advocacy networks have supported, and expanded with, grassroots movements (Staggenborg 2011: 152). Importantly, however, given Olesen's (2005) contentions about transnational activism and globalization (discussed earlier), Cerny (2009: 154) argues 'these advocacy groups do not merely mimic domestic cause groups', for the following three reasons:

> In the first place, they target issues which are international and/or transnational in scope [. . .] Another reason is that they can bring together a range of coalition partners who would not normally be prepared to work closely with each other in a national setting for a variety of structural and historical reasons [. . .] Finally, the Internet and other new communications and information technologies give these coalitions great reach and flexibility in the ways they can target different agents in states, international institutions, academics, the media, and the like.
>
> (Cerny 2009: 154)

Cerny goes on to state that transnational advocacy groups have benefitted from a transformed field of action, which Krieger and Murphy (1998) call the 'transnational opportunity structure'. Essentially, this is the idea of the 'political opportunity structure' we encountered in Chapter 3 transposed into a global context. Hence, Cerny (2009: 154–155) says, while 'the traditional pressure group and social movement literature focuses on the more embedded institutional points of access of the state, commentators on NSMs [new social movements] and NGOs are increasingly pointing to opportunities at the international and transnational level'. Similarly, Tarrow (2005: 25) has talked of the opportunities (and threats) provided by 'internationalism', which he takes to mean 'a dense, triangular structure of relations among states, non-state actors, and international institutions, and the opportunities this produces for actors to engage in collective action at different levels of this system' (see also Smith 2004: 314).

The threats posed by internationalism are very real and well documented, and include threats to sovereignty, equality, and diversity. Intensifying border security and tightening immigration controls are typical state responses here (Martin 2015). However, Tarrow (2005: 25) says, 'internationalism also offers an opportunity space into which domestic actors can move, encounter others like themselves, and form coalitions that transcend their borders'. For Tarrow, international institutions are 'double-edged'. On the one hand, international governance institutions like the World Trade Organization (WTO),

IMF and World Bank are regarded as agents of global capitalism, and thus 'as carriers of threats to ordinary citizens around the world, which is a source of justified resentment and resistance' (Tarrow 2005: 25). On the other hand, international institutions 'offer an opportunity space within which opponents of global capitalism and other claimants can mobilize' (Tarrow 2005: 26). Tarrow alludes to the formation of a global civil society when he says:

> International institutions have emerged at the core of an increasingly complex international society around which NGOs, social movements, religious groups, trade unions, and business groups cluster. They both intrude on domestic politics through their policies and personnel and offer venues where non-state actors and states can take their claims and build coalitions. Not all of these groups directly challenge or work within the ambit of these institutions; many protest against them and others respond only indirectly to their directives and policies. But as in domestic politics, in which states are both targets of resistance and fulcrums for social conflict and coalition building, international institutions, regimes, and practices are 'coral reefs' in a broader sea of complex internationalism.
>
> (Tarrow 2005: 27)

Out of the expanded political opportunities for transnational protest internationalism provides there has emerged what many believe is a genuinely global movement for social justice. This 'global justice movement' can be thought of as a *global* social movement, since it consists of 'supranational networks of actors that define their causes as global and organize protest campaigns that involve more than one state' (della Porta et al. 2006: 18). We will now look at the global justice movement in more detail.

GLOBAL JUSTICE MOVEMENT

Earlier we looked at some possibilities for resisting globalization, which many believe can only happen in a piecemeal way or on a local scale. However, the idea that the juggernaut of global capitalism is unstoppable was subject to serious challenge when, in 1999, anti-capitalist protestors successfully disrupted the WTO ministerial meetings during the Battle of Seattle (see Figure 9.1). We saw in Chapter 7 how the Battle of Seattle caused law enforcement agencies across the world to reconsider the ways they police major protest events. But the Battle of Seattle was not only a watershed moment for the social control of

© David Hoffman Photo Library/Alamy

Figure 9.1 Protest march against the World Trade Organization through Seattle's Capitol Hill before talks began on 27 November 1999

protest; it was also a time when activists realized the potential that might reside in a global movement for social justice.

In her potted history of the global justice movement, Susan Staggenborg (2011: 150) shows how its beginnings can be traced to the neoliberal economic policies that were promoted by the Reagan and Thatcher regimes in the United States and Britain, respectively, during the 1980s and 1990s. Jackie Smith (2004: 313) argues that at this time the important shift was not the rising power of transnational corporations vis-à-vis nation-states, but changing power relations between Western states and non-Western peoples:

> Thus many analysts trace the origins of contemporary resistance to neoliberal forms of economic globalization not to the 1999 World Trade Organization meeting in Seattle, but rather the countless 'IMF riots', or protests in the global South beginning in the 1980s to oppose the economic policies imposed on their governments by the World Bank and International Monetary Fund.
>
> (Smith 2004: 313)

The global justice movement also draws inspiration from the Jubilee 2000 campaign for debt relief (see Box 6.5), as well as Greenpeace's International Day of Action against McDonald's in 1985. However, the more recent incarnation of the movement was inspired by the vision of the Zapatistas, who, it will be recalled from Chapter 7, emerged in 1994 from the jungles of Chiapas, Mexico, fighting for autonomy against the North American Free Trade Agreement (NAFTA), which was a neoliberal reform also representing US neocolonialism in the Central America region.

Subsequently, a coalition calling itself Peoples' Global Action sponsored the first global day of action in May 1998 to coincide with the Group of Eight (G8) meeting held in Birmingham and the WTO meeting held in Geneva. The second global day of action took place when the G8 met in Germany in June 1999, and the third coincided with the WTO meetings in Seattle in November 1999. After the terror attacks of 11 September 2001, the global justice movement also subsumed anti-war activism (Staggenborg 2011: 153), which was directed at another case of neocolonialism, this time in the Middle East: the US-led invasions of Afghanistan and Iraq. The influence and legacy of the global justice movement have been more recently apparent in the protests of Occupy and other movements that sprung up against injustices resulting from the GFC, the bank bailout, and austerity measures (Pickerill and Krinsky 2012: 279; Halvorsen 2012: 429–430).

The global justice movement tells us important things not only about globalization, but also about social movement theory. Global justice activists target economic and cultural globalization as sources of potential threats, including incursions into national cultures and identities; government cuts to social programs; and trade policies, economic projects, and exploitation by corporations of workers and the environment (Staggenborg 2011: 150). However, while activists contest various cultural changes associated with globalization, which have 'created threats to national and ethnic identities and local cultures' (Staggenborg 2011: 150), the fact that these struggles are embedded in broader economic conditions and neoliberal policies highlights the fact that 'old' politics and traditional issues relating to socioeconomic injustice remain relevant. For Cox and Nilsen, though, the global justice movement attempts to defy this type of academic classification. Hence, in opposing the process of neoliberal globalization, what the 'movement of movements' seeks to do is 'challenge and remake the same forms and institutions that the literature takes as its parameters and axioms' (Cox and Nilsen 2007: 426). Moreover:

> By its own bottom–up construction of alternative structures, media and ways of being, it also poses an *implicit* challenge to the world as represented through academic eyes. It is unsurprising, then, that the

primary academic response is one of reasserting the primacy of existing, top-down knowledge.

(Cox and Nilsen 2007: 426–427, original emphasis)

Significantly, the global justice movement exposes the essential ethnocentricity of accounts of social movements in the developed world. For this very reason, Nick Crossley (2003: 300–302) is critical of new social movement theory, which focuses on privileged First World movements concerned with post-material values, yet neglects the material difficulties faced by the majority of the world's population and, importantly, ignores the fact that the prosperity and stability of the First World has been achieved by the exploitation and underdevelopment of the Third World. Crossley looks at the anti-corporate movement, which, as we saw earlier, is a facet of the anti-globalization movement, arguing that what marks this movement as distinctive is that First and Third World campaigners act together to address the problems of the underdeveloped world. Moreover, some Western activists say the central role played by Third World protesters in shaping the tactics and issues of anti-corporatism is what makes it a new and distinctive wave of mobilization, raising the prospect of movements that are even newer than new social movements (Crossley 2003). The Mexican Zapatistas and the Brazilian landless movement, Sem Terra, are two examples of high-profile Third World networks within the anti-corporate movement, which not only predate First World anti-corporate activism by some years, but also have considerable weight, kudos, and symbolic capital within Western anti-corporate culture (Crossley 2003: 301–302).

Martin (2004: 42), too, has argued that the financial imbalance between the rich countries of the north and the poor countries of the south is a principal grievance of anti-capitalist activists, which suggests that 'material and economic concerns continue to be crucial in a globalizing world', which is, in turn, indicative of 'the ethnocentricity of (European) new social movement theory'. For example, while Melucci intimates the emergence of something resembling a global civil society where movements operate independently of the nation-state, and seems able to incorporate globalization into his general thesis about collective identities in complex society, he still appears reluctant to take material issues seriously (Martin 2004: 42). Thus, he says, 'for developing societies the future is still open to development, but they are at the same time entirely involved in the planetary system based on information' (Melucci 1992: 73). Moreover, Melucci sees the world system as a network of relationships between sovereign states, whereas others see it more clearly in terms of a 'global financial apartheid' (Hari 2002: 24).

Finally, Martin (2004: 42) contends that Melucci's work around social movements in a 'planetary society' appears to tells us little about how global collective struggles are played out locally, which is probably because his theory operates at a high level of abstraction.

BOX 9.3 NEW MEDIA AND GLOBAL ACTIVISM

As stated in the introduction to this chapter, a recent development that looks likely to influence global protest into the future is the ubiquity of new media and communication technologies. Earlier we also noted that although much protest derives from disquiet at the negative consequences of globalization or, more specifically, 'global neoliberalism', globalization is not all bad. Thus, a positive aspect of *technological globalization* has been the rise of the Internet, which, among other things, has enabled people to become aware of different world cultures. From a social movement perspective, the Internet now provides activists with an invaluable networking and mobilizing tool and resource.

This was something we looked at in Chapter 8, where we also considered briefly the role of new social media technologies in global activism. We saw, for instance, how information communication technologies such as the Internet have been vital in bringing together activists from across geographically dispersed places. Indeed, in relation to global justice activists' protest at some of the negative cultural consequences of globalization (mentioned earlier), Staggenborg (2011: 150) has said that 'new technologies like the Internet promoted greater awareness of these issues and increased potential for global mobilization'. Olesen (2005: 57), too, has argued that transnational framing processes are highly dependent upon the availability of effective means of communication across considerable physical, social, and cultural distances, which is why, he suggests, 'the Internet makes it easier for distant actors to share everyday experiences and thus to verify empirical credibility and construct experiential commensurability'.

To Olesen (2005: 57), this constitutes 'a qualitative change in the potentials for sharing everyday experiences and constructing a global consciousness through communication media [and] marks a relatively sharp break with traditional forms of communication media' (e.g., television and newspapers), which are characterized by one-way communication where a clear distinction exists between the producers and recipients of information. The Internet blurs this distinction, and is thus one example of new media having a potentially democratizing effect and function, by facilitating, for instance, greater access to information technologies, counterveillance, citizen journalism, and the like (see Chapter 8).

However, as mentioned towards the end of Chapter 8 in relation to Occupy, questions remain as to the effectiveness of new media technologies in enabling international solidarity. In their research into the use of new media by anti-globalization protestors, Van Aelst and Walgrave (2002: 487) found the Internet has indeed provided a basis for collective identity formation and consensus building, allowing activists to frame globalization as an economic problem with negative human and environmental consequences, as well as contest the lack of democratic legitimacy of international organizations as an aspect of political globalization. Moreover, in accordance with what was said in Chapter 8 about the combined importance of online *and* offline activism, by offering general information on the issues, Van Aelst and Walgrave (2002: 487) discovered websites 'actively mobilize people to demonstrate against the symbols of economic globalization'. Thus, they provide an important 'means of support in the mobilization process for all sorts of "real" protest actions' (Van Aelst and Walgrave 2002: 482). In contrast to these arguments, Kevin McDonald (2002b) has suggested the concept of collective identity is redundant in the case of globalization conflicts, which is why, he argues, we should shift focus from solidarity to 'fluidarity'.

Van Laer (2010) believes that because it is used mainly by 'superactivists' – who tend to be highly educated as well as experienced users of digital communication technologies – the Internet reinforces participation inequalities, and thus might prove an inadequate tool to sustain collective action and maintain future movement organizations. Given this, and the widely accepted heterogeneity of the global justice movement, commentators have observed how the Internet is essentially a double-edged sword, simultaneously providing opportunities and constraints for collective action. For instance, in their study of Internet use by global justice activists, della Porta and Mosca (2005: 171) note that although 'the Internet provides social movements with the means for managing logistics, the extent to which it has a leveling effect among social groups is still an open question'. Indeed, they observe, the Internet has given rise to a new form of inequality, or 'digital divide':

> Differences emerge in Internet access between different territorial levels (not only rich regions versus poor ones but also between rich and poor people in wealthy nations), different social classes in the same nation (penalizing those lacking economic and cultural resources), and between social sectors with different degrees of interest in politics (favouring groups of citizens already active and interested in politics).
>
> (della Porta et al. 2006: 98)

We saw something similar in Chapter 8, when we considered how the ubiquity of mobile digital devices, such as camera phones, can have a democratizing effect, although, as Loader and Mercea (2012: 4) observe, the majority of citizen journalists tend to be activists already committed to political causes. In relation to the global justice movement, della Porta (2012) has shown how, regardless of the digital divide, the use of new technologies resonates at a normative level with social movements' vision for *participatory* and *deliberative* democracy. First, beyond their instrumental use in expanding the capacity for communication of social movements, the fast and relatively inexpensive forms of communication permitted by new technologies, like the Internet, for example, 'allows for flexible organisation and more participatory structures' (della Porta 2012: 49).

Second, the communicative value of new technologies also resonates with social movements' critique of representative forms of democracy that are based on principles of delegated authority and majority voting. By contrast, social movements have long been advocates for participatory conceptions of democracy, horizontal forms of internal (and leaderless) organization, and the endorsement of direct citizen involvement in decision making – in other words, decisional processes that are of a deliberative nature, involving 'conditions of equality, inclusiveness, and transparency [and] a communicative process based on reason' (della Porta 2012: 50). The global justice movement is one example of a contemporary social movement that has paid 'attention to values related to communication in an open space, respect for diversity, equal participation, and inclusiveness' (della Porta 2012: 50). Similarly, it has been shown that institutions of global governance have inserted the issue of the digital divide into their agendas (della Porta and Mosca 2005: 172; della Porta et al. 2006: 98).

However, we should be cautious about the extent to which the networking logic of the Internet has enabled movements like the global justice movement to actually practice 'an "open space method" of internal democracy that should produce strength from diversity' (della Porta 2012: 50). Indeed, Martin (2004: 49) has pointed to some of the difficulties faced by the anti-capitalist movement and other contemporary movements, which seek not only independence and autonomy to be part of a genuinely democratic global civil society, but also strive to ensure their own internal organization and structures reflect their democratic ideals. In Chapter 7, too, we saw how there has been some internal division in Occupy, whereby protestors have been reluctant to engage with indigenous peoples' concerns about settler colonialism (Barker 2012).

INTERNATIONAL HUMAN RIGHTS AND PROTEST

Along with the impact of new media and communication technologies, another development that will likely influence future global protest is international human rights norms and law, not least because this highlights a 'democratic deficit' of global institutions:

> While the proliferation of international regimes for human rights, environmental protection, and equitable development both focus transnational movements and expand their opportunities for participation, the neoliberal emphasis on market governance and the expanding influence of international financial institutions has reduced the political power of citizens as it excludes them from decision-making arenas that have increasingly significant implications for their lives.
>
> (Smith 2004: 319)

The contemporary terrain of international human rights has its origins in the formation of the United Nations after the Second World War, which, as noted earlier, was also a period when international NGOs proliferated. However, only relatively recently have social movement scholars and political scientists considered this an area where we might observe global civil society in action. Most of the focus here is on relations and/or interactions between macro (global), meso (national), and micro (local) levels of analysis.

Indeed, in Chapter 3, we looked at Meyer's (2003) case study of the New Zealand anti-nuclear weapons movement to explore some of the ways domestic and international factors interact and how that, in turn, impacts upon social movements. Much in the same way we saw how the 'transnational opportunities structure' (Krieger and Murphy 1988) or 'internationalism' (Tarrow 2005) offers space *and* poses threats for social movements (Tarrow 2005), it will be recalled that Meyer (2003: 19) extends the political opportunity structure concept to argue that national opportunities are *nested* in a broader international environment, which promotes or constrains opportunities for activists within nation-states. This work reflects existing work on global institutions and movements, which 'sees national polities as nested within a much broader system of institutional relations that will vary across issues, time, and place' (Smith 2004: 317).

Similarly, Muñoz (2006: 252) looks at the case of the EZLN (Zapatista Army of National Liberation) to highlight the 'intersection between domestic politics and international negotiations' over the NAFTA. Muñoz argues that although the NAFTA represented the dark side of globalization and had negative effects for people living in the south of Mexico, the international attention it brought to Mexico also created openings for political reforms protecting human rights. In short, he says, 'the formation of human rights norms and economic globalization have created a political opportunity structure that placed the Mexican government in a position where it was unable to either ignore or fully repress EZLN collective action' (Muñoz 2006: 252). Pressure from both international financial interests and human rights groups drastically constrained the Mexican government's military response to the Zapatistas in Chiapas, and the NAFTA played a key role, 'given that its supporters advocated that the agreement would advance human rights and increase political stability' (Muñoz 2006: 262).

While Muñoz (2006: 268) considers the influence of an international political opportunity structure upon state responses to address 'the lack of attention given to the way in which social movements alter the action of their opponents', Kate Nash (2012) argues that state and national law remain important for institutionalizing human rights norms. She, too, uses the 'excellent' but 'exceptional' example of the Zapatistas as a case supporting what 'subaltern cosmopolitans' see as the emancipatory use of human rights and law 'from below' (Nash 2012: 804). By contrast, 'global cosmopolitanism' is a 'top down' approach, which reflects the view that there is a single human rights movement creating international law, such as that enshrined in the Universal Declaration of Human Rights (Nash 2012: 798, 802–803). While there is often suspicion of universal human rights as a form of Western imperialist economic and military power, Nash argues, the middle way of *bringing the state back in* provides both a more fruitful and realistic perspective, albeit one that adds to rather than reduces the complexity of human rights law.

States are the ultimate guarantors of international human rights, which are interpreted contextually by courts in national settings. However, the interpretation and use of human rights is not restricted to national courts, for human rights law is multiscalar by virtue of 'transnational legal pluralism', that is, 'the co-existence of overlapping, local, national and international law within and across states' (Nash 2012: 804). Hence, complexity arises because '[n]ot only can there be more than one jurisdiction through which individuals may claim rights, but there is not necessarily any ultimate judicial authority to adjudicate conflicts' (Nash 2012: 807).

Moreover, even when priorities are clearly set out in domestic legal principles and precedents and national courts become involved, 'state law does not automatically trump local customary law' (Nash 2012: 807). Similarly, international law does not automatically trump state law:

> Although international human rights law is negotiated to make clear requirements of states that have signed treaties and conventions so

that it seems as if the UN is above them as a judicial authority, it is not an authority that can be enforced.

(Nash 2012: 807)

Accordingly, Nash (2012: 808) takes issue not only with global cosmopolitans, but also the multiplicity of social movements that demand human rights 'from below', arguing human rights law is state-centric 'in that it is virtually exclusively through states that international human rights law is made and enforced'. Hence, against subaltern cosmopolitanism, she argues, 'we cannot avoid or ignore the state as it is currently constructed in international law as the guarantor of human rights' (Nash 2012: 808). Indeed, even when human rights are demanded from below, it is the state that tends to address them. Moreover, states do not necessarily adjudicate such matters simply by reference to national law, customary law, or international law. And even when governments sign international human rights treaties, they may not intend to implement them (Smith 2004: 315), which is a form of 'state hypocrisy' that can precipitate the formation of human rights NGOs and movements (Ball 2000: 74). Bringing the state back in therefore complicates matters, such that:

. . . in the complex interplay of definitions of human rights on the part of activists, lawyers and politicians at national and international level, what human rights mean in practice will, for the foreseeable future, involve a patchwork of legal victories, compromises, temporary solutions, and political trade-offs.

(Nash 2012: 808)

At various places in this book we have seen how some social movements demand particular changes in the law or legal system, such as petitioning for the introduction of legalization to protect against discrimination based on race or disability (Chapter 3). We have also seen how, in certain circumstances, social movements may invoke international law or direct their grievances at international institutions. For example, in Chapter 7, we saw how the international indigenous peoples' movement has played a very active role in challenging colonialism (and its legacies), using the language of self-determination and standard setting in international human rights law (Feldman 2002: 42). We also saw how international NGOs and human rights groups have connected the recognition, adoption, and elaboration of international standards relating to indigenous peoples to wider global issues, such as nuclear disarmament and environmental racism (Feldman 2002: 39). In Box 9.4, we look at the case of a network of transnational human rights campaigners who successfully lobbied the UN using international humanitarian law.

BOX 9.4 'COMFORT WOMEN' CHALLENGING INTERNATIONAL LAW

Pak Yong Sim – North Korea: 'I had to service thirty to forty soldiers every-day. One day I was really in pain, and when I didn't respond to the demands of one officer, that bastard beat me with his fists, kicked me with his boots, took a long knife and held it up against my throat and cut me. The blood poured out and soaked my whole body, but that bastard officer went on to satisfy his lust'.

(Sajor 2004: 290)

From 1937 to 1945, the Japanese military established and maintained a 'comfort station' system that was considered vital to the Japanese war effort during the Second World War (Sajor 2004: 303). Comfort stations repre-sented an institutionalized system of rape and sexual slavery wherein 'com-fort women' suffered brutal treatment at the hands of Japanese soldiers: Japanese Imperial Army documents even set out the rules and obligations of women in comfort stations (Sajor 2004: 300).

It took several decades before former comfort women came forward to speak out and tell their stories like the one told by Pak Yong Sim in the extract above. In 2000, former comfort women convened the Tokyo Women's Tribu-nal, which 'brought together women from nine countries in the Asia Pacific region to testify against the Government of Japan, who forced more than two hundred thousand women into sexual slavery during World War Two' (Sajor 2004: 288). The purpose of the tribunal was 'to redress the historic tendency to trivialise crimes against women, particularly sexual crimes committed in war or armed conflict' (Sajor 2004: 289). Specifically, it aimed to hold the Japa-nese government to account in accordance with the principles of international humanitarian law.

Tactics used by former comfort women included filing court cases against the Japanese government, as well as picketing and demonstrating outside Japanese embassies in the cities of Seoul, Manila, Jakarta, Tokyo, Geneva, and New York (see Figure 9.2). Giving voice to their stories also enabled the former comfort women to engage in a process of educating the Japanese people about what had been done to them, which was reflected in the demand 'that their experiences be officially acknowledged in Japanese accounts of history, and taught to students in Japanese schools' (Sajor 2004: 294). The former comfort women also sought an official apology from the prime minister of Japan, individual apologies from soldiers, reparations, and compensation.

The Tokyo Women's Tribunal was tasked with conducting the Women's International War Crimes Tribunal and drawing up a Charter of the Women's

© epa european pressphoto agency b.v./Alamy

Figure 9.2 Filipino Remedios Rocha, 85, joins fellow 'comfort women' of the Second World War in a dance-protest in front of the Japanese Embassy in Pasay City, south of Manila, the Philippines, 12 February 2014, as part of the 'One Billion Rising' for Justice, a global campaign to end violence against women

Tribunal under which the tribunal was granted jurisdiction over crimes committed against women as war crimes and crimes against humanity. However, unlike the 1993 International Criminal Tribunal for the Former Republic of Yugoslavia or the 1995 International Criminal Tribunal for Rwanda, the Tokyo Women's Tribunal lacked the legal authority of an ad hoc tribunal of the UN Security Council. Accordingly, it could neither pass sentence upon individuals nor order reparations. It also diverged from UN Security Council–mandated tribunals, which hear only individual criminal cases, in that it assigned both individual and state criminal responsibility, even indicting Japan's late Emperor Hirohito. Ultimately, the Tokyo Women's Tribunal 'was able to make recommendations backed by the weight of its legal findings and its moral force' (Sajor 2004: 298). On 4 December 2001, a year after the case was heard, the tribunal handed down its judgment in The Hague, holding:

> There is abundant evidence, most notably from victim-survivor testimony, that the Japanese government and military were involved in all aspects of the sexual slavery system. In addition, the evidence provided by experts confirms that Japanese officials at the highest levels participated knowingly in the system of sexual slavery.
>
> (Sajor 2004: 302)

The judgment of the Tokyo Women's Tribunal finally gave the former comfort women a sense of justice and provided recognition of their pain and suffering. Issues about comfort women are now included in Japanese school textbooks, although a nationalist countermovement has campaigned for their removal (Sajor 2004: 302). Lobbying on the part of former comfort women also played a part in preventing Japan from becoming a permanent member of the UN Security Council in 1994 on account of its denial of wartime atrocities (Sajor 2004: 294). The International Labour Organization, too, has recognized comfort women were victims of forced labour, which it prohibits (Sajor 2004: 295).

CONCLUSION

Some of the material presented in this chapter points to the adaptability of the concept of 'political opportunity structure', which, as we have seen, can be transposed into a global context. Indeed, in Chapter 3, we saw how Sarah Soule (2009: 44) has used the idea of 'international political opportunity structure' in relation to anti-corporate activism to argue that social movements against multinational corporations are governed, to a significant degree, by multiple levels of opportunity operating domestically and transnationally. In that chapter, and elsewhere in the book, we have also considered prospects for applying the concept of 'repertoire of contention' on a transnational scale, which has been made possible, in no small part, with the advent of new media, information, and communication technologies. The Arab Spring and Occupy are obvious examples here.

Novel ways of applying concepts like political opportunity structure and repertoire of contention suggest the continued relevance of political process and contentious politics approaches to collective action. So, too, does Nash's argument about *bringing the state back in*, which indicates the ongoing relevance (and resilience) of the nation-state in spite of the apparent fact that globalizing forces strip nation-states of their sovereignty. Moreover, this view also seems to gainsay arguments about social movements ('new' or otherwise) striving to maintain their autonomy by eschewing traditional forms of interest intermediation, such as state politics.

That is not to say, however, that all social movements must connect their demands to 'institutionally immanent possibilities' (Giddens 1991a: 155), or that social movement outcomes are always necessarily synonymous with political, legal, or policy change. For as we have seen at various junctures in this book, social movements can also challenge and influence cultural values and attitudes. Especially in Chapter 5, we saw how movements might do that via emotions and narrative or storytelling, which, in turn, points to the 'cognitive praxis' of social movements, which regards efficacy and success in terms of how influential a movement is 'in spreading its knowledge interests or diffusing its consciousness' (Eyerman and Jamison 1991: 3–4). These elements are clearly evident in the example of comfort women (Box 9.4), who, by *speaking out* and *telling their stories*, not only achieved a sense of justice in legal recognition, but were also successful in spreading their consciousness; now their story is told in school textbooks. As we shall see in the concluding chapter, cognitive praxis is one of the most significant ways social movements bring about change in society.

SUGGESTED READINGS

The following texts and resources can be used to explore issues raised in this chapter.

Books

Smith, J. (2004) 'Transnational Processes and Movements' in D. A. Snow, S. A. Soule, and H. Kriesi (eds.) *The Blackwell Companion to Social Movements*. Oxford: Blackwell, pp. 311–335.

Jackie Smith's book chapter provides a very useful account of some of the most pertinent issues relating to globalization and transnational activism. There are many other books that also look at this, including the following texts:

Cohen, R. and Rai, S. M. (eds.) (2000) *Global Social Movements*. London: Continuum.
della Porta, D. (ed.) (2007) *The Global Justice Movement: Cross-national and Transnational Perspectives*. Boulder, CO: Paradigm.
della Porta, D., Andretta, M., Mosca, L., and Reiter, H. (eds.) (2006) *Globalization from Below: Transnational Activism and Protest Networks*. Minneapolis, MN: University of Minnesota Press.
della Porta, D., Kriesi, H. and Rucht, D. (eds.) (1999) *Social Movements in a Globalising World*. Houndmills: Palgrave Macmillan.
della Porta, D. and Tarrow, S. (eds.) (2005) *Transnational Protest and Global Activism: People, Passions, and Power*. Lanham, MD: Rowman & Littlefield.
Smith, J. (2008) *Social Movements for Global Democracy*. Baltimore, MD: The Johns Hopkins University Press.
Smith, J. and Johnston, H. (eds.) (2002) *Globalization and Resistance: Transnational Dimensions of Social Movements*. Lanham, MD: Rowman & Littlefield.
Tarrow, S. (2005) *The New Transnational Activism*. Cambridge: Cambridge University Press.

Journals

Olesen, T. (2005) 'The Uses and Misuses of Globalization in the Study of Social Movements' *Social Movement Studies* 4(1): 49–63.

This article offers a useful exploration of the relationship between global activism and transnational processes. In addition, the following journal special issues provide more detailed discussion of some of the topics covered in this chapter:

Millennium 23(3) (1994): 'Social Movements and World Politics'.
Mobilization 6(1) (2001): 'Globalization and Resistance'.
Mobilization 13(4) (2008): 'The World Economic Forum Process'.

CHAPTER 10

Conclusion

OBJECTS AND OUTCOMES OF SOCIAL MOVEMENT ACTIVITY

The purpose of this final chapter is to draw together some of the more prominent themes and perspectives that have emerged in the book. To that end, it is probably apt to begin by looking at what is arguably the single biggest aim of any kind of protest, namely to bring about positive social change in the face of perceived wrongs or injustices. Indeed, in Chapter 2, we saw how Turner and Killian (1987 [1957]) believe a sense of injustice is central to *all* social movement activity. Similarly, scholars writing from the framing perspective argue that diagnosing problems and attributing blame are key framing tasks involving the articulation of 'injustice frames', which 'call attention to the ways in which movements identify the "victims" of a given injustice and amplify their victimization' (Benford and Snow 2000: 615). Hence, William Gamson (1992: 68, original emphasis) has said that all 'collective action frames are *injustice* frames'.

However, as noted in Chapter 5, although the framing approach generally succeeds in overcoming the overly rationalistic view of resource mobilization theory, it tends to overstate cognition as a principal factor that motivates people to get involved in protest in the first place. And, in so doing, it fails to recognize that collective action is often *preceded* by emotions, such as a sense of injustice, anger, indignation, fear, or compassion (Polletta and Amenta 2001: 305). Importantly, though, emotions are not only an important motivational force; they can also affect social movement outcomes.

While social movement scholars have tended typically to see movement outcomes in terms of bringing about concrete political, legal, or policy changes, at various points in this book we have seen how the impact and influence of social movements can be far more expansive and wide ranging. For instance, when we looked at the role of narrative and storytelling in Chapter 5, we saw how, as well as functioning internally to cement social bonds and sustain and strengthen activists' sense of commitment to shared organizational goals and a collective identity, storytelling can also have external effects. For example, 'stories of influence' can be a 'spillover effect' of social movement activity (Meyer and Whittier 1994), which can be considered a movement outcome beyond a specific policy goal. Hence, we saw how despite the defeat of the US Equal Rights Amendment in the 1970s, largely because of the influence of the narrative of the women's movement at the time, cultural values and attitudes about women in politics and the workforce were still dramatically transformed for the better during that period (Meyer 2009: 59).

In Chapter 9, we also saw how speaking out and telling their stories was a tactic used by 'comfort women', who sought justice and recognition for the historic sexual crimes they suffered at the hands of Japanese soldiers during the Second World War. Moreover, we considered their success in having their experiences officially acknowledged in Japanese school history books an example of the 'cognitive praxis' of social movements, which 'measures' a movement's success according to how influential it is in diffusing and spreading its knowledge interests or consciousness (Eyerman and Jamison 1991: 3–4). In other parts of the book, too, we have observed the cognitive praxis of social movements. In Chapter 5, we considered the Western media's general support and endorsement of Russian feminist punk band, Pussy Riot, as an example of the operation of cognitive praxis in music and protest, since, according to Seal (2013: 298), it indicates 'the incorporation of elements of feminism and post-feminism into the discourse of the Western news media'. Likewise, in Chapter 7, we saw how Occupy has been successful in spreading its message about the nature of inequality in capitalist societies by the creation and repetition of slogans (e.g., 'we are the 99 percent'), which, regardless of their factual correctness, have 'come to populate the discourse and establish their own truths' (Pickerill and Krinsky 2012: 281).

The idea that social movements can bring about widespread transformation in the ways we think about the world also relates to the performativity of social movements and, in particular, the Quaker tradition of 'bearing witness', which confronts the observer with an issue such that turning a blind eye is not an option. In Chapter 6, we saw how one way social movements resemble religious movements is in their adoption of what might be called 'religious protest repertoires', which include the act of bearing witness. And we looked at the case of Greenpeace's early direct actions as an example of a social movement organization that has been influenced by this religious tradition.

We also saw how the act of bearing witness does not necessarily intend to affect any specific political or policy change, but can constitute a 'symbolic challenge' (Melucci 1984; 1985). Here we considered the example of Argentina's mothers of the disappeared, the *Madres de la Plaza de Mayo*, who, since the 1970s, have walked slowly around the perimeter of a public square in Argentina each Thursday afternoon, dressed in white headscarves and holding pictures of their missing relatives in an act of bearing witness to state oppression (Moser 2003: 188). In Chapter 5, we also considered the creative protest and radical street performance of women's grassroots groups in Peru as an act of bearing witness to government repression and corruption, which, accordingly, posed a symbolic challenge to the incumbent regime.

POLITICAL PROCESS, PROTEST REPERTOIRES, AND OPPORTUNITY STRUCTURES

This discussion highlights the essential adaptability of the concept of 'repertoire of contention', which are essentially the strategies or tactics social movements employ. In Chapter 3, we saw how Charles Tilly (1986: 390) likens activists' use of protest repertoires to the improvisation of jazz artists: 'people know the general rules or performance more or less well and vary the performance to meet the purpose at hand'. Accordingly, at various places in the book we have seen how the concept of repertoire of contention has been variously used to apply to performative protest (Chapter 5), Islamic activism (Chapter 6), and social movements harnessing a variety of media (Chapter 8). Indeed, in Chapter 6, we saw how the use of new forms of social media during the Arab Spring can be seen to have added to the protest repertoire of Islamic activism.

We have seen, too, how, as a result of *technological globalization*, repertoires of contention have altered in scale. As will be recalled from Chapter 3, as originally conceived by Tilly, protest repertoires have evolved over time, shifting from being locally focused to becoming more national in scope. With globalization, we have observed a further shift in scale. The Internet and other new media, information, and communication technologies now provide activists with networking resources that have a transnational reach. However, it is not only movement repertoires that have become more globalized. In Chapter 7, we saw how after the Battle of Seattle and the 9/11 terror attacks, a 'global protest policing repertoire' has emerged particularly in relation to the social control of high-profile international events (Martin 2011b). Indeed, according to Pickerill and Krinsky (2012: 285), this is one of the ways Occupy matters, for it illustrates the degree to which protest policing has evolved and police tactics have diffused transnationally.

The concept of 'political opportunity structure' has also been applied to global activism. So, in Chapter 3, we considered Soule's (2009) arguments about how a transnational political opportunity structure – consisting of international institutions, like the United Nations, World Trade Organization, and World Bank, which make treaties, agreements, and norms – affects the operation of anti-corporate movements. In that chapter, we also looked at Meyer's (2003) study of the New Zealand anti-nuclear weapons movement wherein he explores some of the ways domestic and international factors interact. This, we said in Chapter 9, reflects a more general interest in the relationship between global institutions and movements, which sees national opportunities as *nested* within a broader international environment and system of institutional relations (Smith 2004: 317). And in that chapter we saw how this connects to conceptions of 'global civil society', 'transnational advocacy networks', 'internationalism', and the like, all of which constitute ways of thinking about international opportunities and spaces for international institutions and social movements to coexist and interact.

The notion of political opportunity also has a relationship with that other seemingly versatile concept, 'abeyance structures', which, as we saw in Chapter 4, was originally employed by Verta Taylor (1989) to explain social movement continuity. It will be recalled that Taylor argues social movements are more active (and more visible) when the wider political environment is responsive to their demands and grievances. However, they retreat into quotidian structures and networks when political opportunities are scarce or the prevailing political climate is hostile or unfavourable. In this way, the idea of abeyance provides an answer to the question of what's new about new social movements, since, as Taylor (1989: 761) says, it 'depicts a holding process by which movements sustain themselves in nonreceptive political environments and provide continuity from one stage of mobilization to another'. In Chapter 6, we saw how Taylor's ideas have been applied to 'lifestyle movements', which, argue Haenfler et al. (2012: 13), can act as refuges in hostile political times, serving as abeyance structures until political opportunities improve. And, in Chapter 5, we saw how Taylor has influenced ideas about how stories of the past help sustain social movements in dormant periods (Goodwin et al. 2001: 21; Polletta 2002: 49).

MOVEMENT AUTONOMY AND THE STATE

Towards the end of Chapter 9, we proposed that innovative ways of applying concepts like political opportunity structure and repertoire of contention are indicative of the ongoing relevance of the political process model and contentious politics approach in social movement studies. We also said this, in turn, suggests we ought not dismiss the idea that the state remains a key player in social movement research. We saw, for instance, how Nash's (2012) work highlights the significance of the nation-state (and national courts) for the domestic institutionalization of international human rights, which, we noted, is surprising given arguments about the threat posed to state sovereignty by globalizing processes. Moreover, even when movements such as Occupy refuse to make demands on the state and, instead, strive to provide services (e.g., kitchens, bathrooms, first-aid posts, sleeping areas, educational space) in prefigurative alternative communities, this still raises issues about the role of the state and political parties vis-à-vis social movements. For, as Pickerill and Krinsky (2012: 283) quite rightly ask, 'can we really speak about movements as fully autonomous from the state, and under what conditions does this make sense?' To be sure, during the Arab Spring, the state was an ever-looming and menacing presence, which, as discussed in Chapter 8, sought to censor and repress movements for democracy across the Middle East.

According to the political process model, the criteria for social movement success – or the 'effects' of movement activity – are defined in terms of 'integrating previously excluded issues and groups into the "normal" political process' (Scott 1990: 10), which, as we saw in Chapter 4, is diametrically opposed to the new social movement perspective, since, as Alan Scott (1990: 10) says, '[i]f there is a telos of social movement activity then it is the normalization of previously exotic issues and groups'. The success of a movement 'is thus quite incompatible with, and indeed overlaps, the disappearance of the movement as a movement' (Scott 1990: 10–11). And, in this sense, argue Eyerman and Jamison (1991: 3, 64), talk of social movement 'success' is somewhat paradoxical.

In other terms, Shemtov (1999: 92) has referred to natural-history models of social movements, which 'emphasize the logic of internal structures (e.g. bureaucracy, oligarchy) in predicting that most SMOs [social movement organizations] will displace their radical goals with conservative ones'. So, in Chapter 9, we saw how the global justice movement and Occupy have both struggled to ensure that their internal organization and structure reflect their democratic ideals. We also looked at a related idea in Chapter 6 when we considered how some believe religious movements are necessarily precluded from having a positive, radical, or progressive impact on society because they are, in essence, regressive, conservative, and inward looking.

These ideas, in turn, relate to what we have encountered previously in terms of what has been identified as movements' need to connect their demands to 'institutionally imminent possibilities' (Giddens 1991a: 155). However, while this view seems to dispute new social movement theory in particular, which posits social movements aim to be autonomous of the state and eschew traditional forms of political representation and interest intermediation, as noted earlier, it is nevertheless important not to limit or reduce social movement activity to political, legal, and policy objectives and outcomes. Indeed, as we have seen in various parts of the book, the success of a social movement might be observed in the effective dissemination of its knowledge or consciousness (i.e., its 'cognitive praxis'), or even simply in its awareness-raising activities and lifestyle politics. And this is one of the ways new religious movements and new social movements alike might have an influence in society.

When we looked at this confluence of religious and social movement in Chapter 6, we compared new social movements' quest for autonomy with the search or struggle of religious movements for 'free space' and 'identity spaces' (Beckford 2003: 172). And, in Chapter 7, we looked again at how the idea of identity space relates to indigenous peoples' struggles for autonomy and self-determination. The Zapatistas are often held up as an exemplar of the kind of self-management and autonomy new social movement theorists speak of. In this respect, movements are able to exercise some degree of agency against state interference or systemic intrusion. We saw, too, how in the face of top-down pressures exerted by globalization, the international indigenous peoples' movement has been instrumental in shaping and forcing open international institutions in the global public sphere (Feldman 2002: 42).

This raises the issue of whether it is possible to effectively challenge, or even resist, the seemingly inexorable march of globalization, which brings us back to the initial point made earlier about social movements' central concern with righting wrongs and perceived injustices. In Chapter 9, we saw how some believe the only way of resisting the ill effects of global capitalist neoliberalism is locally, or 'from below'. Others place faith in the global justice movement, which, as we saw, has utilized new information and communication technologies and social media to bring people from geographically dispersed areas together, as well as to promote awareness of the issues. We also identified the use of new media technologies, like the Internet and camera phones, as a key area of potential future social movement research. Indeed, insofar as these new technologies are used by activists as tools or resources for recruitment, mobilization, and the dissemination of information, this demonstrates the enduring relevance of resource mobilization theory.

Moreover, the very existence of the global justice movement constitutes an implied critique of new social movement theory, as it highlights the persistence of material issues and survival struggles. In Chapter 9, we saw how this was a mark of the ethnocentricity of new social movement theory, which emphasizes post-material values and the lifestyle struggles of privileged collective actors in the developed world. Thinking globally, therefore, is not just something activists might do; it is also something social movement scholars must do.

BIBLIOGRAPHY

Adams, J. (2011) 'Occupy Time' *Critical Inquiry*, 16 November 2011, available at: <http://critinq.wordpress.com/2011/11/16/occupy-time>.

Albanese, C. L. (1990) *Nature Religion in America*. Chicago, IL: Chicago University Press.

Alberoni, F. (1984) *Movement and Institution*. New York, NY: Columbia University Press.

Albrow, M. (1992) 'Sine Ira et Studio – or Do Organizations Have Feelings?' *Organization Studies* 13(3): 313–329.

Almeida, P. D. and Lichbach, M. I. (2003) 'To the Internet, From the Internet: Comparative Media Coverage of Transnational Protest' *Mobilization* 8(3): 249–272.

Altheide, D. and Snow, R. (1991) *Media Worlds in the Post-Journalism Era*. New York: Aldine de Gruyter.

Amin, A. (1994) 'Post-Fordism: Models, Fantasies and Phantoms of Transition' in A. Amin (ed.) *Post-Fordism: A Reader*. Oxford: Blackwell.

Anderton, C. (2008) 'Commercializing the Carnivalesque: The V Festival and Image/Risk Management' *Event Management* 12: 39–51.

Angosto Ferrández, L. (forthcoming) 'Indigenous Peoples, Social Movements and the Legacy of Hugo Chávez's Governments' *Latin American Perspectives*.

Annetts, J., Law, A., McNeish, W. and Mooney, G. (2009) *Understanding Social Welfare Movements*. Bristol: Policy Press.

Assies, W. (2003) 'David versus Goliath in Cochabamba: Water Rights, Neoliberalism, and the Revival of Social Protest in Bolivia' *Latin American Perspectives* 30(3): 14–36.

Atton, C. (2003) 'Reshaping Social Media for a New Millennium' *Social Movement Studies* 2(1): 3–15.

Ayres, J. M. (2001) 'Transnational Political Processes and Contention Against the Global Economy' *Mobilization* 6(1): 55–68.

Baker, S. A. (2012) 'Policing the Riots: New Social Media as Recruitment, Resistance, and Surveillance' in D. Briggs (ed.) *The English Riots of 2011: A Summer of Discontent*. Sherfield: Waterside Press, pp. 169–190.

Bakhtin, M. (1968) *Rabelais and His World* (trans. H. Iswolsky). Cambridge, MA: MIT Press.

..., r. (2000) 'State Terror, Constitutional Traditions, and National Human Rights Movements: A Cross-national Quantitative Comparison' in J. A. Guidry, M. D. Kennedy, and M. N. Zald (eds.) *Globalizations and Social Movements: Culture, Power, and the Transnational Public Sphere.* Ann Arbor, MI: University of Michigan Press, pp. 54–75.

Banerjee, T. (2013) 'Media, Movements and Mobilization: Tea Party Protests in the United States, 2009–2010' *Research in Social Movements, Conflicts and Change* 36: 39–75.

Barker, A. J. (2012) 'Already Occupied: Indigenous Peoples, Settler Colonialism and the Occupy Movements in North America' *Social Movement Studies* 11(3–4): 327–334.

Barker, C. (1986) *Festival of the Oppressed: Solidarity, Reform and Revolution in Poland 1980–81.* London: Bookmarks.

Bartholomew, A. and Mayer, M. (1992) 'Nomads of the Present: Melucci's Contribution to "New Social Movement" Theory' *Theory, Culture and Society* 9(4): 141–159.

Bauman, Z. (1998) *Globalization: The Human Consequences.* Cambridge: Polity.

Baumgarten, B., Daphi, P., and Ullrich, P. (eds.) (2014) *Conceptualizing Culture in Social Movement Research.* Houndmills: Palgrave Macmillan.

Beckett, F. (2010) *What Did the Baby Boomers Ever Do for Us? Why the Children of the Sixties Lived the Dream and Failed the Future.* London: Biteback Publishing, Ltd.

Beckett, K. and Herbert, S. (2008) 'Dealing with Disorder: Social Control in the Post-industrial City' *Theoretical Criminology* 12(1): 5–30.

Beckford, J. A. (1989) *Religion and Advanced Industrial Society.* London: Unwin Hyman.

Beckford, J. A. (2003) *Social Theory and Religion.* Cambridge: Cambridge University Press.

Bellah, R. (1970) *Beyond Belief: Essays on Religion in a Post-traditional World.* New York, NY: Harper & Row.

Benford, R. D. (2002) 'Controlling Narratives and Narratives as Control within Social Movements' in J. E. Davis (ed.) *Stories of Change: Narrative and Social Movements.* Albany, NY: State University of New York Press, pp. 53–75.

Benford, R. D. and Hunt, S. A. (1992) 'Dramaturgy of Social Movements: The Social Construction and Communication of Power' *Sociological Inquiry* 62(1): 37–55.

Benford, R. D. and Snow, D. A. (2000) 'Framing Processes and Social Movements: An Overview and Assessment' *Annual Review of Sociology* 26: 611–639.

Berlet, C. (2010a) 'Taking Tea Partiers Seriously' *The Progressive*, 8 March 2010, available at: <www.progressive.org/berlet0210c.html>.

Berlet, C. (2010b) *Tea Bags, Taxes, and Productive Citizens*, available at: <www.zcommunications.org/tea-bags-taxes-and-productive-citizens-by-chip-berlet>.

Billings, D. B. (1990) 'Religion as Opposition: A Gramscian Analysis' *American Journal of Sociology* 96(1): 1–31.

Blaug, R. (2002) 'Engineering Democracy' *Political Studies* 50(1): 102–116.

Blumer, H. (1951) 'Social Movements' in A. M. Lee (ed.) *New Outlines of the Principles of Sociology*: New York, NY: Barnes and Noble, pp. 199–220.

Blumer, H. (1969) 'Collective Behaviour' in A. McClung Lee (ed.) *Principles of Sociology* (3rd ed.). New York, NY: Barnes & Noble.

Bodnar, C. (2006) 'Taking It to the Streets: French Cultural Workers Resistance and the Creation of the Precariat Movement' *Canadian Journal of Communication* 31(3): 675–694.

Bourdieu, P. (1984) *Distinction: A Social Critique of the Judgement of Taste*. Cambridge, MA: Harvard University Press.

Boykoff, J. and Laschever, E. (2011) 'The Tea Party Movement, Framing, and the US Media' *Social Movement Studies* 10(4): 341–366.

Boyle, P. and Haggerty, K. D. (2009) 'Spectacular Security: Mega-events and the Security Complex' *International Political Sociology* 3(3): 257–274.

Brand, R. (2013) '"We No Longer Have the Luxury of Tradition"' *New Statesman*, 25–31 October 2013, pp. 24–29.

Briggs, D. (ed.) (2012) *The English Riots of 2011: A Summer of Discontent*. Sherfield: Waterside Press.

Brophy, E. (2006) 'System Error: Labour Precarity and Collective Organizing at Microsoft' *Canadian Journal of Communication* 31(3): 619–638.

Buechler, S. M. (1993) 'Beyond Resource Mobilization? Emerging Trends in Social Movement Theory' *The Sociological Quarterly* 34(2): 217–235.

Buechler, S. M. (1995) 'New Social Movement Theories' *The Sociological Quarterly* 36(3): 441–464.

Buechler, S. M. (2011) *Understanding Social Movements: Theories from the Classical Era to the Present*. Boulder, CO: Paradigm Publishers.

Calhoun, C. (1994) 'Social Theory and the Politics of Identity' in C. Calhoun (ed.) *Social Theory and the Politics of Identity*. Oxford: Blackwell, pp. 9–36.

Calhoun, C. (1995) '"New Social Movements" of the Early Nineteenth Century' in M. Traugott (ed.) *Repertoires and Cycles of Collective Action*. Durham, NC: Duke University Press, pp. 173–215.

Calhoun, C. (1999) 'Symposium on Religion' *Sociological Theory* 17(3): 237–239.

Carty, V. and Onyett, J. (2006) 'Protest, Cyberactivism and New Social Movements: The Re-emergence of the Peace Movement Post 9/11' *Social Movement Studies* 5(3): 229–249.

Carroll, W. K. and Ratner, R. S. (1999) 'Media Strategies and Political Projects: A Comparative Study of Social Movements' *Canadian Journal of Sociology* 24(1): 1–34.

Castañeda, E. (2012) 'The *Indignados* of Spain: A Precedent to Occupy Wall Street' *Social Movement Studies* 11(3–4): 309–319.

Castells, M. (1983) *The City and the Grassroots: A Cross-Cultural Theory of Urban Social Movements*. Berkeley, CA: University of California Press.

Castells, M. (1996) *The Rise of the Network Society*. Oxford: Blackwell.

Cerny, P. G. (2009) 'Bridging the Transatlantic Divide? Toward a Structural Approach to International Political Economy' in M. Blyth (ed.) *Routledge Handbook of International Political Economy (IPE): IPE as a Global Conversation*. London: Routledge.

Charles, N. (2000) *Feminism, the State, and Social Policy*. Basingstoke: Macmillan.

Chesters, G. and Welsh, I. (2004) 'Rebel Colours: "Framing" in Global Social Movements' *The Sociological Review* 52(3): 314–335.

Chesters, G. and Welsh, I. (2011) *Social Movements: Key Concepts*. London: Routledge.

Cho, W. K. T., Gimpel, J. G., and Shaw, D. R. (2012) 'The Tea Party Movement and the Geography of Collective Action' *Quarterly Journal of Political Science* 7: 105–133.

Cissé, M. (1997) *The Sans-Papiers – A Woman Draws the First Lessons: The New Movement of Asylum Seekers and Immigrants Without Papers in France*. London: Crossroads Books, available at <www.bok.net/pajol/madjiguene2.en.html>.

Clarke, J., Hall, S., Jefferson, T., and Roberts, B. (1976) 'Subcultures, Cultures and Class: A Theoretical Overview' in S. Hall and T. Jefferson (eds.) *Resistance through Rituals: Youth Subcultures in Post-war Britain*. London: Hutchinson, pp. 9–74.

Cohen, J. L. (1985) 'Strategy or Identity: New Theoretical Paradigms and Contemporary Social Movements' *Social Research* 52(4): 663–716.

Cohen, R. and Rai, S. M. (eds.) (2000) *Global Social Movements*. London: Continuum.

Coleman, R. (2005) 'Surveillance in the City: Primary Definition and Urban Spatial Order' *Crime Media Culture* 1(2): 131–148.

Corbin, D. (1981) *Life, Work, and Rebellion in the Coal Fields: The Southern West Virginia Miners, 1880–1930*. Urbana, IL: University of Illinois Press.

Cortez Ruiz, C. (2010) 'The Struggle Towards Rights and Communitarian Citizenship: The Zapatista Movement in Mexico' in L. Thompson and C. Tapscott (eds.) *Citizenship and Social Movements: Perspectives from the Global South*. London: Zed Books, pp. 160–183.

Courser, Z. (2012) 'The Tea "Party" as a Conservative Social Movement' *Society* 49(1): 43–53.

Cox, L. (2014) 'Movements Making Knowledge: A New Wave of Inspiration for Sociology?' *Sociology* 48(5): 954–971.

Cox, L. and Nilsen, A. G. (2007) 'Social Movements Research and the "Movement of Movements": Studying Resistance to Neoliberal Globalization' *Sociology Compass* 1(2): 424–442.

Cresswell, T. (1996) *In Place/Out of Place: Geography, Ideology, and Transgression*. Minneapolis, MN: University of Minnesota Press.

Crist, J. T. and McCarthy, J. D. (1996) '"If I Had a Hammer": The Changing Methodological Repertoire of Collective Behavior and Social Movements Research' *Mobilization* 1(1): 87–102.

Crossley, N. (2002) *Making Sense of Social Movements*. Buckingham: Open University Press.

Crossley, N. (2003) 'Even Newer Social Movements? Anti-Corporate Protests talist Crises and the Remoralization of Society' *Organization* 10(2): 287–305.

Cummings, J. (2008) 'Trade Mark Registered: Sponsorship Within the Australian Indie Music Festival Scene' *Continuum* 22(5): 675–685.

Dale, S. (1996) *McLuhan's Children: The Greenpeace Message and the Media.* Toronto, ON: Between the Lines.

Dalton, R. J., Kuechler, M., and Bürklin, W. (1990) 'The Challenge of New Social Movements' in R. J. Dalton and M. Kuechler (eds.) *Challenging the Political Order: New Social and Political Movements in Western Democracies.* Cambridge: Polity Press, pp. 3–20.

D'Anieri, P., Ernst, C., and Kier, E. (1990) 'New Social Movements in Historical Perspective' *Comparative Politics* 22(4): 445–458.

Davenport, C., Johnston, H., and Mueller, C. (eds.) (2004) *Repression and Mobilization.* Minneapolis, MN: University of Minnesota Press.

Davie, G. (1994) *Religion in Britain Since 1945: Believing Without Belonging.* Oxford: Blackwell.

Davies, W. (2011) 'From New Times to End Times', *New Statesman*, 16 November 2011, available at: <www.newstatesman.com/magazines/2011/11/capitalism-essay-wealth-crisis>.

Davis, J. E. (ed.) (2002a) *Stories of Change: Narrative and Social Movements.* Albany, NY: State University of New York Press.

Davis, J. E. (2002b) 'Narrative and Social Movements: The Power of Stories' in J. E. Davis (ed.) *Stories of Change: Narrative and Social Movements.* Albany, NY: State University of New York Press, pp. 3–29.

Dean, J. (2014) 'Tales of the Apolitical' *Political Studies* 62(2): 452–467.

de Lint, W. and Hall, A. (2009) *Intelligent Control: Developments in Public Order Policing in Canada.* Toronto, ON: University of Toronto Press.

della Porta, D. (ed.) (2007) *The Global Justice Movement: Cross-national and Transnational Perspectives.* Boulder, CO: Paradigm.

della Porta, D. (2012) 'Communication in Movement: Social Movements as Agents of Participatory Democracy' in B. D. Loader and D. Mercea (eds.) *Social Media and Democracy: Innovations in Participatory Politics.* London: Routledge, pp. 39–53.

della Porta, D., Andretta, M., Mosca, L., and Reiter, H. (eds.) (2006) *Globalization from Below: Transnational Activism and Protest Networks.* Minneapolis, MN: University of Minnesota Press.

della Porta, D. and Diani, M. (2006) *Social Movements: An Introduction* (2nd ed.). Oxford: Blackwell Publishing.

della Porta, D. and Fillieule, O. (2004) 'Policing Social Protest' in D. A. Snow, S. A. Soule, and H. Kriesi (eds.) *The Blackwell Companion to Social Movements.* Oxford: Blackwell, pp. 217–241.

della Porta, D., Kriesi, H., and Rucht, D. (eds.) (1999) *Social Movements in a Globalising World.* Houndmills: Palgrave Macmillan.

della Porta, D. and Mosca, L. (2005) 'Global-net for Global Movements? A Network of Networks for a Movement of Movements' *Journal of Public Policy* 25(1): 165–190.

della Porta, D. and Reiter, H. (eds.) (1998) *Policing Protest: The Control of Mass Demonstrations in Western Democracies*. Minneapolis, MN: University of Minnesota Press.

della Porta, D. and Tarrow, S. (eds.) (2005) *Transnational Protest and Global Activism: People, Passions, and Power*. Lanham, MD: Rowman & Littlefield.

Dennis, K. (2008) 'Keeping a Close Watch – The Rise of Self-surveillance and the Threat of Digital Exposure' *The Sociological Review* 56(3): 347–357.

De Sario, B. (2007) '"Precari su Marte": An Experiment in Activism Against Precarity' *Feminist Review* 87: 21–39.

Diani, M. (1992) 'The Concept of Social Movement' *The Sociological Review* 40(1): 1–25.

Diani, M. (1993) 'Themes of Modernity in New Religious Movements and New Social Movements' *Social Science Information* 32(1): 111–131.

Diani, M. (2000) 'Social Movement Networks Virtual and Real' *Information, Communication & Society* 3(3): 386–401.

Diani, M. and Eyerman, R. (eds.) (1992) *Studying Collective Action*. London: Sage.

DiMaggio, A. (2011) *The Rise of the Tea Party: Political Discontent and Corporate Media in the Age of Obama*. New York, NY: Monthly Review Press.

Doerr, N. (2010) 'Politicizing Precarity, Producing Visual Dialogues on Migration: Transnational Public Spaces in Social Movements' *Forum: Qualitative Sozialforschung* 11(2), Art. 30, May 2010.

Doyle, A. (2003) *Arresting Images: Crime and Policing in Front of the Television Camera*. Toronto, ON: University of Toronto Press.

Doyle, T. (2010) 'Surviving the Gang Bang Theory of Nature: The Environment Movement During the Howard Years' *Social Movement Studies* 9(2): 155–169.

Dreier, P. (2012) 'The Battle for the Republican Soul: Who Is Drinking the Tea Party?' *Contemporary Sociology* 41(6): 756–762.

Drury, J. and Reicher, S (2000) 'Collective Action and Psychological Change: The Emergence of New Social Identities' *British Journal of Social Psychology* 39: 579–604.

Durkheim, E. (1962 [1912]) *The Elementary Forms of the Religious Life*. New York, NY: Free Press.

Dwork, D. (1987) *War Is Good for Babies and Other Young Children: A History of the Infant and Child Welfare Movement in England 1898–1918*. London: Tavistock.

Earl, J. (2013) 'Studying Online Activism: The Effects of Sampling Design on Findings' *Mobilization* 18(4): 389–406.

Eder, K. (1985) 'The New Social Movements: Moral Crusades, Political Pressure Groups or Social Movements' *Social Research* 52(4): 869–890.

Eder, K. (1993) *The New Politics of Class: Social Movements and Cultural Dynamics in Advanced Societies*. London: Sage.

Edwards, F. and Mercer, D. (2007) 'Gleaning from Gluttony: An A. Subculture Confronts the Ethics of Waste' *Australian Geographer* 38(3).

Edwards, G. (2014) *Social Movements and Protest.* Cambridge: Cambridge University.

Eisinger, P. (1973) 'The Conditions of Protest Behaviour in American Cities' *American Political Science Review* 67(1): 11–28.

Eltantawy, N. and Wiest, J. B. (2011) 'Social Media in the Egyptian Revolution: Reconsidering Resource Mobilization Theory' *International Journal of Communications* 5: 1207–1224.

Erickson Nepstad, S. (1996) 'Popular Religion, Protest, and Revolt: The Emergence of Popular Insurgency in the Nicaraguan and Salvadoran Churches of the 1960s–80s' in C. Smith (ed.) *Disruptive Religion: The Force of Faith in Social Movement Activism.* New York, NY: Routledge, pp. 105–124.

Erickson Nepstad, S. and Smith, C. (2001) 'The Social Structure of Moral Outrage in Recruitment to the US Central America Peace Movement' in J. Goodwin, J. M. Jasper, and F. Polletta (eds.) *Passionate Politics: Emotions and Social Movements.* Chicago, IL: University of Chicago Press, pp. 158–174.

Erickson Nepstad, S. and Williams, R. H. (2007) 'Religion in Rebellion, Resistance and Social Movements' in J. A. Beckford and N. J. Demerath III (eds.) *The SAGE Handbook of the Sociology of Religion.* London: Sage, pp. 419–437.

Evans, R. J. (2007) (ed.) 'Nazism, Christianity and Political Religion: A Debate' *Journal of Contemporary History* (special issue) 42(1).

Evans, R. R. (ed.) (1969) *Readings in Collective Behaviour* (2nd ed.). Chicago, IL: Rand McNally College Publishing Company.

Eyerman, R. (2005) 'How Social Movements Move: Emotions and Social Movements' in H. Flam and D. King (eds.) *Emotions and Social Movements.* London: Routledge, pp. 41–56.

Eyerman, R. and Jamison, A. (1991) *Social Movements: A Cognitive Approach.* Cambridge: Polity Press.

Eyerman, R. and Jamison, A. (1998) *Music and Social Movements: Mobilizing Traditions in the Twentieth Century.* Cambridge: Cambridge University Press.

Farmer, E. and Boushel, M. (1999) 'Child Protection Policy and Practice: Women in the Front Line' in S. Watson and L. Doyal (eds.) *Engendering Social Policy.* Buckingham: Open University Press.

Fasenfest, D. (2012) 'Radical Politics and the Right' *Critical Sociology* 38(4): 463–465.

Feldman, A. (2002) 'Making Space at the Nations' Table: Mapping the Transformative Geographies of the International Indigenous Peoples' Movement' *Social Movement Studies* 1(1): 31–46.

Fenster, M. (2012) 'Disclosure's Effects: WikiLeaks and Transparency' *Iowa Law Review* 97(3): 753–807.

Fernandez, L. A. (2008) *Policing Dissent: Social Control and the Anti-globalization Movement.* Brunswick, NJ: Rutgers University Press.

Ferrell, J. (2006) *Empire of Scrounge: Inside the Urban Underground of Dumpster Diving, Trash Picking, and Street Scavenging.* New York, NY: New York University Press.

Fetner, T. (2012) 'The Tea Party: Manufactured Dissent or Complex Social Movement?' *Contemporary Sociology* 41(6): 762–766.

Fine, G. A. (1995) 'Public Narration and Group Culture: Discerning Discourse in Social Movements' in H. Johnston and B. Klandermans (eds.) *Social Movements and Culture.* London: UCL Press, pp. 127–143.

Fine, G. A. (2002) 'The Stories Group: Social Movements as "Bundles of Narratives"' in J. E. Davis (ed.) *Stories of Change: Narrative and Social Movements.* Albany, NY: State University of New York Press, pp. 229–245.

Fisher, M. (2009) *Capitalist Realism: Is There No Alternative?* Winchester: Zero Books.

Fitzgerald, S. T. (2009) 'Cooperative Collective Action: Framing Faith-Based Community Development' *Mobilization* 14(2): 181–198.

Flesher Fominaya, C. and Cox, L. (eds.) (2013) *Understanding European Movements: New Social Movements, Global Justice Struggles, Anti-Austerity Protest.* Abingdon: Routledge.

Forsyth, T. (2010) 'Thailand's Red Shirt Protests: Popular Movement or Dangerous Street Theatre?' *Social Movement Studies* 9(4): 461–468.

Foucault, M. (1977) *Discipline and Punish: The Birth of the Prison.* New York, NY: Pantheon Books.

Foweraker, J. (1995) *Theorizing Social Movements.* London: Pluto Press.

Fraser, N. (1995) 'From Redistribution to Recognition? Dilemmas of Justice in a "Post-Socialist" Age' *New Left Review* 212: 68–92.

Freedman, J. and Tarr, C. (2000) 'The *Sans-papières*: An Interview with Madjiguène Cissé' in J. Freedman and C. Tarr (eds.) *Women, Immigration and Identities in France.* Oxford: Berg.

Freud, S. (1945 [1921]) *Group Psychology and the Analysis of the Ego.* London: Hogarth.

Friedman, J. C. (ed.) (2013) *The Routledge History of Social Protest in Popular Music.* London: Routledge.

Funke, P. N. and Wolfson, T. (2014) 'Class In-Formation: The Intersection of Old and New Media in Contemporary Urban Movements' *Social Movement Studies* 13(3): 349–364.

Gaby, S. and Caren, N. (2012) 'Occupy Online: How Cute Old Men and Malcolm X Recruited 400,000 US Users to OWS on Facebook' *Social Movement Studies* 11(3–4): 367–374.

Gamson, W. A. (1992) 'The Social Psychology of Collective Action' in A. D. Morris and C. McClurg Mueller (eds.) *Frontiers in Social Movement Theory.* New Haven, CT: Yale University Press, pp. 53–76.

Gamson, W. A. and Wolfsfeld, G. (1993) 'Movements and Media as Interacting Systems' *Annals of the American Academy of Political and Social Science* 528: 114–125.

Garrett, R. K. (2006) 'Protest in an Information Society: A Review of Literature on Social Movements and New ICTs' *Information, Communication & Society* 9(2): 202–224.

Gerbaudo, P. (2012) *Tweets and the Streets: Social Media and Contemporary A* London: Pluto Press.

Gerges, F. (2011) 'Out of the Shadows' *New Statesman*, 28 November 2011, pp. 26–30.

Gerhards, J. and Rucht, D. (1992) 'Mesomobilization Contexts: Organizing and Framing in Two Protest Campaigns in West Germany' *American Journal of Sociology* 98: 555–596.

Giddens, A. (1991a) *The Consequences of Modernity*. Cambridge: Polity Press.

Giddens, A. (1991b) *Modernity and Self-Identity: Self and Society in the Late Modern Age*. Cambridge: Polity Press.

Gillan, K., Pickerill, J., and Webster, F. (2008) *Anti-War Activism: New Media and Protest in the Information Age*. Houndmills: Palgrave Macmillan.

Gitlin, T. (1980) *The Whole World Is Watching: Mass Media and the Making of the New Left*. Berkeley, CA: University of California Press.

Giugni, M. (1999) 'Introduction – How Social Movements Matter: Past Research, Present Problems, Future Developments' in M. Giugni, D. McAdam, and C. Tilly (eds.) *How Social Movements Matter*. Minneapolis, MN: University of Minnesota Press, pp. xiii–xxxiii.

Giugni, M. (ed.) (2009) *The Politics of Unemployment: Policy Responses and Collective Action*. Farnham: Ashgate.

Giugni, M. and Yamasaki, S. (2009) 'The Policy Impact of Social Movements: A Replication Through Qualitative Comparative Analysis' *Mobilization* 14(4): 467–484.

Giulianotti, R. and Robertson, R. (2004) 'The Globalization of Football: A Study in the Glocalization of the Serious Life' *British Journal of Sociology* 55(4): 545–568.

Goffman, E. (1974) *Frame Analysis*. Cambridge, MA: Harvard University Press.

Goldsmith, A. (2010) 'Policing's New Visibility' *British Journal of Criminology* 50(5): 914–934.

Goodwin, J. and Jasper, J. M. (1999) 'Caught in a Winding, Snarling Vine: The Structural Bias of Political Process Theory' *Sociological Forum* 14(1): 27–54.

Goodwin, J., Jasper, J. M., and Polletta, F. (2000) 'The Return of the Repressed: The Fall and Rise of Emotions in Social Movement Theory' *Mobilization* 5(1): 65–83.

Goodwin, J., Jasper, J. M., and Polletta, F. (2001) 'Introduction: Why Emotions Matter' in J. Goodwin, J. M. Jasper, and F. Polletta (eds.) *Passionate Politics: Emotions and Social Movements*. Chicago, IL: University of Chicago Press, pp. 1–24.

Goodwin, J. and Pfaff, S. (2001) 'Emotion Work in High-Risk Social Movements: Managing Fear in the U.S. and East German Civil Rights Movements' in J. Goodwin, J. M. Jasper, and F. Polletta (eds.) *Passionate Politics: Emotions and Social Movements*. Chicago, IL: University of Chicago Press, pp. 282–302.

Gould, D. (2001) 'Rock the Boat, Don't Rock the Boat, Baby: Ambivalence and the Emergence of Militant AIDS Activism' in J. Goodwin, J. M. Jasper, and F. Polletta (eds.) *Passionate Politics: Emotions and Social Movements*. Chicago, IL: University of Chicago Press, pp. 135–157.

Gould, D. B. (2002) 'Life During Wartime: Emotions and the Development of Act Up' *Mobilization* 7(2): 177–200.

Greer, C. and McLaughlin, E. (2012) '"This Is Not Justice": Ian Tomlinson, Institutional Failure and the Press Politics of Outrage' *British Journal of Criminology* 52(2): 274–293.

Gregory, D. (1994) *Geographical Imaginations.* Oxford: Blackwell.

Gross, J. (2009) 'Capitalism and Its Discontents: Back-to-the-Lander and Freegan Foodways in Rural Oregon' *Food and Foodways* 17: 57–79.

Gueye, A. (2006) 'The Colony Strikes Back: African Protest Movements in Postcolonial France' *Comparative Studies of South Asia, Africa and the Middle East* 26(2): 225–242.

Habermas, J. (1981) 'New Social Movements' *Telos* 49: 33–37.

Habermas, J. (1987) *The Theory of Communicative Action,* vol. 2. Boston, MA: Beacon Press.

Hadden, J. and Tarrow, S. (2007) 'Spillover or Spillout? The Global Justice Movement in the United States After 9/11' *Mobilization* 12(4): 359–376.

Haenfler, R., Johnson, B., and Jones, E. (2012) 'Lifestyle Movements: Exploring the Intersection of Lifestyle and Social Movements' *Social Movement Studies* 11(1): 1–20.

Haggerty, K. D. and Ericson, R. V. (2000) 'The Surveillant Assemblage' *British Journal of Sociology* 51(4): 605–622.

Halebsky, S. (2006) 'Explaining the Outcomes of Antisuperstore Movements: A Comparative Analysis of Six Communities' *Mobilization* 11(4): 443–460.

Hall, J. R. (1978) *The Ways Out: Utopian Communal Groups in an Age of Babylon.* London: Routledge & Kegan Paul.

Halvorsen, S. (2012) 'Beyond the Network? Occupy London and the Global Movement' *Social Movement Studies* 11(3–4): 427–433.

Hamel, P., Lustiger-Thaler, H., and Mayer, M. (eds.) (2000) *Urban Movements in a Globalizing World.* London: Routledge.

Hamilton, C. and Maddison, S. (eds.) (2007) *Silencing Dissent: How the Australian Government Is Controlling Public Opinion and Stifling Debate.* Sydney: Allen & Unwin.

Han, S. (2011) *Web 2.0.* London: Routledge.

Hannigan, J. A. (1990) 'Apples and Oranges or Varieties of the Same Fruit? The New Religious Movements and the New Social Movements Compared' *Review of Religious Research* 31(3): 246–258.

Hannigan, J. A. (1991) 'Social Movement Theory and the Sociology of Religion: Towards a New Synthesis' *Sociological Analysis* 52(4): 311–331.

Hannigan, J. A. (1993) 'New Social Movement Theory and the Sociology of Religion' in W. H. Swatos (ed.) *A Future for Religion? New Paradigms for Analysis.* Newbury Park, CA: Sage, pp. 1–18.

Hardt, M. and Negri, A. (2000) *Empire.* Cambridge, MA: Harvard University Press.

Hargrove, B. (1988) 'Religion, Development, and Changing Paradigms' *Sociological Analysis* 49: S33–48.

Hari, J. (2002) 'Now the Protestors Box Clever' *New Statesman*, 1 April 2002, pp. 23–24.

Harris, K. (2012) 'The Brokered Exuberance of the Middle Class: An Ethnographic Analysis of Iran's 2009 Green Movement' *Mobilization* 17(4): 435–455.

Hart, S. (1996) 'The Cultural Dimension of Social Movements: A Theoretical Reassessment and Literature Review' *Sociology of Religion* 57(1): 87–100.

Harvey, D. (1985) *Consciousness and the Urban Experience*. Baltimore, MD: Johns Hopkins University Press.

Harvey, D. (1990) *The Condition of Postmodernity*. Oxford: Blackwell.

Harvey, D. (2005) *A Brief History of Neoliberalism*. New York: Oxford University Press.

Harvey, N. (1998) *The Chiapas Rebellion: The Struggle for Land and Democracy*. Durham, NC: Duke University Press.

Herbert, S. (1997) *Policing Space: Territoriality and the Los Angeles Police Department*. Minneapolis, MN: University of Minnesota Press.

Hewitt, W. E. (1993) 'Liberation Theology in Latin America and Beyond' in W. H. Swatos (ed.) *A Future for Religion? New Paradigms for Analysis*. Newbury Park, CA: Sage, pp. 73–91.

Hirsch, J. (1988) 'The Crisis of Fordism, Transformations of the "Keynesian" Security State, and New Social Movements' *Research in Social Movements, Conflicts and Change* 10: 43–55.

Holzner, C. A. (2004) 'The End of Clientelism? Strong and Weak Networks in a Mexican Squatter Movement' *Mobilization* 9(3): 223–240.

Howard, P. N. and Hussain, M. M. (2011) 'The Upheavals in Egypt and Tunisia: The Role of Digital Media' *Journal of Democracy* 22(3): 35–48.

Howker, E. and Malik, S. (2010) *Jilted Generation: How Britain Has Bankrupt Its Youth*. London: Icon Books.

Hudson, A. (2005) 'Free Speech and Equality of Arms – The Decision in Steel & Morris v. United Kingdom' *European Human Rights Laws Review* 3: 301–309.

Huey, T. A. (2005) 'Thinking Globally, Eating Locally: Website Linking and the Performance of Solidarity in Global and Local Food Movements' *Social Movement Studies* 4(2): 123–137.

Hug, S. and Wisler, D. (1998) 'Correcting for Selection Bias in Social Movement Research' *Mobilization* 3(2): 141–161.

Hughes, N. (2011) '"Young People Took to the Streets and All of a Sudden All of the Political Parties Got Old": The 15M Movement in Spain' *Social Movement Studies* 10(4): 407–414.

Husu, H-M. (2013) 'Bourdieu and Social Movements: Considering Identity Movements in Terms of Field, Capital and Habitus' *Social Movement Studies* 12(3): 264–279.

Ibrahim, J. (2011) 'The New Toll on Higher Education and the UK Student Revolts of 2010–2011' *Social Movement Studies* 10(4): 415–442.

Inglehart, R. (1971) 'The Silent Revolution in Europe: Intergenerational Change in Post-industrial Societies' *The American Political Science Review* 65(4): 991–1017.

Inglehart, R. (1977) *The Silent Revolution: Changing Values and Political Styles Among Western Publics*. Princeton, NJ: Princeton University Press.

Jacobsson, K. and Lindblom, J. (2012) 'Moral Reflexivity and Dramaturgical Action in Social Movement Activism: The Case of the Plowshares and Animal Rights Sweden' *Social Movement Studies* 11(1): 41–60.

Jasper, J. M. (1997) *The Art of Moral Protest: Culture, Biography, and Creativity in Social Movements*. Chicago, IL: The University of Chicago Press.

Jasper, J. M. (1998) 'The Emotions of Protest: Affective and Reactive Emotions in and Around Social Movements' *Sociological Forum* 13: 397–424.

Jeffries, F. (2011) 'Saying Something: The Location of Social Movements in the Surveillance Society' *Social Movement Studies* 10(2): 175–190.

Jewkes, Y. (2011) *Media and Crime* (2nd ed.). London: Sage.

Johnston, H. (ed.) (2009) *Culture, Social Movements and Protest*. Farnham: Ashgate.

Johnston, H., Laraña, E., and Gusfield, J. R. (1994) 'Identities, Grievances and New Social Movements' in E. Laraña, H. Johnston, and J. R. Gusfield (eds.) *New Social Movements: From Ideology to Identity*. Philadelphia, PA: Temple University Press, pp. 3–35.

Johnston, H. and Klandermans, B. (eds.) (1995) *Social Movements and Culture*. London: UCL Press.

Jones, O. (2014) *The Establishment: And How They Get Away With It*. London: Allen Lane.

Jordan, T. (2007) 'Online Direct Action: Hacktivism and Radical Democracy' in L. Dahlberg and E. Siapera (eds.) *Radical Democracy and the Internet: Interrogating Theory and Practice*. London: Palgrave Macmillan.

Jordan, T. and Taylor, P. A. (2004) *Hacktivism and Cyberwars: Rebels With a Cause?* London: Routledge.

Joseph, L., Mahler, M., and Auyero, J. (eds.) (2007) *New Perspectives in Political Ethnography*. New York, NY: Springer.

Kalyvas, A. (2003) 'Feet of Clay? Reflections on Hardt's and Negri's *Empire*' *Constellations* 10(2): 264–279.

Kane, A. (2001) 'Finding Emotion in Social Movement Processes: Irish Land Movement Metaphors and Narratives' in J. Goodwin, J. M. Jasper, and F. Polletta (eds.) *Passionate Politics: Emotions and Social Movements*. Chicago, IL: University of Chicago Press, pp. 251–266.

Keane, J. (2003) *Global Civil Society?* Cambridge: Cambridge University Press.

Keck, M. and Sikkink, K. (1998) *Activists Beyond Borders: Advocacy Networks in International Politics*. Ithaca, NY: Cornell University Press.

Keith, M. and Pile, S. (1993) 'Introduction Part 2: The Place of Politics' in M. Keith and S. Pile (eds.) *Place and the Politics of Identity*. London: Routledge, pp. 22–40.

Kemp, D. (2001) 'Christaquarianism: A New Socio-religious Movement of Post-modern Society' *Implicit Religion* 4(1): 27–40.

Kemper, T. (2001) 'A Structural Approach to Social Movement Emotions' in J. Goodwin, J. M. Jasper, and F. Polletta (eds.) *Passionate Politics: Emotions and Social Movements*. Chicago, IL: University of Chicago Press, pp. 58–73.

Kenney, S. J. (2010) 'Mobilizing Emotions to Elect Women: The Symbolic Meaning of Minnesota's First Woman Supreme Court Justice' *Mobilization* 15(2): 135–158.

Kerton, S. (2012) 'Tahrir, Here? The Influence of the Arab Uprisings on the Emergence of Occupy' *Social Movement Studies* 11(3–4): 302–308.

Khomeini, A. (1980) *Sayings of the Ayatollah Khomeini: Political, Philosophical, Social and Religious*. New York, NY: Bantam Books.

Klandermans, B. (1991) 'New Social Movements and Resource Mobilization: The European and American Approach Revisited' in D. Rucht (ed.) *Research on Social Movements: The State of the Art in Western Europe and the USA*. Boulder, CO: Westview Press, pp. 17–44.

Klandermans, B. and Staggenborg, S. (eds.) (2002) *Methods of Social Movement Research*. Minneapolis, MN: University of Minnesota Press.

Klandermans, B. and Tarrow, S. (1988) 'Mobilization into Social Movements: Synthesizing European and American Approaches' in B. Klandermans, H. Kriesi, and S. Tarrows (eds.) *From Structure to Action: Comparing Social Movement Research Across Cultures*. Greenwich, CT: JAI Press, pp. 1–38.

Klein, N. (2000a) *No Logo*. London: Flamingo.

Klein, N. (2000b) 'The Tyranny of the Brands' *New Statesman*, 24 January 2000, available at: <www.newstatesman.com/node/136682>.

Kneale, M. (2013) 'The Austerity Pope' *New Statesman,* 18–24 October 2013, pp. 22–24, 26.

Kniss, F. and Burns, G. (2004) 'Religious Movements' in D. A. Snow, S. A. Soule, and H. Kriesi (eds.) *The Blackwell Companion to Social Movements*. Oxford: Blackwell, pp. 694–715.

Krieger, J. and Murphy, C. (1998) 'Transnational Opportunity Structures and the Evolving Roles of Movements for Women, Human Rights, Labor, Development, and the Environment: A Proposal for Research'. Department of Political Science, Wellesley College.

Kriesi, H. (1988) 'The Interdependence of Structure and Action: Some Reflections on the State of the Art' in B. Klandermans, H. Kriesi, and S. Tarrow (eds.) *From Structure to Action: Comparing Social Movement Research Across Cultures*. Greenwich, CT: JAI Press, pp. 349–368.

Kuhn, T. S. (1962) *The Structure of Scientific Revolutions*. Chicago, IL: University of Chicago Press.

Kulick, R. (2014) 'Making Media for Themselves: Strategic Dilemmas of Prefigurative Work in Independent Media Outlets' *Social Movement Studies* 13(3): 365–380.

Koopmans, R. (2004) 'Movements and Media: Selection Processes and Evolutionary Dynamics in the Public Sphere' *Theory and Society* 33(3–4): 367–391.

Kurzman, C. (1994) 'A Dynamic View of Resources: Evidence From the Iranian Revolution' *Research in Social Movements, Conflict and Change* 17: 53–84.

Kurzman, C. (1998) 'Organizational Opportunity and Social Movement Mobilization: A Comparative Analysis of Four Religious Movements' *Mobilization* 3(1): 23–49.

Kurzman, C. (2012) 'The Arab Spring Uncoiled' *Mobilization* 17(4): 377–390.

Langman, L. (2012) 'Cycles of Contention: The Rise and Fall of the Tea Party' *Critical Sociology* 38(4): 469–494.

Leach, D. K. and Haunss, S. (2009) 'Scenes and Social Movements' in H. Johnston (ed.) *Culture, Social Movements and Protest.* Farnham: Ashgate, pp. 255–276.

Le Bon, G. (1960 [1895]) *The Crowd: A Study of the Popular Mind.* New York, NY: Viking Press.

Lefebvre, H. (1979) 'Reconfiguring the Spatiality of Power: The Construction of a Supranational Migration Framework for the European Union' *Political Geography* 16: 123–143.

Lefebvre, H. (1991 [1974]) *The Production of Space* (trans. D. Nicholson-Smith). Oxford: Blackwell.

Leitner, H., Peck, J., and Sheppard, E. S. (eds.) (2007) *Contesting Neoliberalism: Urban Frontiers.* New York, NY: The Guildford Press.

Leizerov, S. (2000) 'Privacy Advocacy Groups Versus Intel: A Case Study of How Social Movements Are Tactically Using the Internet to Fight Corporations' *Social Science Computer Review* 18(4): 461–483.

Lewis, J. (1980) 'The Social History of Social Policy: Infant Welfare in Edwardian England' *Journal of Social Policy* 9(4): 463–486.

Lloyd, F. (1999) 'McLibel: Burger Culture on Trial' *University of Queensland Law Journal* 20(2): 340–344.

Loader, B. D. (2008) 'Social Movements and New Media' *Sociology Compass* 2(6): 1920–1933.

Loader, B. D. and Mercea, D. (2012) 'Networking Democracy? Social Media Innovations in Participatory Politics' in B. D. Loader and D. Mercea (eds.) *Social Media and Democracy: Innovations in Participatory Politics.* London: Routledge, pp. 1–10.

Lofland, J. (1995) 'Charting Degrees of Movement Culture: Tasks of the Cultural Cartographer' in H. Johnston and B. Klandermans (eds.) *Social Movements and Culture.* London: UCL Press, pp. 188–216.

Lofland, J. (1997) 'Systematizing Research Findings on Collective Behavior and Social Movements' *Mobilization* 2(1): 1–20.

Ludlow, P. (2010) 'Wikileaks and Hacktivist Culture', *The Nation*, 15 September 2010, available at: <www.thenation.com/article/154780/wikileaks-and-hacktivist-culture>.

Maddison, S. and Martin, G. (2010) 'Introduction to "Surviving Neoliberalism: The Persistence of Australian Social Movements"' *Social Movement Studies* 9(2): 101–120.

Maheu, L. (ed.) (1995) *Social Movements and Social Classes: The Future of Collective Action*. London: Sage.

Mann, S. (1998) '"Reflectionism" and "Diffusionism": New Tactics for Deconstructing the Video Surveillance Superhighway' *Leonardo* 31(2): 93–102.

Marquand, D. (2014) *Mammon's Kingdom: An Essay on Britain, Now*. London: Allen Lane.

Marston, S. A. (2001) 'Making Difference: Conflict over Irish Identity in the New York City St Patrick's Day Parade' *Political Geography* 21(3): 373–392.

Marston, S. A. (2003) 'Mobilizing Geography: Locating Space in Social Movement Theory' *Mobilization* 8(2): 227–233.

Martin, D. G. and Miller, B. (2003) 'Space and Contentious Politics' *Mobilization* 8(2): 143–156.

Martin, G. (1998) 'Generational Differences Amongst New Age Travellers' *The Sociological Review* 46(4): 735–756.

Martin, G. (2001) 'Social Movements, Welfare and Social Policy: A Critical Analysis' *Critical Social Policy* 21(3): 361–383.

Martin, G. (2002) 'Conceptualising Cultural Politics in Subcultural and Social Movements Studies' *Social Movement Studies* 1(1): 73–88.

Martin, G. (2004) 'New Social Movements and Democracy' in M. J. Todd and G. Taylor (eds.) *Democracy and Participation: Popular Protest and New Social Movements*. London: Merlin Press, pp. 29–54.

Martin, G. (2009) 'Subculture, Style, Chavs and Consumer Capitalism: Towards a Critical Cultural Criminology of Youth' *Crime Media Culture* 5(2): 123–145.

Martin, G. (2011a) 'Why the UK Riots Have More to do With Austerity Than Criminality' *On Line Opinion*, Monday 15 August, available at: <www.online opinion.com.au/view.asp?article=12470>.

Martin, G. (2011b) 'Showcasing Security: The Politics of Policing Space at the 2007 Sydney APEC meeting' *Policing & Society* 21(1): 27–48.

Martin, G. (2013) 'Subcultures and Social Movements' in D. A. Snow, D. della Porta, B. Klandermans, and D. McAdam (eds.) *The Wiley-Blackwell Encyclopedia of Social and Political Movements* (Volume III). Oxford: Wiley-Blackwell Publishing, pp. 1287–1291.

Martin, G. (2014) 'The Politics, Pleasure and Performance of New Age Travellers, Ravers and Anti-road Protestors: Connecting Festivals, Carnival and New Social Movements' in A. Bennett, J. Taylor, and I. Woodward (eds.) *The Festivalization of Culture*. Farnham: Ashgate, pp. 87–106.

G. (2015) 'Stop the Boats! Moral Panic in Australia Over Asylum Seekers' *tinuum*, available at: <http://dx.doi.org/10.1080/10304312.2014.986060>

Martin, G. and Scott Bray, R. (2013) 'Discolouring Democracy? Policing, Sensitive Evidence, and Contentious Deaths in the United Kingdom' *Journal of Law and Society* 40(4): 624–656.

Marx, G. T. (1998) 'Afterword: Some Reflections on the Democratic Policing of Demonstrations' in D. della Porta and H. Reiter (eds.) *Policing Protest: The Control of Mass Demonstrations in Western Democracies.* Minneapolis, MN: University of Minnesota Press, pp. 253–269.

Marx, G. (2007) 'A Tack in the Shoe and Taking Off the Shoe: Neutralization and Counter-neutralization Dynamics' *Surveillance and Society* 6(3): 294–306.

Maslow, A. H. (1943) 'A Theory of Human Motivation' *Psychological Review* 50: 370–396.

Mathiesen, T. (1997) 'The Viewer Society: Michel Foucault's "Panopticon" Revisited' *Theoretical Criminology* 1(2): 215–234.

Matthews, N. (1994) *Confronting Rape: The Feminist Anti-Rape Movement and the State.* New York, NY: Routledge.

Mattoni, A. and Doerr, N. (2007) 'Images Within the Precarity Movement in Italy' *Feminist Review* 87: 130–135.

Mayer, M. (1991) 'Politics in the Post-Fordist City' *Socialist Review* 21(1): 105–124.

Mayer, M. (2007) 'Contesting the Neoliberalism of Urban Governance' in H. Leitner, J. Peck, and E. S. Sheppard (eds.) *Contesting Neoliberalism: Urban Frontiers.* New York, NY: The Guildford Press, pp. 90–115.

McAdam, D. (1982) *Political Process and the Development of Black Insurgency 1930–1970.* Chicago, IL: The University of Chicago Press.

McAdam, D. (1995) '"Indicator" and "Spin-off" Movements: Diffusion Processes in Protest Cycles' in Traugott, M. (ed.) *Repertoires and Cycles of Collective Action.* Durham, NC: Duke University Press, pp. 217–239.

McAdam, D., McCarthy, J. D., and Zald, M. N. (1988) 'Social Movements' in N. J. Smelser (ed.) *Handbook of Sociology.* London: Sage, pp. 695–739.

McAdam, D., McCarthy, J. D., and Zald, M. N. (1996) 'Introduction: Opportunities, Mobilizing Structures and Framing Processes – Towards a Synthetic, Comparative Perspective on Social Movements' in D. McAdam, J. D. McCarthy, and M. N. Zald (eds.) *Comparative Perspectives on Social Movements: Political Opportunities, Mobilizing Structures, and Cultural Framings.* Cambridge: Cambridge University Press, pp. 1–20.

McAdam, D., Tarrow, S., and Tilly, C. (2001) *Dynamics of Contention.* Cambridge: Cambridge University Press.

McAllister Groves, J. (2001) 'Animal Rights and the Politics of Emotion: Folk Constructs of Emotions in the Animal Rights Movement' in J. Goodwin, J. M. Jasper, and F. Polletta (eds.) *Passionate Politics: Emotions and Social Movements.* Chicago: University of Chicago Press, pp. 212–229.

McBain, S. (2014) 'Hacktivists for Democracy' *New Statesman*, 4–10 April 2014, p. 29.

McCammon, H. J. and Campbell, K. E. (2002) 'Allies On the Road to Victory: Coalition Formation Between the Suffragists and the Woman's Christian Temperance Union' *Mobilization* 7(3): 231–251.

McCarthy, J. D. and Zald, M. N. (1977) 'Resource Mobilization and Social Movements: A Partial Theory' *American Journal of Sociology* 82(6): 1212–1241.

McDonald, K. (2002a) '*L'Intervention Sociologique* After Twenty-Five Years: Can It Translate into English?' *Qualitative Sociology* 25(2): 247–260.

McDonald, K. (2002b) 'From Solidarity to Fluidarity: Social Movements Beyond "Collective Identity" – The Case of Globalization Conflicts' *Social Movement Studies* 1(2): 109–128.

McGovern, A. F. (1989) *Liberation Theology and Its Critics*. Maryknoll, NY: Orbis.

McNevin, A. (2006) 'Political Belonging in a Neoliberal Era: The Struggle of the Sans-Papiers' *Citizenship Studies* 10(2): 135–151.

McVeigh, R. (2012) 'Making Sense of the Tea Party' *Contemporary Sociology* 41(6): 766–769.

Melucci, A. (1984) 'An End to Social Movements?' *Social Science Information* 23(4/5): 819–835.

Melucci, A. (1985) 'The Symbolic Challenge of Contemporary Movements' *Social Research* 52(4): 789–816.

Melucci, A. (1988) 'Social Movements and the Democratization of Everyday Life' in J. Keane (ed.) *Civil Society and the State*. London: Verso, pp. 245–59.

Melucci, A. (1989) *Nomads of the Present: Social Movements and Individual Needs in Contemporary Society*. London: Hutchinson Radius.

Melucci, A. (1992) 'Liberation or Meaning? Social Movements, Culture and Democracy' *Development and Change* 23(3): 43–77.

Melucci, A. (1994) 'A Strange Kind of Newness: What's "New" in New Social Movements?' in E. Laraña, H. Johnston, and J. R. Gusfield (eds.) *New Social Movements: From Ideology to Identity*. Philadelphia: Temple University Press, pp. 101–130.

Melucci, A. (1995) 'The Process of Collective Identity' in H. Johnston and B. Klandermans (eds.) *Social Movements and Culture*. London: UCL Press, pp. 41–63.

Melucci, A. (1996) *Challenging Codes: Collective Action in the Information Age*. Cambridge: Cambridge University Press.

Melucci, A. (1997) 'Identity and Difference in a Globalized World' in P. Werbner and T. Modood (eds.) *Debating Cultural Hybridity*. London: Zed Books, pp. 58–69.

Meyer, D. S. (2003) 'Political Opportunity and Nested Institutions' *Social Movement Studies* 2(1): 17–35.

Meyer, D. S. (2004) 'Protest and Political Opportunities' *Annual Review of Sociology* 30: 125–145.

273

Meyer, D.S. (2005) 'Introduction: Social Movements and Public Policy: Eggs, Chicken, and Theory' in D.S. Meyer, V. Jenness, and H. Ingram (eds.) *Routing the Opposition: Social Movements, Public Policy, and Democracy*. Minneapolis, MN: University of Minnesota Press, pp. 1–26.

Meyer, D.S. (2009) 'Claiming Credit: Stories of Movement Influence as Outcomes' in H. Johnston (ed.) *Culture, Social Movements and Protest*. Farnham: Ashgate, pp. 55–75.

Meyer, D.S. and Tarrow, S. (1998) 'A Movement Society: Contentious Politics for a New Century' in D.S. Meyer and S. Tarrow (eds.) *The Social Movement Society: Contentious Politics for a New Century*. Lanham, MD: Rowman & Littlefield, pp. 1–28.

Meyer, D.S. and Whittier, N. (1994) 'Social Movement Spillover' *Social Problems* 41: 277–298.

Miller, B.A. (2000) *Geography and Social Movements: Comparing Antinuclear Activism in the Boston Area*. Minneapolis, MN: University of Minnesota Press.

Monahan, T. (2006) 'Counter-Surveillance as Political Intervention' *Social Semiotics* 16(4): 515–534.

Montagna, N. (2006) 'The De-commodification of Urban Space and the Occupied Social Centres in Italy' *City* 10(3): 295–304.

Mooers, C. and Sears, A. (1992) 'The "New Social Movements" and the Withering Away of State Theory' in W.K. Carroll (ed.) *Organizing Dissent*. Toronto, ON: Garamond Press, pp. 52–68.

Moore, R. and Roberts, M. (2009) 'Do-it-yourself Mobilization: Punk and Social Movements' *Mobilization* 14(3): 273–291.

Morris, A. (1984) *The Origins of the Civil Rights Movement: Black Communities Organizing for Change*. New York, NY: Free Press.

Moser, A. (2003) 'Acts of Resistance: The Performance of Women's Grassroots Protest in Peru' *Social Movement Studies* 2(2): 177–190.

Muir, K. and Peetz, D. (2010) 'Not Dead Yet: The Australian Union Movement and the Defeat of a Government' *Social Movement Studies* 9(2): 215–228.

Muñoz, J.A. (2006) 'International Opportunities and Domestic Protest: Zapatistas, Mexico and the New World Economy' *Social Movement Studies* 5(3): 251–274.

Nash, K. (2000) *Contemporary Political Sociology: Globalization, Politics and Power*. Oxford: Blackwell.

Nash, K. (2002) 'Political Sociology Beyond the Social Democratic Nation-State' *Sociology* 36(2): 437–443.

Nash, K. (2012) 'Human Rights, Movements and Law: On Not Researching Legitimacy' *Sociology* 46(5): 797–812.

Neilson, B. and Rossiter, N. (2006) 'From Precarity to Precariousness and Back Again: Labour, Life and Unstable Networks' *Variant* 25 (Spring 2006): 10–13.

Neilson, B. and Rossiter, N. (2008) 'Precarity as a Political Concept, or, Fordism as Exception' *Theory, Culture and Society* 25(7–8): 51–72.

Nicholls, W., Miller, B., and Beaumont, J. (eds.) (2013) *Spaces of Contention: Spatialities and Social Movements*. Farnham: Ashgate.

Nicholson, M. A. (2000) 'McLibel: A Case Study in English Defamation Law' *Wisconsin International Law Journal* 18(1): 1–144.

Nielsen, K. (1991) 'Towards a Flexible Future – Theories and Politics' in B. Jessop, H. Kastendiek, K. Nielsen, and O. Pedersen (eds.) *The Politics of Flexibility*. Aldershot: Edward Elgar.

Noakes, J. A. and Gillham, P. F. (2006) 'Aspects of the "New Penology" in the Police Response to Major Political Protests in the United States, 1999–2000' in D. della Porta, A. Peterson, and H. Reiter (eds.) *The Policing of Transnational Protest*. Aldershot: Ashgate, pp. 97–115.

Oberschall, A. (1973) *Social Conflict and Social Movements*. Englewood Cliffs, NJ: Prentice-Hall.

Offe, C. (1985) 'New Social Movements: Challenging the Boundaries of Institutional Politics' *Social Research* 52(4): 817–867.

Olesen, T. (2005) 'The Uses and Misuses of Globalization in the Study of Social Movements' *Social Movement Studies* 4(1): 49–63.

Olivera, O. (2004) *¡Cochabamba! Water War in Bolivia*. Cambridge, MA: South End Press.

Olson, M. (1965) *The Logic of Collective Action: Public Goods and the Theory of Groups*. Cambridge, MA: Harvard University Press.

Osa, M. (1996) 'Pastoral Mobilisation and Contention: The Religious Foundations of the Solidarity Movement in Poland' in C. Smith (ed.) *Disruptive Religion: The Force of Faith in Social Movement Activism*. New York, NY: Routledge, pp. 67–85.

Owens, L. (2008) 'From Tourists to Anti-Tourists to Tourist Attractions: The Transformation of the Amsterdam Squatters' Movement' *Social Movement Studies* 7(1): 43–59.

Parker, M. (2000) 'The Sociology of Organizations and the Organization of Sociology: Some Reflections on the Making of a Division of Labour' *The Sociological Review* 48(1): 124–146.

Parkin, F. (1968) *Middle Class Radicalism: The Social Bases of the British Campaign for Nuclear Disarmament*. New York, NY: Praeger Publishers.

Pascall, G. (1998) 'Social Movements and Social Policy: Gender and Social Policy' in N. Ellison and C. Pierson (eds.) *Developments in British Social Policy* (1st ed.). Basingstoke: Macmillan, pp. 191–204.

Peterson, P. (1987) 'Flag, Torch and Fist: The Symbols of Anarchism' *Freedom* 48(11): 8.

Pichardo, N. A. (1997) 'New Social Movements: A Critical Review' *Annual Review of Sociology* 23: 411–430.

Pickerill, J. and Krinsky, J. (2012) 'Why Does Occupy Matter?' *Social Movement Studies* 11(3–4): 279–287.

Plotke, D. (1990) 'What's So New About the New Social Movements?' *Socialist Review* 90(1): 81–102.

F. (1998a) 'Contending Stories: Narrative in Social Movements' *Qualitative logy* 21(4): 419–446.

Polletta, F. (1998b) '"It Was Like a Fever . . ." Narrative and Identity in Social Protest' *Social Problems* 45(2): 137–159.

Polletta, F. (2002) 'Plotting Protest: Mobilizing Stories in the 1960 Sit-Ins' in J. E. Davis (ed.) *Stories of Change: Narrative and Social Movements*. Albany, NY: State University of New York Press, pp. 31–51.

Polletta, F. and Amenta, E. (2001) 'Conclusion: Second That Emotion? Lessons from Once-Novel Concepts on Social Movement Research' in J. Goodwin, J. M. Jasper, and F. Polletta (eds.) *Passionate Politics: Emotions and Social Movements*. Chicago, IL: University of Chicago Press, pp. 303–316.

Purdue, D., Dürrschmidt, J., Jowers, P., and O'Doherty, R. (1997) 'DIY Culture and Extended Milieux: LETS, Veggie Boxes and Festivals' *The Sociological Review* 45(4): 645–667.

Pusey, M. (1991) *Economic Rationalism in Canberra: A Nation-Building State Changes Its Mind*. Cambridge: Cambridge University Press.

Putnam, R. (1995) 'Bowling Alone: America's Declining Social Capital' *Journal of Democracy* 6(1): 65–78.

Rasmussen, S. and Schoen, D. (2010) *Mad as Hell: How the Tea Party Movement is Fundamentally Remaking Our Two-Party System*. New York, NY: Harper.

Reygadas, L., Ramos, T., and Montoya, G. (2009) 'Pandora's Box: The Implications of Social Movements on Development. Lessons from the Lacandona Jungle in Chiapas' *Social Movement Studies* 8(3): 225–241.

Ritzer, G. (1993) *The McDonaldization of Society*. Thousand Oaks, CA: Pine Forge Press.

Roberts, J. M. (2008) 'Expressive Free Speech, the State and the Public Sphere: A Bakhtinian-Deleuzian Analysis of "Public Address" at Hyde Park' *Social Movement Studies* 7(2): 101–119.

Rodgers, K. (2010) '"Anger Is Why We're All Here": Mobilizing and Managing Emotions in a Professional Activist Organization' *Social Movement Studies* 9(3): 273–292.

Rolfe, B. (2005) 'Building an Electronic Repertoire of Contention' *Social Movement Studies* 4(1): 65–74.

Romanos, E. (2014) 'Evictions, Petitions and *Escraches*: Contentious Housing in Austerity Spain' *Social Movement Studies* 13(2): 296–302.

Rosello, M. (1998) 'Representing Illegal Immigrants in France: From *Clandestins* to *L'affaire des Sans-Papiers de Saint-Bernard*' *Journal of European Studies* 28(1): 137–151.

Rosenkrands, J. (2004) 'Politicizing *Homo Economicus*: Analysis of Anti-corporate Websites' in W. van de Donk, B. D. Loader, P. G. Nixon, and D. Rucht (eds.) *Cyberprotest: New Media, Citizens and Social Movements*. London: Routledge, pp. 57–76.

Ross, A. (2008) 'The New Geography of Work. Power to the Precarious?' *Theory, Culture and Society* 25(7–8): 31–49.

Roszak, T. (1970) *The Making of a Counter Culture*. London: Faber & Faber.

Rothe, D. L. and Steinmetz, K. F. (2013) 'The Case of Bradley Manning: State Victimization, Realpolitik and Wikileaks' *Contemporary Justice Review* 16(2): 280–292.

Rothschild-Whitt, J. (1979) 'The Collectivist Organization: An Alternative to Rational-bureaucratic Models' *American Sociological Review* 44: 509–527.

Roy, O. (2012) 'The Islamic Counter-revolution' *New Statesman*, 23 January 2012, pp. 24–22, 27, 29.

Rucht, D. (2005) 'Appeal, Threat, and Press Resonance: Comparing Mayday Protests in London and Berlin' *Mobilization* 10(1): 161–182.

Ruggiero, V. (2001) *Movements in the City: Conflicts in the European Metropolis*. Harlow: Prentice Hall.

Sajor, I. L. (2004) 'Challenging International Law: The Quest for Justice of the Former "Comfort Women"' in S. Pickering and C. Lambert (eds.) *Global Issues, Women and Justice*. Sydney: Sydney Institute of Criminology Series, pp. 288–306.

Salter, L. and Boyce Kay, J. (2011) 'The UWE Student Occupation' *Social Movement Studies* 10(4): 423–430.

Sampedro, V. (1997) 'The Media Politics of Social Protest' *Mobilization* 2(2): 185–205.

Sandbrook, D. (2012) *Seasons in the Sun: The Battle for Britain, 1974–1979*. London: Allen Lane.

Sassen, S. (2001) *The Global City*. New York: Princeton University Press.

Sawer, M. (2007) 'Wearing Your Politics on Your Sleeve: The Role of Political Colours in Social Movements' *Social Movement Studies* 6(1): 39–56.

Sbicca, J. and Perdue, R. T. (2014) 'Protest Through Presence: Spatial Citizenship and Identity Formation in Contestations of Neoliberal Crises' *Social Movement Studies* 13(3): 309–327.

Schehr, R. C. (1997) *Dynamic Utopia: Establishing Intentional Communities as a New Social Movement*. Westport, CT: Bergin & Garvey.

Scott, A. (1990) *Ideology and the New Social Movements*. London: Unwin Hyman.

Scott, A. and Street, J. (2000) 'From Media Politics to E-protest: The Use of Popular Culture and New Media in Parties and Social Movements' *Information, Communication & Society* 3(2): 215–240.

Scott Bray, R. (2013) 'Paradoxical Justice: The Case of Ian Tomlinson' *Journal of Law and Medicine* 21(2): 447–472.

Seal, L. (2013) 'Pussy Riot and Feminist Cultural Criminology: A New "Femininity in Dissent"?' *Contemporary Justice Review* 16(2): 293–303.

Sennett, R. (1998) *The Corrosion of Character: The Personal Consequences of Work in the New Capitalism*. New York, NY: W. W. Norton & Company.

Shackle, S. (2011) 'Canon Chancellor of St Paul's Cathedral resigns' *New Statesman*, 27 October 2011, available at: <www.newstatesman.com/blogs/the-staggers/2011/10/fraser-notice-protest>.

Shapiro, M. (1999) 'Triumphant Geographies' in M. Featherstone and S. Lash (eds.) *Spaces of Culture: City, Nation, World*. London: Sage.

Sharpe, E. K. (2008) 'Festivals and Social Change: Intersections of Pleasure and Politics at a Community Music Festival' *Leisure Sciences* 30: 217–234.

Shaw, M. (1994) 'Civil Society and Global Politics: Beyond a Social Movement Approach' *Millennium* 23(3): 647–667.

Shemtov, R. (1999) 'Taking Ownership of Environmental Problems: How Local Nimby Groups Expand Their Goals' *Mobilization* 4(1): 91–106.

Shimazono, S. (1999) '"New Age Movement" or "New Spirituality Movements and Culture"?' *Social Compass* 46(2): 121–133.

Sieder, R. (2005) 'Challenging Citizenship, Neo-liberalism and Democracy: Indigenous Movements and the State in Latin America' *Social Movement Studies* 4(3): 301–307.

Sklair, L. (1995) 'Social Movements and Global Capitalism' *Sociology* 29(3): 495–512.

Skocpol, T. and Williamson, V. (2012) *The Tea Party and the Remaking of Republican Conservatism*. Oxford: Oxford University Press.

Smelser, N. J. (1962) *Theory of Collective Behaviour*. London: Routledge & Kegan Paul.

Smelser, N. J. (1964) 'Theoretical Issues of Scope and Problems' *The Sociological Quarterly* 5(2): 116–122.

Smith, A. (2008) *Native Americans and the Christian Right: The Gendered Politics of Unlikely Alliances*. Durham, NC: Duke University Press.

Smith, C. (1996a) 'Correcting a Curious Neglect, or Bringing Religion Back In' in C. Smith (ed.) *Disruptive Religion: The Force of Faith in Social Movement Activism*. New York, NY: Routledge, pp. 1–25.

Smith, C. (ed.) (1996b) *Disruptive Religion: The Force of Faith in Social Movement Activism*. New York, NY: Routledge.

Smith, J. (2004) 'Transnational Processes and Movements' in D. A. Snow, S. A. Soule, and H. Kriesi (eds.) *The Blackwell Companion to Social Movements*. Oxford: Blackwell, pp. 311–335.

Smith, J. (2008) *Social Movements for Global Democracy*. Baltimore, MD: The Johns Hopkins University Press.

Smith, J. and Johnston, H. (eds.) (2002) *Globalization and Resistance: Transnational Dimensions of Social Movements*. Lanham, MD: Rowman & Littlefield.

Smith, J. Harvey (1978) 'Agricultural Workers and the French Wine-Growers' Revolt of 1907' *Past and Present* 79: 101–125.

Smith, R. L. (1984) 'Creating Neighbourhood Identity through Citizen Activism' *Urban Geography* 5(1): 49–70.

Smith, R. L. (1985) 'Activism and Social Status as Determinants of Neighbourhood Identity' *Professional Geographer* 37(4): 421–432.

Snell, L. (2008) *Protest, Policing, Protection: The Expansion of Police Powers and the Impact on Human Rights in NSW – The Policing of APEC as a Case Study.* Sydney: Combined Community Legal Centres Group (NSW) and Kingsford Legal Centre.

Snow, D. A. (2004) 'Social Movements as Challenges to Authority: Resistance to an Emerging Conceptual Hegemony' in D. J. Myers and D. M. Cress (eds.) *Authority in Contention.* Amsterdam: JAI Press, pp. 3–25.

Snow, D. A. and Benford, R. D. (1988) 'Ideology, Frame Resonance, and Participant Mobilization' *International Social Movement Research* 1: 197–218.

Snow, D. A. and Benford, R. D. (1992) 'Master Frames and Cycles of Protest' in A. D. Morris and C. McClurg Mueller (eds.) *Frontiers in Social Movement Theory.* New Haven, CT: Yale University Press, pp. 133–155.

Snow, D. A., Burke Rochford, E., Worden, S. K., and Benford, R. D. (1986) 'Frame Alignment Processes, Micromobilization, and Movement Participation' *American Sociological Review* 51(4): 464–481.

Soja, E. and Hooper, B. (1993) 'The Spaces that Difference Makes: Some Notes on the Geographical Margins of the New Cultural Politics' in M. Keith and S. Pile (eds.) *Place and the Politics of Identity.* London: Routledge, pp. 183–205.

Soldatic, K. and Chapman, A. (2010) 'Surviving the Assault? The Australian Disability Movement and the Neoliberal Workfare State' *Social Movement Studies* 9(2): 139–154.

Soule, S. A. (2009) *Contention and Corporate Social Responsibility.* Cambridge: Cambridge University Press.

St John, G. (2008) 'Protestival: Global Days of Action and Carnivalized Politics in the Present' *Social Movement Studies* 7(2): 167–190.

Staggenborg, S. (1988) 'The Consequences of Professionalization and Formalization in the Pro-Choice Movement' *American Sociological Review* 53(4): 585–605.

Staggenborg, S. (2011) *Social Movements.* Oxford: Oxford University Press.

Standing, G. (2011) *The Precariat: The New Dangerous Class.* London: Bloomsbury.

Stein, A. (2001) 'Revenge of the Shamed: The Christian Right's Emotional Culture War' in J. Goodwin, J. M. Jasper, and F. Polletta (eds.) *Passionate Politics: Emotions and Social Movements.* Chicago, IL: University of Chicago Press, pp. 115–131.

Steinmetz, G. (1994) 'Regulation Theory, Post-Marxism, and the New Social Movements' *Comparative Studies in Society and History* 36(1): 176–212.

Sutton, P. W. and Vertigans, S. (2006) 'Islamic "New Social Movements"? Radical Islam, Al-Qa'ida and Social Movement Theory' *Mobilization* 11(1): 101–115.

Swatos, W. H. (ed.) (1993) *A Future for Religion? New Paradigms for Analysis.* Newbury Park, CA: Sage.

Tarrow, S. (1983) *Struggling to Reform: Social Movements and Policy Change During Cycles of Protest.* Western Societies Paper No. 15. Ithaca, NY: Cornell University.

Tarrow, S. (1991) 'Comparing Social Movement Participation in Western Europe and the United States: Uses and a Proposal for Synthesis' in D. Rucht (ed.) *Research on*

Social Movements: The State of the Art in Western Europe and the USA. Boulder, CO: Westview Press, pp. 392–420.

Tarrow, S. (1992) 'Mentalities, Political Cultures, and Collective Action Frames: Constructing Meanings Through Action' in A. D. Morris and C. McClurg Mueller (eds.) *Frontiers in Social Movement Theory*. New Haven, CT: Yale University Press, pp. 174–202.

Tarrow, S. (1994) *Power in Movement: Social Movements and Contentious Politics* (1st ed.). Cambridge: Cambridge University Press.

Tarrow, S. (1995) 'Cycles of Collective Action: Between Moments of Madness and the Repertoire of Contention' in M. Traugott (ed.) *Repertoires and Cycles of Collective Action*. Durham, NC: Duke University Press, pp. 89–115.

Tarrow, S. (1998) *Power in Movement: Social Movements and Contentious Politics* (2nd ed.). Cambridge: Cambridge University Press.

Tarrow, S. (2005) *The New Transnational Activism*. Cambridge: Cambridge University Press.

Taylor, P. A. (2005) 'From Hackers to Hacktivists: Speed Bumps on the Global Superhighway?' *New Media and Society* 7(5): 625–646.

Taylor, V. (1989) 'Social Movement Continuity: The Women's Movement in Abeyance' *American Sociological Review* 54(5): 761–775.

Taylor, V. (1999) 'Gender and Social Movements: Gender Processes in Women's Self-help Movements' *Gender and Society* 13(1): 8–33.

Taylor, V. and Rupp, L. J. (2002) 'Loving Internationalism: The Emotion Culture of Transnational Women's Organizations, 1888–1945' *Mobilization* 7(2): 141–158.

Taylor, V. and Van Willigen, M. (1996) 'Women's Self-help and the Reconstruction of Gender: The Postpartum Support and Breast Cancer Movements' *Mobilization* 1(2): 123–42.

Tazreiter, C. (2010) 'Local to Global Activism: The Movement to Protect the Rights of Refugees and Asylum Seekers' *Social Movement Studies* 9(2): 201–214.

Thomas, S. (2010) 'Do Freegans Commit Theft?' *Legal Studies* 30(1): 98–125.

Thompson, K. (1996) *Key Quotations in Sociology*. London: Routledge.

Thompson, M. J. (2012) 'Suburban Origins of the Tea Party: Spatial Dimensions of the New Conservative Personality' *Critical Sociology* 38(4): 511–528.

Thorson, K., Driscoll, K., Ekdale, B., Edgerly, S., Gamber Thompson, L., Schrock, A., Swartz, L., Vraga, E. K., and Wells, C. (2013) 'YouTube, Twitter and the Occupy Movement: Connecting Content and Circulation Practices' *Information, Communication & Society* 16(3): 421–451.

Tilly, C. (1979) 'Repertoires of Contention in America and Britain, 1750–1830' in M. Zald and J. McCarthy (eds.) *The Dynamics of Social Movements*. Cambridge, MA: Winthrop, pp. 125–155.

Tilly, C. (1986) *The Contentious French*. Cambridge, MA: Harvard University Press.

Tilly, C. (1995) 'Contentious Repertoires in Great Britain, 1758–1834' in M. Traugott (ed.) *Repertoires and Cycles of Collective Action*. Durham, NC: Duke University Press, pp. 15–42.

Tilly, C. (2006) *Regimes and Repertoires*. Chicago, IL: University of Chicago Press.

Tormey, S. (2006) '"Not in My Name": Deleuze, Zapatismo and the Critique of Representation' *Parliamentary Affairs* 59(1): 138–154.

Tormey, S. (2013) *Anti-Capitalism: A Beginner's Guide* (revised ed.). London: Oneword Publications.

Touraine, A. (1978) *Lutte Étidiante*. Paris: Seuil.

Touraine, A. (1981) *The Voice and the Eye*. Cambridge: Cambridge University Press.

Touraine, A. (1985) 'An Introduction to the Study of Social Movements' *Social Research* 52(4): 749–87.

Tremayne, M. (2014) 'Anatomy of Protest in the Digital Era: A Network Analysis of Twitter and Occupy Wall Street' *Social Movement Studies* 13(1): 110–126.

Tucker, K. H. (1991) 'How New Are the New Social Movements?' *Theory, Culture and Society* 8(2): 75–98.

Turner, B. S. (1986) *Citizenship and Capitalism: The Debate over Reformism*. London: Allen and Unwin.

Turner, B. S. (2013) *The Religious and the Political: A Comparative Sociology of Religion*. Cambridge: Cambridge University Press.

Turner, R. and Killian, L. (1987 [1957]) *Collective Behaviour*. Englewood Cliffs, NJ: Prentice-Hall.

Turner, R. and Killian, L. (1988) 'Behaviour Without Guile: Chicago in the Late 1940s' *Sociological Perspective* 31: 315–324.

Tyson, D. (2009) 'Questions of Guilt and Innocence in the Victorian Criminal Trial of Robert Farquharson and the Fact Before Theory Internet Campaign' *Current Issues in Criminal Justice* 21(2): 181–204.

Uitermark, J. and Nicholls, W. (2012) 'How Local Networks Shape a Global Movement: Comparing Occupy in Amsterdam and Los Angeles' *Social Movement Studies* 11(3–4): 295–301.

Van Aelst, P. and Walgrave, S. (2002) 'New Media, New Movements? The Role of the Internet in Shaping the "Anti-globalization" Movement' *Information, Communication & Society* 5(4): 465–493.

van de Donk, W., Loader, B. D., Nixon, P. G., and Rucht, D. (eds.) (2004) *Cyberprotest: New Media, Citizens and Social Movements*. London: Routledge.

Van der Heijden, H-A. (2006) 'Globalization, Environmental Movements, and the International Political Opportunity Structure' *Organization and Environment* 19(1): 28–45.

Van Laer, J. (2010) 'Activists Online and Offline: The Internet as an Information Channel for Protest Demonstrations' *Mobilization* 15(3): 347–366.

Vidal, J. (1997) *McLibel: Burger Culture on Trial*. London: Macmillan.

Vitale, A.S. (2005) 'From Negotiated Management to Command and Control: How the New York Police Department Polices Protest' *Policing & Society* 15(3): 283–304.

Waddington, D. and King, M. (2007) 'The Impact of the Local: Police Public Order Strategies During the G8 Justice and Home Affairs Ministerial Meetings' *Mobilization* 12(4): 417–430.

Walgrave, S. and Verhulst, J. (2006) 'Towards "New Emotional Movements"? A Comparative Exploration into a Specific Movement Type' *Social Movement Studies* 5(3): 275–304.

Walgrave, S. and Verhulst, J. (2011) 'Selection and Response Bias in Protest Surveys' *Mobilization* 16(2): 203–222.

Wallace, A. (1956) 'Revitalization Movements' *American Anthropologist* 58: 264–281.

Wallerstein, I. (1976) *The Modern World-System: Capitalist Agriculture and the Origins of the European World-Economy in the Sixteenth Century.* New York, NY: Academic Press.

Wallis, R. (1984) *The Elementary Forms of the New Religious Life.* London: Routledge & Kegan Paul.

Walter, M. (2010) 'Market Forces and Indigenous Resistance Paradigms' *Social Movement Studies* 9(2): 121–137.

Weber, M. (1978 [1922]) *Economy and Society: An Outline of Interpretive Sociology* (eds. G. Roth and C. Wittich). Berkeley and Los Angeles, CA: California University Press.

Weber, M. (1947 [1922]) *Theory of Social and Economic Organization.* New York, NY: The Free Press.

Webster, F. (ed.) (2001) *Culture and Politics in the Information Age: A New Politics?* London: Routledge.

Welch, M. (2011) 'Counterveillance: How Foucault and the Groupe d'Information sur les Prisons Reversed the Optics' *Theoretical Criminology* 15(3): 301–313.

White, R. C. and Howard Hopkins, C.; with an essay by Bennett, J. C. (1976) *The Social Gospel: Religion and Reform in Changing America.* Philadelphia, PA: Temple University Press.

Wieviorka, M. (2005) 'After New Social Movements' *Social Movement Studies* 4(1): 1–19.

Wiktorowicz, Q. (2004) 'Introduction: Islamic Activism and Social Movement Theory' in Q. Wiktorowicz (ed.) *Islamic Activism: A Social Movement Theory Approach.* Bloomington, IN: Indiana University Press, pp. 1–33.

Wilby, P. (2012) 'Alan Rusbridger: The Quiet Evangelist' *New Statesman,* 4 June 2012, pp. 32–37, 39, available at: <www.newstatesman.com/media/media/2012/05/guardian-editor-alan-rusbridger-peter-wilby>.

Willetts, D. (2010) *The Pinch: How the Baby Boomers Took Their Children's Future – and Why They Should Give It Back.* London: Atlantic Books.

Williams, R. H. (2000) 'Introduction: Promise Keepers: A Comment on Religion and Social Movements' *Sociology of Religion* 61(1): 1–10.

Williams, R. H. (2004) 'The Cultural Contexts of Collective Action: Constraints, Opportunities, and the Symbolic Life of Social Movements' in D. A. Snow, S. A. Soule, and H. Kriesi (eds.) *The Blackwell Companion to Social Movements*. Oxford: Blackwell Publishing, pp. 91–115.

Williams, R. H. (2006) 'Collective Action, Everyday Protest, and Lived Religion' *Social Movement Studies* 5(1): 83–89.

Willis, P. (1978) *Profane Culture*. London: Routledge & Kegan Paul.

Wilson, D. and Serisier, T. (2010) 'Video Activism and the Ambiguities of Counter-surveillance' *Surveillance and Society* 8(2): 166–180.

Wouters, R. (2013) 'From the Street to the Screen: Characteristics of Protest Events as Determinants of Television News Coverage' *Mobilization* 18(1): 83–105.

Yates, J. J. and Hunter J. D. (2002) 'Fundamentalism: When History Goes Awry' in J. E. Davis (ed.) *Stories of Change: Narrative and Social Movements*. Albany, NY: State University of New York Press, pp. 123–148.

Young, A. (1990) *Femininity in Dissent*. London: Routledge.

Young, M. P. (2001) 'A Revolution of the Soul: Transformative Experiences and Immediate Abolition' in J. Goodwin, J. M. Jasper, and F. Polletta (eds.) *Passionate Politics: Emotions and Social Movements*. Chicago, IL: University of Chicago Press, pp. 99–114.

INDEX

Abengoa 170
abeyance structures: lifestyle movements as 139, 253–4; and political opportunity 253; and resource mobilization 199; and social movements 67, 86–9, 106; and social welfare 89–90; and women's activism 90
abolitionism 128
Aboriginal peoples *see* indigenous peoples; indigenous peoples' movements
abortion issues 128, 147, 164, 182; and the Tea Party 173
accumulation, intensive vs. flexible 75
acting crowd, 13; *see also* crowd behaviour; crowd psychology
action, collective *see* collective action
activists and activism: AIDS 114; animal rights 101–2, 155; anti-corporate 44–5, 110, 171, 203; anti-globalization 103, 186, 211; anti-sweatshop 203, 226; anti-war 237; black 32, 41, 52; Christian conservative 146; collective 1, 3; couch potato 197, 219; effects of on public policy 55; Facebook 218; feminist 86, 88, 90, 94, 117; global 239–41, 253; global justice 223; global/transnational 50, 155, 239–41; grassroots 59, 118–19; Islamic 128, 129, 216, 252; lesbian and gay (LGBT) 32, 77; media 207; middle-class 64–5; mob 214; neighborhood

156; offline 219; optical 207; peace 117, 161; professional 114; pro-life 128, 146; social movement 55; storytelling as 109; student 113; Tea Party 176; transnational 9, 222–5, 231, 234; union (labour) 141; use of music in 141–2; use of new social media in 194–5; video 193–4, 210; *see also* hacktivism; social movements
activity, instrumental-strategic 93
actors: collective 7, 28, 53, 69, 100, 118, 128, 137, 194, 228, 256; contemporary 69–70; deliberate 112; established 4; media 193; non-state 234, 235; plurality of 39; political 8, 45, 67, 68, 160; rational collective 8, 35, 36, 100 social 62, 65, 224; women 119
Adbusters 203
Afghanistan, US invasion of 129, 237
Africa: Arab Spring in 216; former colonies in 159–60; religious protest in 127
aged movement 57
agency: and globalization 224; human 215, 219; and the repertoire metaphor 46; state 166, 170
agitation 16, 23
Aguas del Tunari 170–1
Al Jazeera 217
Albert, Marcelin 47
Alexander, Cecil F. 142
Ali, Muhammad 149

Ford, Henry 74
Fordism 73, 74–5, 81, 85, 90; *see also*
    post-Fordism
Foucault, Michel 67, 206, 207
Fourth World 165
frame alignment 56, 100, 101, 108, 109
frame analysis 55
Frame Analysis (Goffman) 56
frames and framing 29–30, 36, 58, 64,
    94, 98, 100, 118, 161, 250; in animal
    rights activism 101–2; collective
    action 56–7, 112; control of 107;
    criticism of 108, 110; cultural 50, 57;
    diagnostic 56; and geography 161;
    and globalization 224; influences on
    109; master 57; by media 195; non-
    emotional 101–2; perspective of 123;
    processes of 58; social movement 161;
    spatiotemporal 163; theories of 112,
    113; transnational 224–5, 239; *see also*
    injustice frames
France: film and television industries
    in 79; human rights issues in 159;
    industry workers in 83; McDonald's
    in 230; popular action in 47–50;
    relationship with former African
    colonies 159–60; social movements
    in 6; undocumented immigrants in
    157–60
Francis (pope) 149
Fraser, Giles 172
Fraser, Nancy 78
free market economies 2, 159, 227
free rider problem, 30–2, 219
free space 140–2, 164, 255
free speech 117, 186
free trade 226, 227
free will 8, 11–12
freedom of expression 117
freedom of speech 117
freegan movement 155
French Revolution 103
French syndicalism 70

Freud, Sigmund 10, 12–13
Friedan, Betty 20
fringe benefits 31
Fujimori, Alberto 118, 119, 129
Fulana 207–8
fundamentalism: Christian 145–6;
    Islamic 136, 144–5; religious 144;
    Shi'ite Muslim 128

Gay and Lesbian Mardi Gras 120–1
gay and lesbian movements 19, 161,
    228; *see also* homosexuality; LGBT
    activism and rights; queer politics
gay and lesbian pride 32, 104, 105
gay community, in San Francisco 157
gay marriage 173
Geldof, Bob 149
gendered issues 68, 78, 161
General Motors 200
gentrification 207
geography 153; critical 164; of
    movement support 157; and the
    Occupy movement 178, 180–2;
    and political opportunity 162;
    of recruitment 161; and social
    movement studies 9; and social
    movement theory 153, 156–7; and
    the Tea Party 177
Germany, under the Nazis 99, 104, 125
Gitlin, Todd 193
global activism: and new media 239–41;
    and political opportunity structure 253
global consciousness 225
global day of action 17
global financial crisis (GFC) 3, 86, 91–2,
    172, 173, 227, 237
global institutions 228
global justice movements: activism
    50, 223; and culture jamming 208;
    effects of 3; examination of 9; and
    hacktivism 202; history of 235–7; on
    neoliberal globalization 90; protests
    118; on social movement theory